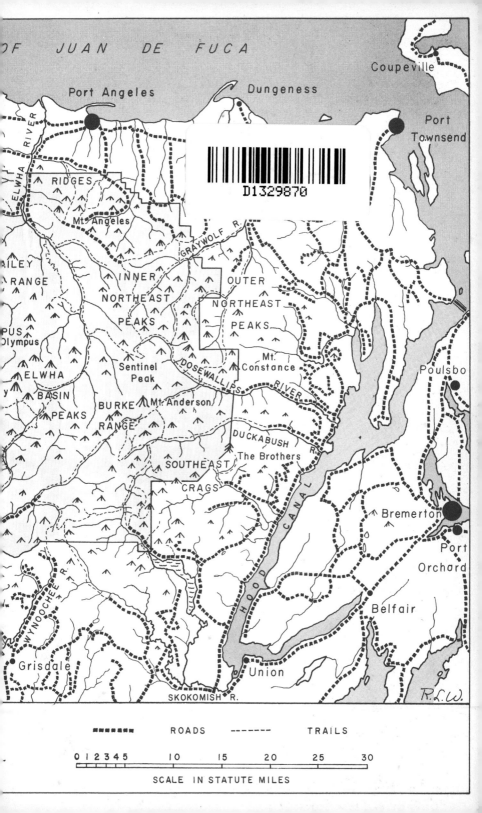

Trail Country

OLYMPIC NATIONAL PARK

The Mountaineers
Seattle

The Mountaineers, with groups based in Seattle, Everett, Tacoma, and Olympia (and groups elsewhere in the planning stage), invite the membership of all lovers of outdoor life who sympathize with the purposes of the organization and wish to share in its activities.

Publication of this book suggests the importance of the club role in conservation education and action in regard to the Olympics. In other areas are other concerns. If you share these concerns, your membership is particularly desired and needed.

Preservation, though, is only one side of the coin; the other is using and enjoying the back country.

The Mountaineers sponsor a year-round program of climbing, hiking, camping, ski-touring, and snowshoeing. Hundreds of outings are scheduled each year, ranging from single-day walks to trips lasting two weeks or more. On a typical weekend as many as thirty or forty excursions may be offered, from Pacific Ocean beaches to the summit of Mount Rainier. In addition, members engage in countless privately-organized trips of all kinds; perhaps a major value in belonging to an outdoor organization (The Mountaineers or any other) is the opportunity to meet other people with similar interests, to make new friends.

For further information on club activities and how to join, write The Mountaineers, P.O. Box 122, Seattle, Washington 98111.

Trail Country

OLYMPIC NATIONAL PARK

by

Robert L. Wood

Foreword by John Osseward

The Mountaineers

Organized 1906

To explore and study the mountains, forests, and watercourses of the Northwest;

To gather into permanent form the history and traditions of this region;

To preserve by the encouragement of protective legislation or otherwise, the natural beauty of Northwest America;

To make expeditions into these regions in fulfillment of the above purposes;

To encourage a spirit of good fellowship among all lovers of outdoor life.

First edition, 1968
Copyright 1968 © by
The Mountaineers, Seattle, Washington 98111
P.O. Box 122

Library of Congress Catalog Card Number 68–16316

To him who in the love of Nature holds
Communion with her visible forms

. . . William Cullen Bryant, Thanatopsis

FOREWORD

As I look westward through my office window, the Olympics have shed themselves of soft clouds before a gentle, dry north wind. Each of the peaks I have known for long years will be there for time beyond our count. To the east the peaks survey the entire Puget Sound basin with its timbered slopes under harvest to supply the hungry mills. To the west lie waves of wild mountain ranges, meadows, and valleys of primeval forests. By sheer luck the wilderness of Olympic National Park has been spared to serve a higher purpose than commerical exploitation.

All living things react to their environment. Americans have put up with the deterioration of their natural environment for some sixty years or more. Increasingly, however, forthright public demands have resulted in greater legal protection of lands needed for public enjoyment and recreation. Preservation of adequate recreational land from the blight of commercialism has now become a part of our federal land-use policy. Meanwhile,

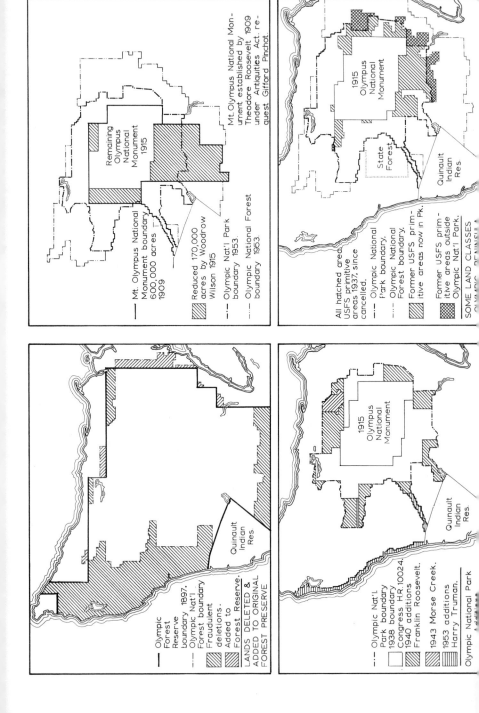

Mt.Olympus National Monument boundary 600,000 acres 1909

Remaining Olympus National Monument 1915

Mt.Olympus National Monument established by Theodore Roosevelt 1909 under Antiquities Act. request Gifford Pinchot.

Reduced 170,000 acres by Woodrow Wilson 1915

Olympic Nat'l Park boundary 1953.

Olympic National Forest boundary 1953.

1915 Olympus National Monument

State Forest

Quinault Indian Res.

All hatched area: USFS primitive areas 1937, since cancelled.

Olympic National Park boundary.

Olympic National Forest boundary.

Former USFS primitive areas now in Pk.

Former USFS primitive areas outside Olympic Nat'l Park.

SOME LAND CLASSES

Olympic Forest Reserve boundary 1897.

Olympic Nat'l Forest boundary 1915.

Fraudulent deletions.

Added to Forest Reserve.

Quinault Indian Res.

LANDS DELETED & ADDED TO ORIGINAL FOREST PRESERVE

1915 Olympus National Monument

Quinault Indian Res.

Olympic Nat'l. Park boundary 1938 boundary Congress H.R.10024.

1940 additions Franklin Roosevelt.

1943 Morse Creek.

1953 additions Harry Truman.

Olympic National Park

the long neglect of urban environment creates a situation that becomes more explosive each year. Any provision for the protection of our natural heritage of wilderness is an aid to efforts aimed at remedying our urban and rural living problems. It is simply not true that man must surrender the quantity and quality of his environment because it contains material resources which will be needed to supply our future needs. Professor James Bonner of the California Institute of Technology, in an essay entitled "The Ultimate Limit of Our Resources," has said in part:

"The time must inevitably come when high-grade resources, rich deposits of this or that, magnificent stands of timber, water flowing in the streams of our mountains, will no longer suffice for the requirements of an expanding industrial society. We have to learn how to get along without these high-grade resources, and to use low-grade ones instead. We know that we can in principle get along with low-grade resources for an essentially infinite time into the future.

"The pressure today for the despoliation and utilization of our natural areas in order to obtain from them material resources such as ores, trees, or fuel is immense. As high-grade resources become ever more scarce the pressure to exploit and utilize the last little remnants will become ever more intense. There is, however, no logical reason why our society should yield to these pressures. The amount of any material resource obtainable by the despoliation of a natural area today is insignificant in comparison with the future requirements of our nation or of the world as a whole. To maintain a natural area in its native state will at the most delay but a second in time the moment when we must depend upon the lowest grades of materials anyway. Let us, therefore, resist those pressures for the despoliation of natural areas, pressures based upon the argument that the material resources which they contain are essential to the welfare of our culture. Let us maintain a portion of the surface of our earth in its original state. By doing so we do not cheat mankind of anything which is essential to his well-being, we merely hasten very slightly the day which must inevitably come anyway, the day when industrial civilization must live upon rock, seawater and air."

Olympic National Park is predominantly a wilderness park, despite the ten roads built on its periphery when the area was under the jurisdiction of the United States Forest Service. The future of this park, as it was conceived, lies in preserving its wilderness character and use from the pressures to "improve" it. This policy cannot be compromised, for each piecemeal concession weakens the conservation concept. Our goals and decisions are affirmed in terms of the conservation ideal.

People from all walks of life have recognized in the Olympic National Park the last remnant of the Pacific Northwest ocean-oriented wilderness, a unique heritage of seashore, primeval forests reaching to alpine meadows, mountain ranges, and glaciers. Few areas can match the variety of unspoiled natural splendor contained in this park.

For thirty years, resolute determination on the part of conservation organizations and an aroused public has repeatedly thwarted efforts of the wood products industries to commercially exploit the rain forests in the park. Equally unavailing have been the efforts of those who would despoil the remaining wild ocean strip with roads, those who want the present valley stub roads extended, and those who advocate a trans-mountain road through the heart of the park. Roads, and the inevitable developments that follow, cannot by law be included in wilderness classification. To preserve this wilderness these nonconforming developments must be curbed.

In spite of the successful outcome to date, the Olympic National Park wilderness will reach the crossroads of decision when its lands are recommended for segregation into several of six classes provided for in the Wilderness Act. The new Master Plan now being formulated for Olympic National Park will be the basis for recommending its lands for wilderness and other classifications. The park is unique in many respects, and planning for the future, as in the past, should be objectively oriented to its wilderness resources. General classification rules applicable to other parks could be disastrous here.

Recommendations at the forthcoming classification hearings likely to be held in 1968 or 1969 could even provide for deleting certain park lands and reclassifying them as a National Recreation Area, an idea recently advanced by an Olympic Study Committee. Being of lesser significance than a national park, the dominant purpose of a National Recreation Area is mass all-purpose recreational use with road access. No part of Olympic National Park could stand the indignity of aerial tramways, helicopters, more roads, and other inappropriate developments.

Because of its timely, far-reaching importance, something should be said of national park land classification. The Wilderness Act provides for six classes of federal public use lands. The classification must be accomplished within ten years of the Wilderness Bill's enactment date.

Class I designates high-intensity recreation areas; Class II, general outdoor recreation areas; Class III, natural environment areas (called "wilderness threshold" by the National Park Service); Class IV, outstanding natural areas; Class V, primitive wilderness; and Class VI, historic and cultural areas. Classes IV and V are wilderness designations. Classes I and II lands are reserved for "administrative facilities, formal campgrounds, lodges, etc., of varying intensities." The Director of the National Park Service continues, "Class II lands serve a special purpose in relation to national park wilderness . . . These are the lands that provide the 'setting' or 'buffer' for the wilderness—we prefer to identify these lands as the 'wilderness threshold.' The only development allowed in these wilderness threshold areas is the minimum required for public enjoyment, health, safety, preservation and protection of the features, but even then such limited developments must be in complete harmony with the natural environment." (In this connection let's not overlook the monstrosity at Mount Rainier National Park, the brand new "round house" lodge.) The type of developments permitted in Class III lands, he says, are, "for example, one-way motor nature trails, small overlooks, informal picnic sites, short nature walks, etc." [1]

Ample areas lie along existing roads and their endings for Class II and III land use in Olympic National Park. These areas include the mouth of the Ozette River, Mora near LaPush

[1] "National Park Wilderness Planning Procedures," by George Hartzog, Director, National Park Service, August 1, 1966.

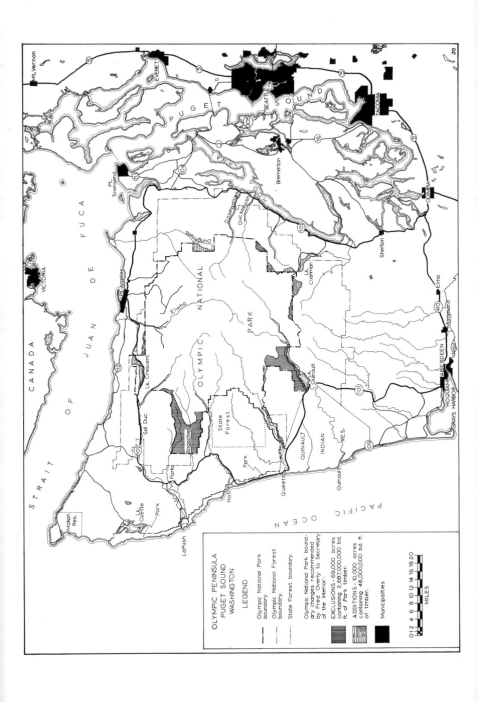

OLYMPIC PENINSULA
PUGET SOUND
WASHINGTON

LEGEND

Olympic National Park
boundary.

Olympic National Forest
boundary.

State Forest boundary.

Olympic National Park boundary changes recommended
by Fred Overly to Secretary
of the Interior:.

EXCLUSIONS—69,000 acres
containing 2,687,000,000 bd.
ft. of Park timber.

ADDITIONS—10,000 acres
containing 48,000,000 bd. ft.
of timber.

Municipalities

0 1 2 4 6 8 10 12 14 16 18 20
MILES

on the ocean coast, and the thirteen miles along the ocean beach from the Queets River to Ruby Beach. Some thirteen other locations in the park are available for Class II and III uses. On the north are Sol Duc Hot Springs, parts of Lake Crescent, Olympic Hot Springs, the Elwha entrance, Hurricane Ridge, Obstruction Point, and Deer Park. On the east is the Dosewallips entrance; to the south, the Lake Cushman entrance. The southwest offers the Lake Quinault area, the North Fork of the Quinault, and Graves Creek. On the west are the Queets Campground and the Hoh entrance. Special study should seek to locate accommodations outside the park. The ultimate National Park Service recommendations should be viewed critically where undue encroachments invade de facto wilderness in the park.

The master-planning of national parks would present few problems if the number of visitors were stabilized. Planning is complicated, however, because visitation increases at an accelerated rate. Increased park attendance requires amplified facilities. Present planning must be conceived in terms of ultimate future aims, guided by criteria that conform to mandated park standards. Major accommodations should be dispersed as much as possible to private and federal lands outside the parks; otherwise, the quality of visitor experiences will be impaired by congestion, as is already the case in some parks. Increasing visitor density will regulate enforcement at service centers, on trails, lakes, and highways, in order to educate the public and preserve park resources for their proper use.

There is no doubt about the sincerity of the National Park Service, confronted as it is with serious dilemmas involving park uses. However, there appears to be a lack of research and criteria on which to base judgments. The best use of the Pacific Ocean Strip is an example. Judgments have vacillated for some thirty years as to whether it should remain in its wild state or be traversed by roads, which would ruin it. Other serious errors have occurred. Millions of board feet of Olympic National Park timber were cut as "salvage" until public wrath stopped the practice, which had been approved by the National Park Service. Recommendations of the Quinault Study Report of 1962 have been largely ignored by the Senate Interior Committee and the Park Service. While the Service is willing to contemplate the expenditure of millions for a road on the ocean strip and has spent some $900,000 to acquire Sol Duc Hot Springs, its archaic fiscal policy prevents a timely means of acquiring private lands offered for sale to the Park Service. Motorboating on Lake Crescent is another example of permitted misuse in Olympic National Park. The National Park Service, at the public Congressional hearings at Lake Crescent in 1947, approved the deletion of 59,000 acres of rain forest from the Bogachiel and Quinault valleys! An identical deletion was proposed again, early in 1966, by Fred Overly, a former superintendent of the park. For the second time the proposal was vigorously denounced. These judgment errors impose hardship on park superintendents, who are exposed to intense local pressures for resource exploitation, roads, and other development.

There is one school of thought in the National Park Service oriented toward recreational activity development and more roads. The question is development versus preservation. Strong pressures are also exerted by sportsmen to permit hunting in our parks. This new thinking stems from an attempt to rationalize the purpose of national parks, as stated in the 1916 National Park Act, the essential provision of which is that national parks are to be used by people, "but that their use is to be regulated by such means and measures . . . as will leave them unimpaired for the enjoyment of future generations." Obviously, parks cannot be used and still be left unimpaired, but this does not mean that parks are to be choked with people and development until their impairment is assured.

The time will soon arrive when some form of reservations will be required to visit national parks when they become congested, as we normally have to do at hotels. It has been said that national parks bear the seeds of their own destruction. The increasing population densities of the west and the rapidly growing Puget Sound basin, located at the very backdoor of Olympic National Park, will pose a serious park accommodation problem, if policy is not formulated now to cope with it in the future. It is necessary to calculate saturation capacities now if planning is to be effective.

Parks are for people to enjoy, but not on their own terms. A golfer should not expect to play golf in national parks,

since more appropriate areas are available for this type of recreation. Nor should a motorcyclist expect to ride national park
trails. Are visitor limitations to be forced on park management
only after there is no more space to be black-topped? During
the congested times of the year it may be necessary to provide
parking areas outside parks and use specially-designed bus con-
veyance into the parks. Already, trailer and camping space along
the thirteen miles of ocean beach cannot meet demands. Re-
locating Highway 101 back from its present close proximity to
the beach will provide much-needed space in this high-density
service area. Even then, the saturation point is in sight.

Planning must be coordinated with other federal, state,
local, and private agencies so they can share the responsibility
of providing complementary services, recreation, and accommodations which may not be appropriate in a national park.

For some time, revolutionary methods of research and
systems analysis have become standard tools for the solution of
complex problems in the fields of business, manufacturing, engineering, federal, state, and local governments. The program-
ming of these systems has become excitingly sophisticated and
successful. Parks and their problems might provide a limited
research field for computer use, which properly programmed,
would compel a more realistic confrontation of our national
park problems. Caution would be in order, however, for some
park problems cannot be dealt with as simulated models subject to mathematical formula solutions. "The greatest good for
the greatest number" is often used by resource exploiters to
justify their ends. This overused quote cannot be evaluated exclusively within an economic frame of reference. National parks,
wilderness areas, and wildlife refuges are simply not ordered by
profits, per se. Preservation of such lands is a mandate of the
Congress. All such uses of lands are costly, but the social and
economic costs of misused and over-exploited commercial land
are much greater.

The values of national parks and wilderness land use
are concerned with a variety of important interdependent intangibles, which cannot be measured in quantity-terms, as most
engineering problems can. Such human feelings as appreciation
of beauty or pleasing environments, more often than not, can

only be expressed by intuition. Though these intangibles defy quantitative measure, the public has demonstrated its concern for them in recent years.

Again, the criteria so necessary for balanced land-use judgments must be determined by all the disciplines concerned with land use—ecology, biology, sociology, long-term environmental planning, and a modern concept of responsible custodianship for commercial land exploitation.

Thus, the broad principles and methodology used to define and approach problems of public land use are, in many respects, as important as the problems themselves. The desired ends of balanced land use, both esthetic and commercial, should be sought in some commonly accepted measurement criteria, such as the ratio of recreational land preserved to the total amount of land. Such a basis would employ a common measurement and would not involve intangibles. Data is available for such an approach, to measure the adequacy of land which should be used for public enjoyment.

The future integrity of Olympic National Park demands a recognition of the existing old growth timber and, equally important, the pulp resources potentially useful for thinning in the large areas of second growth outside the park. Only five states possess more saw timber than do the four counties on the Olympic Peninsula. How vital is the need to cut timber in Olympic National Park, when in 1966 Washington and Oregon exported over a billion board feet of unprocessed logs, principally to Japan? Forty per cent of the logs exported from the state of Washington were shipped from the ports of Aberdeen and Port Angeles, communities adjacent to the park.

Conservationists need not apologize for the size of Olympic National Park. The entire land area of the forty-eight conterminous states set aside in national parks, wilderness, state, county, and municipal parks amounts to less than three per cent of the total land area of the United States. More, not less, of our land is essential for this type of public use, measured in terms of present and future needs to properly balance use of the land for living environment and industrial needs.

Congress, in establishing Olympic National Park, limited its acreage to 892,000. Consequently, some areas of superb beauty were left outside its boundaries—areas that elsewhere would have become national parks in their own right. The eastern boundary excluded land that was then classified as primitive areas by the Forest Service, since the boundary team wished to preserve some 56,000 acres for a future ocean strip. One such area, the upper Dungeness Basin, should be preserved as a wild area by the Forest Service. Another boundary adjustment from Lower Lena Lake to The Brothers should also be made by the Forest Service to provide protection from cutting. Because of a lack of funds, the nine mile seascape north of the present ocean strip boundary was omitted; this area includes the Point of Arches and Shi Shi beach. For the same reason, only the western shores of Lake Ozette were included in the park. This was a tragic error. Under the present situation none of the water uses on the lake may be regulated.

It is not generally known that the actual ocean beaches abutting the fifty-six miles of Olympic National Park belong to the State of Washington. In 1941 the Department of the Interior was acquiring these beaches from the state by condemnation when funds were depleted. The suit was dropped in exchange for a document known as a Declaration of Policy, signed by the then governor of the state and his public land commissioner providing that the uses of the tidelands would not be in detriment to the national park land. Nonetheless, violations have occurred on several occasions, under the jurisdiction of the Department of National Resources. The situation eased considerably this year when the ocean beaches were placed under the administration of the State Park Commission. These tidelands are an integral part of Olympic National Park and should eventually become part of it.

Many unsolved problems remain in Olympic National Park. Olympic Park Associates, Inc., of which The Mountaineers and other conservation groups are members, backed by a strong public interest and concern, keeps a watchful vigil over the wilderness integrity of this unique park.

Robert L. Wood is eminently qualified to share with others the mysteries and grandeur of the trails of Olympic National Park. His book is a major contribution to the better understanding and enjoyment of this superb wilderness.

John Osseward

AUTHOR'S PREFACE AND ACKNOWLEDGMENTS

This book is intended primarily for two groups of persons—"armchair adventurers" who wish to visit the mountains and seashore vicariously, by reading about them; backpackers, who desire to explore the Olympics personally and find pleasure in their wonders and beauties firsthand.

Over the years I have met many people, both in the mountains and in the cities, who were just beginning to learn the art of backpacking; others, experienced wilderness travelers, who did not know the Olympics. Invariably, these people have asked about places to go—where and why. This book was written to supply the answer, and emphasizes the why. Why visit Honeymoon Meadows or the Enchanted Valley? Why climb Olympus? Why hike the Bogachiel?

TRAIL COUNTRY is a book that has evolved slowly. In order to explain how it came into being, I must necessarily relate some personal history.

In the fall of 1946 I moved to the State of Washington from mid-Western United States, and found myself living almost within the shadow of the snow-clad Olympic Mountains. Caught in the magic web of their enchantment, I began reading everything I could find—there wasn't much in those days—concerning the Olympic Peninsula. The following summer I made my first trip to the mountains—in an automobile, to the end of the Dosewallips River road. Then, in the summer of 1948, came my first experience on the forest trails, hiking in the vicinity of Lake Quinault.

In August, 1950, I first began making notes for a book on Olympic National Park (as an outgrowth of two term papers prepared while attending the University of Washington). However, the first draft of the manuscript was not completed to my satisfaction until nearly six years later. During this time I went on a number of backpack trips into the park's interior. Then, in 1954, I attended the Basic Campcraft class conducted by Olympic College in the rain forests and high country on the western side of the park. On this trip I made my first mountain climb—an ascent of Mount Olympus. The following year I was a student in the college's climbing course and climbed several peaks in the eastern Olympics.

The manuscript completed in 1956 was never published. However, I continued to hike and climb in the Olympic Mountains, and in 1957 joined The Mountaineers, an outdoor organization with headquarters in Seattle, Washington.

In May, 1961, Harvey Manning, a member of The Mountaineers, inquired about my manuscript (then gathering dust on a shelf), and after reviewing what I had written requested that I revise and update it, with a view toward publication by The Mountaineers. The revision was completed in February, 1964. However, new problems developed, and this second major draft remained unpublished. Then, later in 1964, Mr. Manning again asked that I revise the manuscript, particularly with a view toward shortening it. At that time Murrell Boyd agreed to act as literary editor, and assisted me in reducing the manuscript's length.

TRAIL COUNTRY, the book now in hand, is the result—the third and final draft of a manuscript that has literally evolved over the years. Although it has been written primarily from my personal experience hiking and climbing in the Olympic Mountains and walking the Olympic Seashore, I am, needless to say, indebted to a number of persons for their help in making this book a reality. Without the help of Mr. Boyd (who very ably assisted me in reducing the manuscript's length about thirty per cent without loss of relevant material) and the unrelenting encouragement and inspiration of Mr. Manning, this book would still be only a manuscript.

I also wish to express particular appreciation to Jesse Epstein, President of The Mountaineers, and to John Osseward, Vice President of Olympic Park Associates. Mr. Epstein constantly encouraged me in my efforts, especially in the formative years of the first draft, and without his encouragement I might never have finished the original manuscript. Mr. Osseward, an outstanding conservationist, wrote the Foreword for this book, and also prepared the two maps accompanying the Foreword.

A number of others have been helpful in one way or another, and I wish to acknowledge their assistance: Frank L. Atkinson; the late Irving M. Clark (Wilderness Society); Floyd L. Dickinson (National Park Service); Leo Gallagher; Kent Heathershaw; Ward Irwin; Harlean James (American Planning & Civic Association); Ruth Jewell; Fannie Johnson; Lois Bliss Layton; Preston P. Macy (former Superintendent, Olympic National Park); Dorothy McKinney (Clubroom Secretary, The Mountaineers); Dale Petite; Jim Richardson; Harry K. Sanders (National Park Service); Robert Scott; Frank O. Shaw; Helen Walcott.

The photographs appearing in this book came from several sources, and I wish to acknowledge the assistance of those who made it possible to illustrate this book with a representative display of the Olympic scene: Charles L. Allyn; Anna M. Ibbotson (acting librarian, Washington State Historical Museum); George W. Martin; Jerry Matchett; Knute F. Melsom (Pacific Aerial Surveys, Inc.); Bob and Ira Spring.

All maps in this book, except the two accompanying the Foreword which were drawn by John Osseward, were prepared by myself, and all are oriented so that north is to the top, south to the bottom, east to the right, and west to the left.

I would also like to acknowledge my appreciation to

Mrs. Joyce Kachergis, who designed this book; and to sundry anonymous members of the Literary Fund Committee of The Mountaineers, and of the staff of the Seattle Public Library, who have helped toward its publication.

It is probable that I have overlooked others whom I should acknowledge. If I have, I hope they will forgive me.

Robert L. Wood

Seattle, Washington
November, 1967

TABLE OF CONTENTS

LIST OF ILLUSTRATIONS

Between pages 102 and 103

LIST OF MAPS

The two maps accompanying the foreword were prepared
by John Osseward; the other maps were prepared by the
author. All maps are oriented to the compass with north to
the top, south to the bottom, east to the right, and west to
the left.

PACIFIC NORTHWEST
■ OLYMPIC NATIONAL PARK

Book I

The Olympic Peninsula

Pioneers in the Pacific Northwest found the Olympic Peninsula a strange, wild land. Nature was prolific on a grand scale, and the vast resources, seemingly impossible of exhaustion, were an open invitation to the exploitative instincts of "civilized man." Except for the lofty mountains in the interior, the whole region was heavily forested. Towering evergreen trees, the result of mild temperatures and heavy rainfall, stretched in unbroken ranks from salt water beaches to the snows of the mountain peaks. These primeval forests so impressed the men of the U. S. Coast Survey that, in their 1858 report, they referred to "the immeasurable sea of gigantic timber coming down to the very shores." Spruce and cedar grew upon the river bottoms; the uplands were covered by stately stands of Douglas fir and hemlock. Many trees exceeded ten feet in diameter and rose skyward more than two hundred and fifty feet. On the moss-carpeted ground beneath them grew luxuriant ferns, vine maple and rhododendron. Wildlife was abundant, with the mammals ranging in size from mice to elk. Trout and salmon filled the swift, icy rivers; the tide-washed beaches teemed with oysters, clams and crabs.

This rich land was not unclaimed, however, because seafaring Indians resided along the shores in dwellings shadowed by the towering trees. These primitive people fished the coastal waters. They cruised the ocean in cedar dugouts in quest of seals or the Tyee salmon, and sometimes the hunters ventured far out to sea to harpoon whales.

In the winter the land was gloomy and forbidding. Gray storm clouds darkened the skies for weeks, and continuous rains left the forests soaked and dripping. Then the mountains enrobed themselves in cloud and fog, withdrawing from the sight of man. But the long summer days were often cloudless, and the mountain snows gleamed with distant, dreamlike purity. Unspoiled, the land had for centuries lain undisturbed by the white man's exploitation, its landscape a scene of serene natural beauty.

Chapter I

The Wilderness Mountains

The Olympic Peninsula

Bordered by the sea on three sides and almost an island, the rain drenched Olympic Peninsula displays an array of natural features worthy of a continent. This isolated corner of Washington State is a land of contrasts. Although its perimeter has been changed by civilization, the interior is still primitive, one of the wildest regions in the United States. Here towers glacier-studded Mount Olympus, guarded on all sides by snowy ramparts of lesser peaks. Only sixty miles away is Seattle, city of more than half a million people.

Roughly quadrangular, about eighty miles across, the peninsula has an area of some sixty-five hundred square miles, of which three thousand square miles are covered by the Olympic Mountains, a cluster of precipitous peaks cut by chasms and festooned with glaciers and snowfields. Surrounding the mountains is a belt of low, broken country generally less than four hundred feet above sea level. This belt is about twenty miles wide on the west and south, five to ten miles on the north and east.

The peninsula is connected to the mainland only on

the south where foothills of the Olympic Mountains fade into alluvial bottomlands along the Chehalis River. On all other sides the sea encroaches. For a hundred miles on the west, from Cape Flattery to Grays Harbor, the Pacific Ocean washes a coast characterized by broad beaches and offshore rocks and pinnacles. On the north the tide-swept Strait of Juan de Fuca edges the land for another hundred miles from the Pacific to Puget Sound, whose sheltered coves and inlets limit the land on the east. Here a portion of the peninsula, known as the Kitsap Peninsula, is separated from the main area, like a thumb from its hand, by fiord-like Hood Canal, a salt water channel seventy miles long and one to two miles wide.

Climate

The Pacific Ocean dominates the weather pattern on the peninsula. Maritime air masses lie over the region most of the time, resulting in an essentially marine climate. Temperatures are therefore mild throughout the year, especially for a land lying closer to the North Pole than to the Equator. Winter is the wet season, rainfall being abundant from November to June. The summers are cool and generally damp.

The peninsula lies within the storm tracks of the "prevailing westerlies" which sweep across the northern hemisphere throughout the year. These winds are strongest during winter and spring, when the Aleutian low pressure system dominates the North Pacific and spawns cyclonic storms along the "polar front." The storms travel eastward across the sea, then inland over the Pacific Northwest. The marine air becomes unstable, because it is warmer than the land surface over which it moves. The result is raininess, overcast skies and high humidity.

In summer the North Pacific high pressure system displaces the Aleutian low. Northwest winds predominate, moving air which is cooler than the land, therefore stable and of low humidity. Skies are generally clear, rainfall considerably diminished, and sea breezes prevail along the coast. The days are pleasantly cool, the temperature seldom rising to ninety degrees.

If the Olympic Mountains did not exist, the peninsula would have an annual rainfall of approximately fifty inches, rather evenly distributed. However, the mountains form an effective barrier to the passage of storms and influence the rainfall pattern. When warm, moisture-laden air masses from the sea strike the windward slopes they must rise in order to move inland. This cools the air, thus reducing its capacity to retain water vapor. Consequently, rainfall is heavy on the western and southern sides of the peninsula, about one hundred and forty inches falling annually at the base of the mountains, still more on seaward-facing slopes above the valleys. Higher up, most of the precipitation occurs in the form of snow, coming as it does in the winter. Thus the loftier, ocean-oriented peaks receive one of the world's heaviest snowfalls.

Fifty miles away, however, on the leeward side of the mountains, precipitation is meager, because the so-called "rain shadow" shelters this area. As the air masses descend the northeastern slopes, they are warmed by compression and their capacity to retain water vapor is increased. The result is greatly reduced precipitation. This is the driest area on the Pacific coast north of San Francisco, with an annual rainfall of only fifteen to twenty inches, and were it not for the northerly latitude evaporation would make it an arid land. In fact, farmers in this district irrigate their fields.

Dry air masses from the continental interior occasionally invade the peninsula, but this is the exception rather than the rule. Foehn winds accompany the invasion, bringing cold, winter weather and warm, clear summer days.

The Olympic Mountains

Nearly surrounded by the sea, the Olympics stand alone, isolated from other mountains. Starting close to the water's edge, forested foothills extend upward to timberline like staircases, and above them rise rocky, snow-flecked peaks sharply etched against the sky. The mountains are actually a directionless jumble, but appear to be a precipitous range paralleling whichever coastline the viewer faces. Hence, different peaks and directional trends are noted, depending upon whether the vantage point is Puget Sound, the Strait of Juan de Fuca or the Pacific Ocean. These apparent lines of peaks visible from the surrounding seas present a broken appearance, cut as they are by deep canyons which swift rivers have sliced through spurs and ridges.

The peninsula's pioneer settlers made the mistake of believing the various "ranges" enclosed a large central valley that drained to a great inland lake. But these mountains are deceptive, and the apparent ranges are only the higher peaks along whichever edge of the uplift is nearest the viewer. Beyond each "edge" extend similar peaks and ridges for fifty miles.

The Olympics are not unique by reason of their isolation or because they rise from low coastal plains and overlook the sea. Most Americans are accustomed to mountain ranges that stand atop high plateaus, the peaks strung out like pearls on a necklace. In the Olympic jumble no point lies more than thirty miles from the sea, and from bases only a few feet above tidewater the peaks sweep sharply upward to altitudes approaching eight thousand feet. This is not lofty as mountains go, but these peaks rise as far above the nearby sea as do most summits in the Rockies over the Great Plains.

The early settlers thought the peaks were higher than they are. Because the pioneers came into the region from the continental interior, they had not seen mountains standing out boldly against the sea. Then, too, they often saw the Olympics veiled by mist and fog. This made them appear higher than when viewed against cloudless skies. Together with the Indians' fear of the unknown interior, this veiled effect gave to the mountains a halo of mystery—one that prevails to this day even though the region has been thoroughly explored.

Geology

The terrain of the Olympic Mountains impedes the study of their geological history, because dense vegetation on the lower slopes and perpetual fields of snow and ice at higher elevations screen the rock formations from the geologist's eye. Nevertheless, the record of the rocks has revealed salient features of the region's complicated geology.

Over a period of about one hundred and twenty million years most, if not all, of the Olympic Peninsula has lain beneath the sea at least five times, with intervening elevations above the surface. Wave-cut terraces along the Pacific are an indication of fluctuation in the level of the land.

Although the lowlands surrounding the mountains are composed of marine sediments, the base of the mountains is probably granite. The only granitic rocks that have been found, however, are erratics brought down from Canada by the continental glacier. The rock structures of the mountains reveal much folding and some faulting. The axis of folds in the interior is generally northwest to southeast and the general dip of the beds is strong to the southwest, while the northern and eastern bedding commonly dips to the northeast. Toward the center of the peninsula the rocks become increasingly deformed and crystalline, the oldest so warped and shattered it is impossible to tell whether they are right side up. In fact, the summit pinnacles of many high peaks show almost vertical strata.

This inner core of mountains is composed of weakly metamorphosed and closely folded sedimentary rocks— primarily schist, quartzite, slate and graywacke (a dark sandstone)—bordered by a prominent band of volcanics on all sides except the west. The band of submarine extruded volcanics, containing a few unmetamorphosed limestone sediments, wraps around the central mountains like a horseshoe. Essentially a steeply dipping or overturned monocline, the band begins near Lake Crescent and circles around the mountains to the east, to terminate in the southwest near Lake Quinault. At its widest in the east where it parallels Hood Canal, the band includes the high eastern peaks of the Olympics. North of this horseshoe of volcanics is another series, mostly well-fossilized sedimentary sandstones and shales.

Creation of the Olympic Mountains began early in the Cretaceous Epoch of the Mesozoic Era, about one hundred and twenty million years ago. Where the peninsula now stands a shallow sea occupied a great depression in the earth's crust. This trough-like depression or geosyncline was bordered on the east, approximately where the Cascade Range presently rises, by the western margin of North America. West of the depression, in what is still part of the Pacific, a chain of islands probably paralleled the coastline.

For millions of years streams carried sediments into the

geosyncline from the land. These marine sediments accumulated on the ocean bottom to estimated depths ranging from ten thousand to twenty-five thousand feet. Pressure from their own weight compacted them into stratifications or layers of interbedded shale, sandstone and graywacke. Near the shore, breccia and conglomerate formed in shallow water.

Stresses and strains in the earth's crust apparently created fissures in the sea floor, and molten lava poured through these breaks. The lava cooled rapidly in the salt water, thus forming pillow-like masses on top of the accumulating sediments. These lavas were in turn buried by later sediments, and they combined with calcium carbonate to form impure, lens-shaped beds of limestone, the "red rocks" found today in the Olympics.

Pressure from the Pacific Basin eventually compressed the sediments, causing folding, crumpling and buckling, and elevating the area far above the sea. This occurred about one hundred million years ago, late in the Cretaceous Epoch. Folded and crumpled as they were by pressure, and "baked" by the resultant heat, the rocks underwent metamorphic changes—fossils were destroyed, shale became slate, and the sandstone became harder, some of it being altered to quartzite.

The newly uplifted land was gradually lowered by erosion during the millions of years remaining in the Cretaceous, toward the end of which the last North American epeiric sea invaded the continent. Geologists believe, however, that the cycle of erosion continued into the first epoch of the Cenozoic Era, some sixty million years ago.

By the beginning of the second epoch of the Cenozoic, about four million years later, the land had been reduced by erosion nearly to sea level. Apparently it then subsided and what is now western Washington was once again submerged beneath a shallow sea. Considerable non-explosive volcanic activity occurred and enormous quantities of basaltic lava flowed from fissures in the ocean floor. The lava cooled quickly in the sea, forming massive pillow-like structures. These so-called "pillow lavas" today stand nearly vertical.

The lava flows spread out in layers generally one to two thousand feet thick, and attained a maximum depth of about five thousand feet in a broad belt on the eastern side of the peninsula. On the contact line between the volcanic rocks of the east and the sediments of the west, the upwelling volcanics thrust against the sediments, thus amplifying the buckling and folding processes at work on these rocks. The later flows of molten magma lacked the pillow structure (an indication that they probably occurred above the surface of the sea) and formed a matrix for the huge balls of lava formed by the initial outpouring.

Several hundred feet of sediments were deposited on this lava before the "second sea" withdrew. In the northeastern Olympics lava outpourings on the sea floor alternated with deposits of sandstone, shale and conglomerate. Following the deposition of volcanic and sedimentary rocks during the Eocene Epoch rhythmic advances and retreats of the shallow continental sea occurred. This fluctuation was caused by several risings and sinkings of the land that now forms the peninsula.

The sea again invaded the land in the Oligocene Epoch, about thirty-six million years ago, and spread eastward across western Washington as the land subsided. Sedimentary deposits again accumulated atop the older rocks, and the region was subjected to a gentle uplift.

About ten million years later, in the Miocene Epoch, the land was uplifted for the fourth time, with simultaneous folding, creating a northwest-southeast trending mountain range, the first Olympic Mountains. The areas to the north and south of this ancestral range were depressed, and remain so to this day as the Strait of Juan de Fuca and the Chehalis valley. Today's Olympic Mountains stand upon the remnants of these first Olympics created fifteen to twenty million years ago.

During the late Pliocene and early Pleistocene—a time of mountain building all over the earth—a fifth uplift took place. This involved the western portion of the old Olympics, and formed the mountains we know today. Concurrently, the Puget Sound Basin was depressed, thus leaving lowlands on all sides of the mountains.

The Olympic Mountains were extensively sculptured by glacial ice during the Pleistocene Epoch or Ice Age. Apparently the ice made two great advances, separated by an interglacial epoch. The continental glacier from Canada covered the large basin lying between the Cascades and Olympics, and pushed one stream of ice westward along the Strait of Juan de Fuca, another southward through the Puget Sound trough. This northern ice crushed its way up the river valleys on the northern and eastern slopes of the Olympics. When the ice tongues retreated, boulders of Canadian granite were left behind. These "glacial erratics" are found as high as three thousand feet above sea level. Previous to the advance of the northern ice, alpine glaciers descended from the mountain center and left pebbles from the Olympic rocks in the Puget Sound Basin.

The mountains continued to rise during the Pleistocene and reached their present level. Grays Harbor and Puget Sound were connected by tidewater, and the Puget Sound lobe of the continental glacier drained to the sea via the Chehalis River valley. Thus the Olympics were isolated from the mainland. When the continental glacier receded some twenty thousand years ago, huge alpine glaciers were left in the mountains. These formed an icecap on the higher peaks.

For three thousand years following the Ice Age, temperatures were excessively warm, and subtropical conditions existed as far north as Canada. The alpine glaciers gradually retreated up the valleys, post-glacial erosion occurred and vegetation began to grow upon the land. During the last four thousand years, however, a rebirth of glaciation has occurred, but on a much smaller scale. Geologists sometimes call this period the "little Ice Age of historic times." During this glacial rebirth, the ice has alternately advanced, stagnated, and receded, leaving small moraines parallel to the larger ones created during the Pleistocene.

Erosion by wind, water and ice gradually wears away the mountains, but the result is countered by unseen tectonic forces within the earth that uplift the land. It may be that the Olympics are still being slowly elevated. Evidence suggests that mountain building forces are now working in the region, for orogenic movement is indicated by earthquakes having epicenters in the Olympic country. Gently folded and tilted glacial clays, sands and gravels in the northern part of the peninsula also reflect recent movement. Obviously, much remains to be learned about the geology of the Olympic Mountains.

Of particular interest are studies made by Dr. Z. F.

Danes, a geophysicist, whose findings indicate that folding and faulting in the earth's crust is causing the Olympic Peninsula to move northeastward. The movement is so slow it amounts to but a fraction of an inch each year. If this movement continues for millions of years, however, the land will shift many miles.

Present Day Topography

The classic formation of mountains is long, irregular rows. The pattern of the Olympics, however, is an exception to the rule. In place of rows are clustered peaks and ridges strewn in a confusing jumble, apparently with little regard for order. Twisting valleys and canyons break the continuity of the knife-edge ridges, and no one peak, not even Mount Olympus, dominates the wild tangle. The mountain mass contains not only isolated summits and spurs but also several short "ranges," the whole enclosing dozens of hidden valleys and lakes.

The mountains are remnants of an anticline, a dome-like mass uplifted by forces within the earth. This dome had its apex near the center of the peninsula, where the highest elevations still occur. The mountains slope steeply downward along their northern and eastern periphery, less abruptly on the southern and western. No central culminating point exists, but a discernible directional trend extends northwest from Hood Canal toward Cape Flattery. This is the residual of a line of ancient peaks which stretched across western Washington in that direction.

What at first glimpse seems unpatterned chaos becomes a "spiral nebula" from the proper distance. The mountain mass is roughly circular, with rivers, intervening ridges and peaks spiraling outward from the center. This spiral effect is centered primarily around Mount Olympus, the core of the "nebula," from which canyon-enclosed rivers radiate in all directions. The analogy is somewhat inexact, but graphic, illustrating that the chaos is only apparent.

Pleistocene ice sharpened the outlines of the Olympics, and since the ice retreated the forces of erosion have had insufficient time to grade down the deeply dissected labyrinth. Thus, narrow gorges and canyonlike valleys extend far into the interior. Some of the valleys are broader and reveal the u-shaped profile characteristic of glacial carving.

The Olympics impress the mountain climber as a region of rough crags, pinnacles and serrated ridges dominated by snow-clad peaks shining above the dark depths of unbroken conifer forests. Plateaus are nonexistent, as is a main or central divide. Instead, irregular ice-sculptured divides or arêtes separate the canyons and stream heads from each other. The larger divides branch out to form ridges and spurs truncated by glacial action. Some of the ridges are long and unbroken, others have been eroded into groups of semi-isolated peaks harboring cirques and hanging valleys. These cirques were scooped in the mountainsides by ancient glaciers, and some still function as points of glacial origin. Most, however, are only reminders of an age when ice fields were more numerous. Many contain permanent snowfields that sustain creeks and rivers. In others the snow melts out completely during the summer, and small alpine lakes, often bordered by marshland, occupy the recesses.

Glaciation effects are noticeable far down the mountainsides in the form of moraines, polished rock, striations, tarns and beds of clay filled with boulders. Glacial outwash is found on the lowlands at the base of the mountains.

The summits of the higher peaks are usually masses of splintered rocks where rainbow-hued wildflowers cling to rock crevices in the summer. From these vantage points overlooking green valleys and foothills the mountaineer can see the waters surrounding the peninsula—the Pacific, the Strait of Juan de Fuca and Puget Sound. On the eastern horizon the long chain of the Cascades is surmounted in several places by volcanic cones that appear to float, suspended in the sky.

Glaciers and Ice Fields

The Olympic Mountains, rising abruptly as they do from coastal lowlands, intercept winter storms and alter their own weather pattern. Their moderate elevation places them squarely within the zone of heavy cloud formation, five to nine thousand feet above sea level. On the higher summits facing the ocean, the annual precipitation of one hundred and fifty to two hundred inches falls mostly during the winter in the form of snow, with the maximum amount occurring above five thousand feet. On peaks and ridges not directly exposed to the sea winds the amount is less, from seventy-five to one hundred and twenty inches. During the coldest winter weather snow sometimes falls at sea level, but the "snow line" is usually up several hundred feet, and when spring arrives this line retreats upward until, in late summer, it disappears entirely. However, many fields of snow, particularly those on northern slopes, last from one winter to the next. Technically, the "snow line" is the elevation above which snow persists the year around. In the Olympics this is about six thousand feet, the lowest snow line in the United States, excluding Alaska.

The snow pack reaches its maximum depth in late winter, when cornices project forty feet or more on the leeward sides of ridge crests. The snow, consolidated by its own weight, often lies ten to twenty feet deep. Still greater depths are measured in catchment basins on the highest peaks, but this results partially from avalanche and wind accumulations. All this snow cannot melt during the cool summers, and that which remains at the end of the ablation or melting season is gradually transformed into ice. Over long periods of time this has resulted in formation of glaciers and permanent snowfields. These are found throughout the loftier part of the mountains, chiefly on northern slopes. The glaciers alone cover about thirty square miles. Counting the tiny "glacierets" and stagnant ice fields, more than one hundred ice masses are recessed in the mountainsides. At least half of these are active, pulled downward by their own weight. Only a few, however, are large enough to be called "ice rivers." These are valley glaciers with low, dynamically active tongues. The smaller ones are cirque glaciers or ice aprons similar to those in Glacier National Park.

Most of the glaciers, including all the larger, active ones, are found on the windward side of the Olympics, principally on the Mount Olympus, Bailey and Burke ranges and on peaks near the head of the Quinault. Because of the heavy snowfall, glaciers occur here at lower elevations than in other mountains at this latitude, beginning at six thousand to eight thousand feet above sea level and terminating between thirty-five hundred and forty-five hundred feet. The largest glaciers are two to three miles long, small compared to those found in high latitude lands.

The small cirque glaciers of the Olympics were probably created during the "Little Ice Age" of the last four thousand years, for it is unlikely they could have survived the period of excessive warmth which followed the Pleistocene. Geologists believe, however, the large ice streams on Mount Olympus and Mount Anderson are Ice Age relics that have persisted continuously since Pleistocene time.

The upper parts of the glaciers are replenished each winter by heavy snowfall and by snow avalanching into the catchment basins. Because they project to rather low altitudes, the glacier snouts lose more by melting than they receive from winter snows, but they are sustained by ice masses descending from above.

For a decade scientists have studied the glaciers on Mount Olympus, particularly the Blue Glacier, in an effort to determine climatic trends, among other things. Because of their low altitude, the glaciers in the Olympic Mountains are particularly sensitive to slight changes in temperature and precipitation. This is manifested in expansion or shrinkage of the ice. Thus the ice fields are long-range climatic indicators. During the past century winters have become somewhat milder and drier, and this has resulted in a general recession of glaciers around the world. However, recent studies made by the University of Washington indicate that most glaciers in the Pacific Northwest have stopped receding and are either stabilized or growing. This change is apparently the result of a trend which began about 1944 toward a cooler, wetter climate. It would be premature, however, to forecast an end to the long period of glacial recession, because this growth may be only a minor interruption in the major trend which has threatened glaciers with extinction.

Rivers of the Olympics

The drainage pattern of the Olympics is radial, partly because the mountains constitute a domelike uplift with the highest elevations toward the center and lower peaks trailing along the periphery. The rivers spiral outward from the interior, tending to curve counter-clockwise as they flow through the mountains, then straightening their courses as they cross the surrounding lowlands.

The rivers originate in glaciers and snowfields on the higher peaks toward the center of the mountains, where a multitude of tributary brooks and creeks tumble down from the snow-covered heights, sometimes plunging over cliffs in ribbon-like cascades. The most spectacular waterfalls are in the isolated Enchanted Valley, near the headwaters of the Quinault's east fork.

In their first few miles the rivers descend sharply to the bottoms of deep, narrow canyons, there to flow rapidly toward the sea amid obstructions of boulders and drift logs. The canyon floors are usually only a few hundred feet above sea level, but the mountainsides rise sharply, reaching elevations of five thousand or six thousand feet along ridge crests a mile or two away. Farther downstream the valleys broaden to form deep troughs. These are usually v-shaped, but valleys like the Hoh and Queets are more spacious, displaying the u-shape, level floor and truncated lateral spurs characteristic of glaciated country. On the relatively wide bottomlands of these glacial valleys the rivers meander, as on a flood plain, and display braided channels.

None of the rivers can be called large, but they are powerful by reason of the tremendous quantities of water they carry from the mountains to the sea. During the winter they are sustained by heavy rainfall, in summer by melting snowfields. Because the rivers flow steadily, the pioneers were prone to believe a great lake existed in the center of the mountains. With the exception of the glacial streams, the rivers are of unsurpassed clarity.

Although the rivers flow rapidly, they seldom flood, but do so occasionally, especially after unusually heavy rains. Then bridges may be washed out, log jams carried to sea, trails obliterated and roads destroyed.

The rivers on the peninsula flow toward the four compass points. Those flowing to the north, east and west originate deep in the mountainous interior, but the streams that trace their way southward, and are tributary to the Chehalis River, originate along the southern flank of the mountains. The most important of these tributaries are the Humptulips, the Wynoochee and the Satsop.

Five rivers flow eastward through the mountains and debouch into Hood Canal—the Skokomish, Hamma Hamma, Duckabush, Dosewallips and Quilcene. Because the mountains drop more sharply on the east, these streams are shorter than those flowing north and west, and also are more tortuous, winding as they do in the depths of narrow, close-walled canyons. They break the continuity of the eastern ridges, giving to the Olympics their jagged appearance as viewed from Puget Sound.

The rivers flowing west to the Pacific—the Quinault, Queets, Hoh, Bogachiel and Soleduck—travel a longer distance, over shallower gradients. The Hoh and Queets originate in the glaciers of Mount Olympus; the others have their sources in glaciers or snowfields of nearby high peaks. A few miles from the coast the Bogachiel and Soleduck unite to form the short Quillayute.

Only two rivers of consequence flow northward through the mountains to the Strait of Juan de Fuca. The Elwha, perhaps the best known stream on the peninsula, drains the vast central portion of the Olympics; the Dungeness, together with its large tributary, the Graywolf, flows through the northeastern part of the mountains.

The Mount Olympus Range

Mount Olympus, focal point of the tangle of mountains, stands near the geographic center of the peninsula, about twenty-five miles south of the Strait of Juan de Fuca and slightly northwest from the center of the Olympics. Not quite eight thousand feet high and surpassed in elevation by more than a hundred other Washington peaks, it outranks most in grandeur with its glittering mantle of ice. Together with Mount Tom, Olympus dominates the rugged chain of spurs, crags and pinnacles known as the Mount Olympus Range.

Although it is the peninsula's loftiest peak, Olympus is hidden from distant viewing by intervening high peaks. Thus it is not well known outside mountaineering circles. However, climbers have long considered it one of Washington's major summits. In all the United States, excluding Alaska, only Mount Rainier and Mount Baker (in the Cascade Range) have larger icecaps.

Olympus is actually a massive cluster of rock peaks that poke upward through a sprawling cloak of ice. This ice appears, at the end of summer, when thinnest, to be several hundred feet thick. The greatest known depth of the ice is nine hundred feet, on the Blue Glacier near the base of the icefall.

The heaviest precipitation on the peninsula occurs on Mount Olympus—upward of two hundred and fifty inches near the summit, mostly in the form of snow. The resulting glaciers are the largest in the Olympics, and several vary in length from one to three miles.

Several of the rock peaks that thrust upward from the ice fields, thus constituting the mountain's summit, approach the eight thousand foot level, far above the fingers of fog crawling through surrounding canyons. The highest is West Peak (7976), a wedge of broken, weather-torn rock. Nearly as high are Middle Peak (7930) and East or Sphinx Peak (7780). Other high points include Athena or South Peak, and several false summits collectively known as Five Fingers Peak.

The icecap on Olympus covers more than twelve square miles, about forty per cent of the perpetual ice in the Olympic Mountains. The largest glaciers—the Blue, White and Hoh—flow down the mountain's northern and eastern slopes and contain two-thirds of the ice. On the sunnier southern and western slopes are smaller glaciers—the Jeffers, Hubert and Humes—covering slightly more than three square miles. The Ice River and Mud glaciers, together with several unnamed ice fields, lie in cirques recessed between the major ice streams.

The glaciers are deeply entrenched in the mountain's flanks and separated by high combs of rock. They display crevasses, icefalls and other features characteristic of the larger ice masses found in Alaska and Canada. The forests of the lower slopes extend upward almost to the edge of the ice and, in some places, grow above the ice on steep ridges.

In winter the upper part of the mountain is often torn by winds exceeding a hundred miles per hour, accompanied by heavy snow. During the winter of 1957–58 an International

Geophysical Year team remained on the Snow Dome, fifteen hundred feet below the summit, and measured precipitation averaging an inch a day during the three month period beginning in mid-December. This was snow, usually heavy and dense since it fell at a relatively high temperature. The total snowfall on the Snow Dome during this three months exceeded forty feet. The resulting snowpack after consolidation and packing was about twenty feet, with depths of thirty to thirty-five feet in the accumulation basin above the Blue Glacier.

West of Olympus rises the bulk of remote, seldom-climbed Mount Tom (7048), and beyond it to the southwest the Mount Olympus Range is studded with unnamed glaciers and capped by nameless peaks that have never been climbed. Viewed from the summit of Olympus, the range appears to be a solid wall of rock, ice and snow, almost bare of trees. This is one of the wildest, most inaccessible parts of the Olympic Mountains.

The Bailey Range

Closely linked with Olympus is the Bailey Range, a long, curving chain of snow-capped summits named in 1890 by the Press Expedition for William E. Bailey, proprietor of the *Seattle Press*. The range constitutes the divide between the Elwha and Hoh rivers and extends from Bear Pass in a northerly direction, unbroken as far as Cat Creek. Beyond this stream are lesser peaks, among them the sharp crests of Cat Creek Ridge. Both sides of the range plunge abruptly. The western slope, together with the Olympus massif, walls in the upper Hoh canyon, and the eastern side is nearly as precipitous, leading down to the Elwha and Goldie rivers. At its southern terminus the Bailey Range ties in with the Mount Olympus Range and other peaks near Bear Pass, topographic center of the Olympic Mountains.

More than a dozen peaks in the Bailey Range exceed six thousand feet elevation. This is not high, but the range is nonetheless impressive, for the peaks rise more than a mile above the deep valley of the Hoh and remain snow-clad well into summer. Mount Carrie (7020) is the highest point. Other important summits are Mount Fitzhenry (6105), Stephen Peak (6430), Mount Ferry (6157), Mount Pulitzer or Snagtooth (6283), Mount Childs (6205) and Mount Scott (5905), an outlier, plus several unnamed peaks approaching seven thousand feet.

Snowfall is very heavy on the Bailey Range, probably second only to Mount Olympus. Because the axis of the range trends generally from northwest to southeast, the southwestern slopes face the prevailing winds and much of the snow is blown to the shaded northeastern side. Consequently, except upon the plateau-like southern part of the range, the larger snowfields and glaciers are found on the leeward side. None of the glaciers are named. The largest, more than a mile long, occupies a cirque on the eastern flanks of Mount Carrie. Avalanche paths scar the steeper mountainsides, and small lakes dot subalpine basins almost encircled by the peaks. Probably the best known tarn is Cream Lake. In the summer, large numbers of elk frequent these basins.

The Bailey Range is isolated, wild and rugged. The Press Expedition called it the "backbone of the Olympics," an apt description. These peaks do lie toward the center of the mountains. Because of the long slope of foothills to the west, however, the range is not located in the center of the mass of higher peaks. Instead, together with the Mount Olympus Range, it guards the western frontier of this region of high, open country. Although travel is not difficult, the range is visited only by the seasoned hiker because of the necessity of strenuous cross-country backpacking beyond the trails. This region constitutes the primitive core of Olympic National Park, and most persons who have visited the range feel it should remain free of man-made trails and other developments.

Elwha Basin Peaks

South of the Bailey Range a cluster of precipitous, glaciated peaks surrounds the Elwha Basin and abuts the eastern terminus of the Mount Olympus Range. These peaks do not form a range, but are broken into clumps by the headwaters of the Elwha, Quinault and Goldie rivers. Snow-covered, wild and windswept, they lack the continuity of the Bailey and Olympus ranges.

Located near the center of the Olympic Mountains, this area is inaccessible to the weekend hiker. However, the peaks have been climbed on numerous occasions. In 1907 The Mountaineers held their first summer outing in the central Olympics, and most of these peaks were first climbed at that time.

These are mountains individual in character, not easily mistaken for others. Their elevation is comparable to the Bailey Range. Because of heavy snowfall, small glaciers and perpetual snowfields adorn the peaks. The loftiest summits are Mount Queets (6480), Mount Meany (6695), Mount Seattle (6246), Mount Dana (6209) and Mount Christie (6177 and 6122). Lesser peaks include Mount Barnes (6041 and 5993), Mount Frazier (5428) and Mount Wilder (5925).

Mount Anderson and the Burke Range

A conspicuous landmark, Mount Anderson occupies a nearly central position in the mountains several miles east of the Elwha group of peaks. This lofty block is the nucleus of a north-south extension of high ridges that tend, pincer-like, to embrace the western Olympics. The southern arm of this crescent-shaped band is the Burke Range; the northern, a series of high, unbroken ridges that extend many miles and finally terminate as Hurricane Ridge and the Elwha River Range.

The peaks and spurs of Mount Anderson are well exposed to storms sweeping inland from the sea. Winter snowfall is therefore heavy, and the mountain is covered with glaciers and snowfields. Next to Olympus, this peak has the most extensive glacial system in these mountains, and because it marks the hydrographic apex of the Olympics, meltwater from its snowpack flows to the three seaward sides of the peninsula. The peak is situated at the head of the Quinault's east fork and is nearly encircled by two branches of the Dosewallips. The West and East peaks (7365 and 7321) are the highest points. They are separated by Flypaper Pass (6500), the col between the Eel and Anderson glaciers.

Mount Anderson has been extensively eroded by ice. Several active glaciers scar its rough sides, but the ice has receded greatly from its former extent. The largest glaciers are the Eel and the Anderson, respectively on the northern and southern sides. Each is more than a mile long and nourishes a river. The Eel drains via Silt Creek, a tributary of the Dosewallips. The Anderson serves as the source field of the Quinault's east fork. The other glaciers are much smaller, and are unnamed.

The Burke Range, also called the Anderson Range, extends from Muncaster Mountain (5910) to Diamond Mountain (6800), and includes Mount Anderson. Essentially a high, inaccessible ridge paralleling the East Fork Quinault and capped by a succession of precipitous peaks, the range forms the north wall of Enchanted Valley, noted for its multitude of cascades. In addition to Mount Anderson, important peaks are Crystal Peak (6896), Mount Watterson (6400), Mount Medill (6700), Chimney Peak (6900) and Mount Norton (6319). The range was named in 1890 for Judge Thomas Burke of Seattle.

The massive spur extending northeast from Mount Anderson and dominated by Diamond Mountain and Piro's Spire (6301) is actually a part of the Burke Range. Another spur, also part of the Burke Range, extends from Crystal Peak to Mount Norton. Northward from Mount Anderson a high ridge, with elevations in excess of six thousand feet, continues unbroken to Sentinel Peak, near the headwaters of the Dosewallips.

The Southeastern Crags

Two clusters of rugged peaks comprise the southeastern part of the Olympic Mountains. These peaks are lower than those to the north, but are alpine in character. One cluster tends to encircle the headwaters of the Duckabush River; the other wraps around the upper course of the Hamma Hamma and is, in turn, embraced by the Skokomish's north fork and the midsection of the Duckabush. These peaks are separated from the remainder of the Olympics by the Quinault's east fork and West Creek, a tributary of the Dosewallips.

In spite of their location on the east side of the peninsula, these clusters have a windward orientation and therefore receive heavy snowfall from winter storms sweeping across the mountains from the south. The elevation is low, generally between six thousand and sixty-five hundred feet, resulting in formation of snowfields rather than glaciers. Timberline meadows, dotted with alpine lakes, sprawl over large areas, and the steeper mountainsides are scarred by avalanche paths. The largest of the alpine pools is Heart Lake (sometimes spelled Hart), near the head of the Duckabush.

The highest summits in the group of peaks near the source of the Duckabush River are Mount Steel (6200), Mount Duckabush (6233), Mount Hopper (6114), White Mountain (6412), Mount LaCrosse (6417) and Mount Elklick (6517).

The group of mountains surrounding the upper Hamma Hamma is a jumble of peaks threaded by deep gorges, with perpetual snowfields on northern slopes. Dominant in this cluster is The Brothers (6866 and 6800), a prominent landmark from many points on Puget Sound. Other notable peaks are Bretherton (5960), Mount Lena (5995), Mount Skokomish (6434), Mount Cruiser (6104), Mount Washington (6255), Mount Pershing (6154) and double-peaked Mount Stone (6612 and 6605).

Included in this group is the Sawtooth Range, only three miles long, its picturesque pinnacles and horns rising sharply from green meadows and steep snowfields. Together with The Needles in the Graywolf area, the Sawtooth affords the best rock climbing in the Olympics.

The Inner Northeast Peaks

In the northeastern Olympics, shielded from visibility on the lowlands by other high peaks, is an interesting area containing many unnamed mountains. This region is best known, however, for a cluster of five named peaks surrounding the headwaters of the Dosewallips River. These are Wellesley Peak (6758), Lost Peak (6515), Mount Claywood (6836), Mount Fromme (6650) and Sentinel Peak (6592). Immediately southwest of the latter is a companion peak (6301) sometimes called Sentinel's Sister. Between Fromme and Sentinel lies Hayden Pass (5847), through which a trail passes from the Dosewallips to the Elwha valley.

Northeast of Lost Peak, Cameron Ridge rises far above the Dosewallips valley. The ridge has an average elevation of seven thousand feet and forms the watershed between the upper Dosewallips and the northward flowing Graywolf River and Cameron Creek. The twin summits of McCartney Peak (6784 and 6728), enclosing the Lillian Glacier, constitute the western terminus of the ridge, and Graywolf Pass (6150) marks the eastern end. The ridge has many high points. At its greatest elevation, nearly seventy-two hundred feet above sea level, the ridge is surmounted by jagged, unnamed pinnacles. Below them, on the northern side of the ridge, are the Cameron Glaciers, small ice fields lying in cirques.

Other ridges and spurs extend north and northwest from Cameron Ridge, all dominated by unnamed summits exceeding sixty-five hundred feet elevation.

The Outer Northeast Peaks

Also on the northeastern side of the Olympics is a horseshoe-shaped loop of barren peaks surrounding the upper Dungeness River. These basaltic mountains are among the highest in the Olympics, loftier than the peaks of sedimentary rock, with the lone exception of Olympus. Many of the peaks exceed seven thousand feet elevation; a few approach eight thousand. The group is flanked on the south by the deep valley of the Dosewallips, on the west by Graywolf River.

This area lies on the leeward side of the mountains, thus is protected from winter storms. Precipitation is comparatively light, but the region is far from arid. The snowfall is not heavy enough, however, to produce extensive glaciation, and permanent snowfields are not widespread, most of them occurring on northern slopes. Despite the altitude, only a few small glaciers are present. Instead, lofty barren ridges, high timberlines, and a few alpine lakes are the rule. The lower valleys are forested, but lie largely outside the national park and have been badly scarred by logging operations.

Among the more important peaks of the loop are

Mount Deception (7788), Mount Mystery (7631), Little Mystery (6941), Mount Constance (7743), Inner Constance (7654), Warrior (7300), Buckhorn (6988) and Iron Mountain (6956). A number of peaks are unnamed. Part of the loop is capped by The Needles, a series of rough pinnacles and crags varying in elevation from seventy-three hundred to seventy-six hundred feet, including Mount Clark (7528) and Mount Walkinshaw (7378). Several outliers, all more than six thousand feet high, stand detached. The highest is Mount Fricaba (7134).

Mount Deception is the second highest peak on the peninsula, exceeded only by Olympus. Better known, however, and far more conspicuous is Mount Constance, one of the most beautiful peaks in the Olympic Mountains, with pillow lavas and fierce precipices frequented by mountain goats. Visible from many points on Puget Sound, this peak is often mistaken for Olympus by the uninformed.

The Northern Ridges

Along the northern edge of the Olympics a number of high ridges roughly parallel the Strait of Juan de Fuca. Marine and mountain air mix readily here, for these ridges lie generally within ten miles of the coast and overlook the lowlands. They are heavily timbered below four thousand feet. East of the Elwha the ridges extend into the zone of mountain meadowlands, but those to the west are, for the most part, forested to their summits.

Baldy, Happy Lake and Aurora ridges rise west of the Elwha, and are of moderate height, generally between four and five thousand feet. Happy Lake Ridge exceeds five thousand feet in places, the highest point being Lizard Head (5351). Aurora Ridge parallels the southern shore of Lake Crescent. Mount Storm King (4534), the western terminus of Baldy Ridge, southeast of Lake Crescent, is the best known peak in this area.

East of the Elwha are the Elwha River Range, Hurricane Ridge and Mount Angeles (6454). The latter stands only seven miles from tidewater, thus is visible for miles from the Strait of Juan de Fuca.

Hurricane Ridge, probably the best known part of the

Olympic Mountains, overlooks the strait as well as the mountains toward the peninsula's interior. The ridge is noted for its smooth slopes and sweeping meadowlands, similar to the land east of the Cascade Mountains. In late summer the brown, rolling meadows appear to be, and are, an almost arid land. Hikers traversing the ridge at that time find it difficult to believe they are in the snowy Olympics.

The general elevation of Hurricane Ridge is between five thousand and six thousand feet in the west, and from fifty-five hundred to sixty-five hundred feet in the east. The highest point is Elk Mountain (6764).

Chapter II

The Botanical Pattern

The Infinite Forest

The Olympic Peninsula amazed the first European explorers who sailed along its coast, for the land appeared to be covered by endless primeval forests. Spanish seafarers called the region "an infinity of trees," and those who came later were equally impressed. Today, after tremendous destruction from cutting and burning, forests still dominate the land and extend over a much larger area than do the meadows, snowfields, glaciers and barren country of the mountainous interior.

The densest forests grow upon the lowlands—the bottomlands, benches and low ridges between the mountains and the seas. Dark stands also sweep up the mountainsides, the trees gradually diminishing in density and height with increasing altitude until at timberline the trees relinquish sovereignty over the land to low-growing plants. Here clumps of thick-skirted subalpine species are scattered over the grassy meadows, and beyond the tree line are tundra-like meadows, bleak cliffs, snowfields and glaciers.

Heavy snowfall in the mountains keeps the timberlines at relatively low altitudes, varying from four to six thousand feet

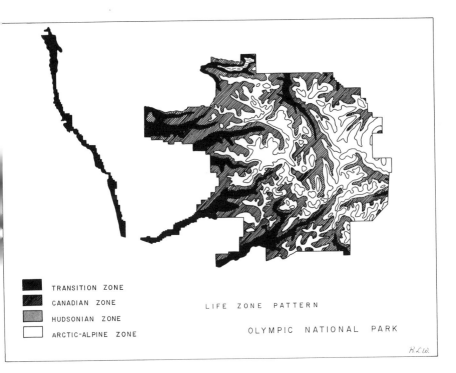

TRANSITION ZONE
CANADIAN ZONE
HUDSONIAN ZONE
ARCTIC-ALPINE ZONE

LIFE ZONE PATTERN

OLYMPIC NATIONAL PARK

H.L.W.

above sea level, but generally between five thousand and fifty-five hundred. Because the snows are heavier on the windward side of the mountains, timberlines are lower on the western slope.

On the margins of the forest, ocean shoreline and timberline in the high mountains, the trees struggle to exist and are often gnarled and weatherbeaten. Strong winds have left their mark. "Wind shear" has torn limbs from the coastal trees, sometimes stripping away all branches except those that point to the lee of the prevailing westerlies. A similar condition exists among the tenacious trees found on the crests of windswept mountain ridges. In addition, barren soils and the harshness of the winter climate at higher altitudes, with its low temperatures and deep snows, have stunted and distorted the trees at the upper limits of the forest.

Most of the virgin forest viewed by the pioneers has

been cut, especially on the accessible lowlands. The logged-off land is now covered with farms and second-growth forest, or else lies bleak and barren. Huge, blackened stumps stand as desolate reminders of the forest's former glory, and vividly illustrate the power of man to alter the surface of the earth. In fact, two factors have exerted enormous influence on the flora of the peninsula—the Ice Age, which ended some twenty thousand years ago, and the recent invasion of the white man. Only time will reveal which has been the more destructive.

Life Zones

In the mountains dramatic changes of climate often occur within short distances, the temperatures becoming more subject to extremes with increasing altitude, the rainfall patterns varying with exposure to moisture-laden winds. This is true not only in the temperate belts but also in arctic and tropical regions. Accompanying the climatic differences are conspicuous variations in the flora, fauna and general appearance of the landscape.

Geographers call this phenomenon "altitudinal zonation." More often, however, the various patterns noted are referred to simply as "life zones." These are natural biotic units with their own distinctive kinds of plants and animals. In reality, they are variations of the latitudinal zones present on the continents, thus comparable in many ways to the variations observed at different latitudes on the earth. As the altitude increases in the mountains, temperatures decrease and the climate changes radically. Sometimes this is gradual, more often abrupt. The greater the altitude the stronger the resemblance to conditions of northerly latitudes, until in high mountains, even in the tropics, the landscape becomes arctic in nature.

Climatic differences, especially temperature variations, create noticeable changes in the floral pattern. Certain groups of species tend to dominate each zone, within which exists a general sameness of flora, fauna and topography, and this is primarily the result of climatic similarity. In fact, some plant and animal species adapted to the climatic conditions of a particular altitude apparently are unable to extend their range to higher or lower elevations because of limiting factors of temperature, precipitation or exposure.

Seven "life zones" or latitudinal belts occur in North America. These are the Tropical, Lower Austral, Upper Austral, Transition, and the three Boreal zones—Canadian, Hudsonian and Arctic. In mountain regions the latter is called the Arctic-Alpine. Four of the seven zones occur on the Olympic Peninsula—those corresponding roughly to the various latitudinal belts north of 45° latitude. The *Transition* (humid phase) occurs from sea level to altitudes of about 1500, occasionally 2000, feet; the *Canadian* ranges from the upper limits of the Transition to approximately 3500 feet; the *Hudsonian* is found generally between 3500 and 5000 feet; and the *Arctic-Alpine* reaches upward from about 5000 feet to the summits of the highest peaks, nearly 8000 feet above the sea. On the peninsula the three latter zones are confined to the mountains, because the surrounding lowlands lie wholly within the Transition zone.

The boundaries are somewhat arbitrary because the zones actually blend into each other in an irregular manner and lack sharp lines of demarcation. However, conditions within a given zone are fairly distinct, with little overlapping into adjacent areas. The irregularity of the boundaries is best illustrated by timberline, the division between the Hudsonian and Arctic-Alpine zones. The subalpine trees of the Hudsonian extend farther up the ridges than in the valleys between, the dividing line thus being sinuous rather than straight.

In the Olympic Mountains a thousand foot gain in elevation is roughly comparable to three hundred miles difference in latitude at sea level so far as climate and vegetation are concerned. Thus in climbing a peak from river bottom to summit, the mountaineer experiences a variation in landscape equivalent to a sea level journey from Puget Sound to the Arctic Circle.

Within Olympic National Park a fine balance exists between the respective life zones. Transition zone forests cover approximately fourteen per cent of the main body of the park (excluding the ocean strip and the Queets Corridor), Canadian zone forests forty-one per cent, the Hudsonian zone forests and meadows comprise thirty-one per cent, and the rocks, ice and snow of the Arctic-Alpine zone about fourteen per cent.

Botanists have long been interested in the Olympics because of their isolation from other mountains. In the latter part of the nineteenth century and early twentieth century, they made extensive studies of the flora, but found fewer endemic species than had been anticipated.

The Transition Zone

The only phase of the Transition zone represented on the peninsula is the *humid*, which prevails at low altitudes along the Pacific coast from northern California into southeastern Alaska. Luxuriant virgin forests once covered this entire region, but fire and lumbering operations have destroyed most of the big trees. Only remnants of virgin forest still exist, occupying chiefly the remote, relatively inaccessible regions. On the peninsula the finest stands are found in the foothills and valleys, particularly on the seaward slope of the Olympic Mountains.

This life zone, the lowest on the peninsula, contains seventy per cent of the flora and covers about two and one-half million acres of land surrounding the mountains. Within the mountains this zone is restricted to narrow fingers of lowland, the bottomland along the larger rivers.

In this zone of low elevation, characterized by abundant rainfall and mild temperatures throughout the year, the vegetation of the Pacific Northwest exhibits its greatest luxuriance. Not only are the trees taller and of greater girth than those at higher elevations, but also many kinds of shrubs and wild flowering plants are present, including numerous evergreen species.

When forest growth occurs on "new" land—i.e., where glacial ice has retreated, or where the previous vegetative cover has been destroyed by fire, wind or other cause—a succession of species takes place until the forest reaches a level of stability known as the "climax." Such a forest then dominates the landscape until it, in turn, is destroyed by some natural phenomenon. On the peninsula two climax forests are found within the Transition zone. The *spruce-hemlock* type covers the lowlands between the mountains and the sea. Inland from the coast is the *hemlock-cedar* climax, and associated with it are extensive sub-climax forests of *Douglas fir*, the great timber tree of the Pacific Northwest.

In the ecological cycle, the Douglas fir forests are the stage of forest succession immediately preceding the *hemlock-cedar* climax. Because of its intolerance to shade, Douglas fir develops on open, sunny areas. Upon reaching maturity, however, the stands of fir gradually suffer from encroachment by other species, particularly hemlock. Nevertheless, before lumbering operations began on the peninsula, Douglas fir probably composed seventy-five per cent of the low altitude forest. Today this species dominates the sub-climax forests on the eastern slopes of the mountains. Some splendid stands of Douglas fir are also found on the seaward side, but they are not extensive.

The *spruce-hemlock* climax forest is restricted to the "fog belt" between the mountains and the sea. The eastern limits of the spruce are the heads of the deep mountain valleys which drain to the Pacific. Sitka spruce and western hemlock, the dominant trees, thrive in the mild, wet climate. Associated with them are western red cedar, lodgepole pine and some Douglas fir.

Although the ubiquitous hemlock is abundant throughout the peninsula, this tree reaches its best development where the rainfall is greatest. The spruce, however, exhibits a definite preference for the valleys facing the rain and fog of the sea winds, and is seldom found more than fifty miles from the ocean or where the yearly rainfall is less than seventy inches. On the other hand, western red cedar, also a moisture loving species, grows in all parts of the peninsula, particularly on wet lowlands and swampy places. However, the most extensive stands of cedar are located near the coast.

In the *spruce-hemlock* forests the most common shrubs are willow, elder, salmonberry, salal, currant, and the blue, red and false huckleberries. Oregon grape, an attractive evergreen with prickly, holly-like foliage, often covers the forest floor, adding a festive touch.

Inland from the inward limits of the *spruce-hemlock* forest is the *hemlock-cedar* climax, which covers lowlands north, east and south of the mountains, and climbs the lower slopes to elevations of 1500 to 2000 feet. The dominant trees are western hemlock and western red cedar. Associated species include western white pine, western yew and grand fir, one of the true firs. Within this climax forest are remnants of ancient Douglas fir forests that once were dominant.

The most noticeable shrubs of the *hemlock-cedar* and Douglas fir forests are rhododendron, salal, Oregon grape, Scouler willow, Oregon boxwood, Devil's-club, wild rose, currant, red evergreen and false huckleberries.

Numerous deciduous trees flourish in the Transition zone, primarily on bottomlands where they mingle with the larger conifers. Most abundant is red alder, a short-lived species which monopolizes new land, often forming pure stands on abandoned stream channels. In the mountains, presence of a lichen often causes the alders to have bark with a bleached appearance, similar to that of beech trees. Bigleaf maple usually grows in small groves along the streams, but sometimes as isolated specimens. The largest deciduous tree is the black cottonwood, which approaches two hundred feet in height and ten feet in diameter. In the drier eastern Olympics, Pacific dogwood splashes conspicuously white in May, the cascara buckthorn grows singly or in clumps on the bottomlands, and the crooked limbs of the red-barked madrona brighten the conifer-covered mountainsides.

Undergrowth along bottomland stream banks often forms a wall-like barrier, sometimes difficult to penetrate. This ground covering consists of vine maple, swamp currant, Indian plum, willow, and the attractive Devil's-club, with large leaves, poisonous thorns, and clusters of red berries.

Wild flowering plants grow profusely in this zone. Early blooming species include the white trillium, starflowers and waxen-gold buttercups. Skunk cabbage colors the swamps with streaks of yellow and fills the air with a pungent odor. The lowland trails are sometimes lined with unbroken expanses of the lavishly blooming twinflower, its dainty pink, bell-like flowers exuding an elusive fragrance. Other plants common to the damp lowlands include lily of the valley, Solomon's-seal, deerfoot vanillaleaf, cowparsnip, bleeding heart, longtube twinflower, beadruby and fireweed. The colorful spires of foxglove—an exotic which has adapted itself to openings in the forest—glow against the green background.

Many ferns thrive in the shaded dampness, often forming unbroken carpets beneath the trees. Among these are the western sword fern, the kind collectors gather for the Christmas trade. Throughout the "rain forests" it grows luxuriantly on moist hillsides. Also plentiful, but inconspicuous because of its smallness, is the deer fern, so named because the spore frond bears a resemblance to deer antlers. The tiny fronds are bright green, and the tall fruiting stalk or spore frond reaches heights of eighteen to twenty-four inches. The deer fern is strictly a forest plant and disappears from land where the trees have been cut. Western maidenhair ferns decorate damp clefts with their fragile greenery, massing themselves along moist stream banks, or covering rock walls through which the mountain streams plunge, spraying as they fall. The fronds of this delicately-structured fern have been compared to the chubby fingers of a baby's hand; the name is derived not from its delicate beauty, however, but from the black, hairlike roots.

Less common ferns finding a habitat among the lowland forests include the brake fern or bracken, occasionally found growing head high along the trails; the lady fern; the swamp fern, with circular tufts and fronds similar to those of the bracken; the licorice-root fern, whose home is mossy rocks, tree trunks and fallen trees; and the oak fern, with fronds resembling oak leaves, and whose total height seldom exceeds twelve inches.

Two important vegetal variations in the Transition zone merit special attention. The first is a very narrow strip along the Pacific coast; the second, the famous "rain forests" of the western Olympic valleys.

The Narrow Ocean Belt

Bordering the Pacific Ocean from Cape Flattery south to the vicinity of Point Grenville are steep bluffs and cliffs varying in height from fifty to three hundred feet. The cliff faces are often bare, their crests banded by storm-dwarfed trees, usually spruce or hemlock, sometimes cedar, occasionally lodgepole pine. Buffeted by the fierce winds of winter gales, the trees appear to have been carefully trimmed on their windward sides, but are ragged and unkempt to the leeward.

The dense coastal undergrowth is composed of shrubby species such as crab apple, blackberry, salal, false huckleberry, evergreen huckleberry and salmonberry. On the tide-soaked rocks are found surf and eel grass, and the beaches are often strewn with brown and red seaweed and the giant kelp. In swampy areas back from the immediate coastline, sphagnum, rushes and skunk cabbage grow profusely.

In sand dune areas along the coast are found a range of small grasses which maintain a meager existence. These include rye, beach, and beard grasses, and such plants as sand verbena, pepper cress, sand-bur, lupine, and morning glory.

The "Rain Forests"

The Olympic forest attains its most spectacular development on the western flanks of the mountains where the spruce-hemlock and hemlock-cedar climax forests merge. Nurtured by an annual rainfall exceeding twelve feet, and protected by the mountain barrier from temperature extremes, the forest has here achieved a luxuriance comparable to the vegetation of wet equatorial lands and ecologists term it a temperate zone rain forest.*

This rain forest, unique in North America, is confined to the narrow river bottoms where giant Douglas fir, Sitka spruce and western red cedar have been growing for hundreds of years. The oldest of these primeval giants were living when King John signed the Magna Carta. The largest exceed twelve or thirteen feet in diameter, and the tallest tower three hundred feet or more above the ground. Most of the trees, however, are from three to ten feet in diameter, and heights of two hundred fifty feet are average.

With trunks set close and their branches interlocking, the firs lift rough, wind-torn crowns high above the earth. The

* Similar forests are found in southern Chile and in New Zealand. Technically, "rain forest" is a term given to tropical forests where, throughout the year, temperatures are uniformly high and precipitation heavy, the rainfall distributed more or less evenly, so no marked dry season exists. The term "rain forest" is without precise definition as applied to temperate zone forests.

giant shafts, resembling fluted columns, are frequently free of limbs for one hundred to one hundred fifty feet. The massive, bell-bottomed spruces sometimes grow as tall as the firs and often support shaggy, spreading crowns, with limbs closer to the ground. Unlike the firs, the spruces are characterized by pronounced root flares. This gives a deceptive impression of sturdiness when, in fact, they are shallow rooted and easily subject to windthrow if neighboring trees are removed. The cedars are also heavily buttressed and of large diameter, but are usually of lesser height.

The conifers overshadow smaller deciduous trees, although the bigleaf maples and black cottonwoods often reach large proportions. Below the cottonwoods, maples and alders is still another understory of shrubs and low growing trees. Most prominent here is the vine maple, with its crooked and sprawling limblike trunks.

The rain forest owes its strange appearance primarily to thick growths of mosses, liverworts, ferns and lichens. These adorn the trees and cover the ground with a resilient carpet, softly outlining the forest. In some of the valleys the forest aisles are cloaked with yellow-green and brownish lichen, and the fallen trees—the "nurse logs" for new forest growth—are upholstered with mosses and oxalis. Tree trunks are cushioned with moss; almost every branch is draped with long, pendent festoons. Tropical-looking ferns grow in profusion—on the ground, on fallen trees and on tree limbs a hundred feet above the winding footpaths.

Botanists have estimated that more than one hundred fifty varieties of mosses thrive in the dampness of the Olympic rain forest. The colors are varied: green, gray, golden-yellow, emerald and brown. Some kinds are feathery, forming plumelike sprays; others resemble ferns. Most conspicuous is selaginella, a clubmoss with reindeer-horn sprigs. Dark draperies of this plant decorate the bigleaf maples and the slender arches of the vine maples.

The mosses and ferns generally prefer deciduous trees to conifers as a habitat, and exhibit a decided affinity for the maples. On sunny days the golden-green of the mosses contrasts vividly with the bright green of the maple leaves, and dark moss pads accentuate the whiteness of alder trunks in dense stands on the river bars. Lichens occur commonly along water courses, or on rocky outcroppings. Usually they are dull shades of gray, umber or tan. Lichens also beard the hemlock, spruce and cedar trees and, together with the mosses, cover the forest floor, thus enabling the hiker to walk through an unbroken stillness.

The Canadian Zone

The somber evergreen forests of the Canadian life zone clothe the lower mountainsides constituting the steep valley sidewalls rising above the river bottoms. The vegetation here resembles that found at sea level at the latitude of southern Canada. Heavy forest growth often masks rough, precipitous slopes, causing terrain broken by cliffs and ravines to appear deceptively smooth when viewed from a distance.

The upper and lower limits of this zone are indistinct and irregular, varying according to local conditions. The lower boundary occurs anywhere from one thousand to two thousand feet above sea level, but most generally at fifteen hundred feet where the Canadian zone forests merge imperceptibly with those of the Transition zone. The upper limit is generally about thirty-five hundred feet. Sometimes this zone extends higher on slopes and ridges, lower where tongues of subalpine growth extend down the intervening valleys because cold air from the snowfields descends the defiles.

Most of the trees are conifers. Pacific silver fir and western hemlock form the climax forests, but generous sprinklings of western white pine, Douglas fir and western red cedar are also present. One of the most common trees is the Pacific silver fir, a true fir with upright purple cones that are never shed, but sometimes cut loose by squirrels. The straight, columnar hemlocks grow 150 to 250 feet tall, often in nearly pure, closely packed stands. Many rise free of branches for half their height, and their crowns create a canopy so dense that even in summer the light reaching the forest floor is soft and indirect, and the air is cool, fragrant and moist. In fact, this evergreen covering is so thick it intercepts the first winter snows, and they often melt, on warm succeeding days, never having reached the ground.

The Canadian zone is heavily forested in its lower levels, but higher up the trees become smaller and the stands thinner. On the steeper mountainsides are stands of pistol-butted trees which grew that way as a result of ground creep or, more often, because heavy snow burdened them when they were young. Mosses and ferns cover the cliffs above, from which the snow avalanches down.

Undergrowth in the Canadian zone forests is sparser than in the Transition zone, and the forest floor is more apt to be open. However, a wide variety of shrubs and numerous saprophytic plants grow upon the ground. Vine maple flourishes in moist spots, salal and blue and black huckleberry grow thickly in many places, and the Sitka alder and Devil's-club are found along streams. Other shrubs include the mountain ash, ocean spray and salmonberry. In the drier eastern part of the mountains rhododendrons bloom lavishly in late spring. Low-growing plants include the bunchberry, violet, pipsissewa and the rare phantom orchid. Several species of wintergreen exhibit fragrant waxen blossoms along snow-fed streams; white and green bog-orchids bloom in marshy places. One of the most spectacular plants is bear grass, its tall white plumes a striking feature in the upper parts of this zone where the forest is sometimes broken by open glades.

The saprophytic plants reach their greatest abundance in the Canadian zone. Among them are the Indian pipe, coral-roots, pinesap and the barber pole. The shelf-like bracket fungus grows on the trunks of dead trees. Usually it is cream-colored, but sometimes displays brilliant shades of reddish orange.

The silent forests of this life zone are frequently considered a zoological desert. Although animal life is less abundant than on the bottomlands below or the meadows above, many species of birds and small animals do make their homes here, among them woodpeckers, owls, thrushes, grouse, chipmunks and Douglas squirrels. The elk herds of the Olympics are transient visitors, for they must pass through this zone when traveling from their summer home in the high country to the lowlands where they spend the winter.

The Hudsonian Zone

In the Olympic Mountains the Hudsonian zone usually occurs between thirty-five hundred and five thousand feet. This belt occupies the summits of the lower peaks and ridges, and the "shoulders" of the higher mountains. This, the highest timbered zone, is not heavily forested. Primarily this is a region of luxuriant meadows, subalpine forests, glacial lakes and small swamps and bogs, markedly similar to the sea level pattern at the latitude of Hudson Bay.

The scenic beauty of the subalpine forests is outstanding. They have little commercial value, but protect the watersheds by retarding heavy snow melt runoffs which otherwise would seriously erode the thin mountain soils. Few natural openings are found below four thousand feet in these forests, which blend gradually into the denser stands of lower elevations. Throughout most of the Hudsonian zone, however, the forest is broken by open meadows edged by scattered clusters of spire-pointed trees.

The distinctive trees of this zone are all conifers, principally subalpine fir, mountain hemlock and Alaska cedar. Many are bearded with brownish-yellow lichen. The mountain hemlock is essentially a timberline tree, associated with subalpine fir and frequently found on the northern slopes of exposed ridges. Mountain juniper, more a shrub than a tree, sprawls across rocky slopes and ridges, and extends above the upper limits of this zone. Pacific silver fir and western white pine are common near the lower margin of this zone.

The trees growing at this altitude have adapted themselves well to the environment. The subalpine firs and mountain hemlocks grow straight and rigid, and thus are resistant to breakage from the deep winter snows. The Alaska cedars, however, are limber, and shed the snow after allowing it to accumulate to a certain depth. The yellow-green foliage of this tree droops in long, limp streamers from branches that curve gracefully.

Timberline is the border between this zone and the treeless Arctic-Alpine zone. Here the clusters of firs and hemlocks give way to individual, wind-torn specimens that cling precariously to rocky, storm-swept ridges and ledges. These lone trees have fought hard for survival, and often are twisted into grotesque shapes. Contorted trees, their growth stunted by deep snow, thin rocky soils and winter cold, may be centuries old. Some are only a few inches in diameter, and no taller than a child. On exposed ridges the trees tend to become prostrate, with low matted branches spreading along the ground.

Numerous shrubs grow in the Hudsonian zone. Willows and slide alder crowd the stream banks; blueberry and huckleberry bushes cover many slopes and ridges. Other shrubs found in abundance include white and red mountainheath, mountain currant, spirea, kinnikinnick and mountain azalea. Also present is the mountain ash, usually a shrub but sometimes assuming the size of a small tree.

Most of the meadows, the characteristic trademark of this zone, are not found upon the ridge tops. More often they occupy flat basins or depressions in the mountainsides, and commonly extend into the Arctic-Alpine zone, well above timberline, right up to the bare rock and ice. Snow covers the meadows for eight or nine months of the year, and after it melts the lands become richly carpeted with grasses and ferns. Grasses grow profusely along the margins of lakes and bordering rocky streams. Ferns found in the meadows include the delicate bladder fern, the parsley fern, cliff brake, twisted sword fern, lace fern, and the holly or narrow sword fern.

Splendid as the subalpine trees, grassy meadows, azure lakes and snowfields are, they are climaxed by the riot of wild flowering plants that bloom with a sudden rush at the height of the brief summer season. Although wildflowers are found at all elevations in the mountains, lining valley trails and clinging to crevices in high cliffs, they reach their glory in the meadowlands. Here the floral display attains its peak—usually in late July and early August—when hundreds of kinds blossom, exhibiting every color and hue, and flooding the mountainsides with vivid color.

The heavy snows protect the wild flowering plants from the winter cold and provide moisture in the spring and summer. Nurtured by the long summer daylight, the plants grow profusely and with compelling intensity. The flowers bloom first at the lower elevations, then appear on higher slopes as the season progresses and the snowdrifts recede.

Some ninety-five genera of wild flowering plants grow in this zone. With the single exception of *polygonum minimum*, a member of the buckwheat family, they are all perennials. The fawnlilies, both the white avalanche and the glacier lily, bloom beside the melting snowbanks, even pushing their stems upward through thin layers of snow. Great masses of these flowers cover the open meadows. Later, when most of the snow has disappeared, lupine and scarlet paintedcup streak the mountainsides with blue and red, displaying a bright welter of color. However, the lupine is the characteristic flower of the high country in late summer. Conspicuous on open slopes are the creamy-white blossoms of the pine lily—also known as bear or squaw grass. The flowers, borne at the ends of tall spikes, are greenish toward the bottom.

Interspersed among the grasses and sedges are many others that compete for attention. Among them are buttercups, violets, shooting stars, anemones, bluebells, daisies, monkey flowers, elephanthead, asters, blue gentian, larkspur, phlox, columbine, goldenrod, mountain buckwheat and douglasia. Particularly attractive are the ribbed leaves of the false hellebore; the white-and-gold globeflower, with its maple-like leaves; the rich blue blossoms of the dwarf pentstemon; and the white, starlike flowers, and leathery green leaves of the saxifrage.

Other flowering plants abundant in this zone include the sedum, usually noted on rocky outcroppings where its orange blooms add a touch of brightness; the purple campion, found in mossy clumps alongside the perpetual ice of glaciers; the Columbia lily, a splash of brilliant orange; the marshmarigold, washed by the spray of cascades; and the pioneer violet, bleeding heart, fireweed and alpine speedwell.

Four of the plants which grow in this zone are found only in the Olympics—two varieties of paintedcup, a locoweed and an agoseris.

The Arctic-Alpine Zone

The Arctic-Alpine, the highest life zone in the Olympic Mountains, lies above the timberline. The lower limit is variable, generally around five thousand feet, and the zone extends upward to the tops of the loftiest crags.

This is a region of tundra-like meadows intermingled among permanent snowfields, glaciers, cliffs, and rocky, barren country. Most of the year this inhospitable region lies under a deep blanket of snow, and appears as desolate and isolated as the polar regions. During the winter even the mountain goats forsake the high cliffs and move to lower elevations.

Plant growth is sparse due to shallow soils and the short growing season that results from the snow, cold and constant wind. Night frosts occur even during the summer, and the only plants that survive are those able to withstand freezing temperatures. Consequently, fewer species are found in this zone than in the Hudsonian, with its more favorable conditions for plant growth. The plants, all low-growing perennials, only a few of which are evergreen, are mostly hardy alpine grasses, sedges, rushes, and a few low-growing shrubs and flowers. Many are found on the talus slopes, or lodged in rock crevices. They must blossom hurriedly, and their seeds are scattered by the winds of the first autumn storm.

Many plants living in the Arctic-Alpine zone are identical with those of Alaska, northern Canada, Greenland, and northern Eurasia. Among these are phlox, goldenrod, bluebell, purple campion and Alaska spirea. In the lower parts of this zone are found species such as Olympic onion, marshmarigold, harebell, lomatium and the necklace erysimum. Higher up are hardier species, including eriogonum, phlox, agoseris, siversia, buttercup, red mountainheath, arctic lupine, pleated gentian, yellow heather and alpine speedwell. Dwarf arctic willows hug the ground at the bases of jagged pinnacles. On glacial moraines, anemones and douglasia add touches of color to the rocky terrain. Saxifrages and the shrub-like cinquefoil, with its golden blossoms, are also to be found.

Some flowers grow above the snowfields on cliffs too steep to retain a mantle of ice, and where it appears no sustaining soil could possibly be lodged. Numerous examples can be found of Alfred Lord Tennyson's "flower in the crannied wall." One of the finest is Piper's harebell, with bright, clear blue flowers and grayish leaves. Unlike the other harebells, this one turns its face upward to the sky instead of drooping.

Ferns are rarer here than in the Hudsonian zone. In addition to the alpine lady fern, two alpine species, the mountain licoriceroot fern and the lace fern, find a habitat here. The licoriceroot fern prefers cliffs or rocky peaks, and the lace fern forms a tangled mat of dark green fronds on exposed rocks and ledges.

At the extreme upper limits of plant life grow such species as bent, reed, timothy and squirreltail grasses; mosses and lichens thrive in recesses in the rock walls.

Ten of the twenty endemic plants of the Olympic Peninsula are found in the Arctic-Alpine zone, chiefly in areas not glaciated by Pleistocene ice. Among these are the Olympic rock cress, Henderson's spirea, Flett violet, alpine dandelion, Piper's harebell and the fleabane daisies.

Chapter III

Children of the Wilderness

The Olympic Wildlife

The wilderness within Olympic National Park is one of our finest wildlife sanctuaries. Because the area is large enough to include the annual migratory range of many species, the birds and mammals live their life cycles according to nature's design, undisturbed by man. Even the maligned "predators" are protected from the red-hatted hunter and his thunderstick, the park thus providing refuge for a complete biotic unit.

Observing the wild animals of the Olympic Mountains is not difficult, although the dense vegetation provides protective camouflage for man and animal alike. Hikers who roam along the trails, moving on from day to day, will often come upon the tracks of elk, deer and bear, and even those of the elusive Olympic mountain lion, but are not as likely to see the animals as are experienced outdoorsmen who hike into a promising area and camp. The latter have found that patient waiting in the quiet solitudes is rewarded by the appearance of wildlife, large and small. Such powerful predators as bear and cougar, usually shy of man, may be thus observed.

Foremost among the big mammals is the Olympic or

Roosevelt elk. Other ungulates are the Columbia black-tailed deer and mule deer. The latter is not native but was introduced some years ago, as was the mountain goat. Although the mule deer has not adapted itself well to the Olympics, the mountain goat is thriving and has spread across the eastern part of the national park. The habitat is ideal for the goats, and their absence in the native state was probably due to the isolation of the Olympics from other mountains. The larger predators include the black bear and several carnivores—the Olympic mountain lion, wildcat and coyote. The Olympic wolf, once numerous, is believed to be extinct, a victim of ruthless persecution before the park was established.

Among the smaller animals are the Olympic marmot, Douglas squirrel, chipmunk, raccoon and the mountain beaver.

A tendency toward darker coloration in animals often prevails in regions where rainfall is heavy, and less than average amounts of sunshine the rule. This is true on the Olympic Peninsula, where almost all the animals are much darker than similar species elsewhere. This may explain why the "cinnamon phase" of the black bear has never been reported in these mountains.

The Olympic Elk

The Olympic elk, the largest mammal living on the peninsula, is the second largest member of the deer family in America, surpassed only by the moose. This animal formerly roamed the coastal region from northern California into southern British Columbia. With the exception of a small herd in the redwood country, however, it has disappeared from all areas except the Olympic Peninsula.

These animals are stately, graceful and well-proportioned. Full grown bulls stand five feet high at the shoulder and may weigh more than six hundred pounds. The cows are somewhat smaller. The animals shed their dark, tawny-brown coats during the summer. Mature bulls discard their antlers annually, usually in late winter, and the young bulls lose theirs a bit later during early spring. The new antlers that soon follow are soft, hairy, full of blood, and clublike in appearance.

During this "velvet stage" the bulls expose their antlers to the sun to harden them, and rub them against objects for smoothing and polishing. This is usually accomplished by the middle of August.

The elk are equally at home in the forested lowlands or in the high mountain meadows where they move from basin to basin. Although present at all seasons in the river valleys (their normal winter range), they tend to practice a "vertical migration," moving up with the receding snowline in the summer to the subalpine country. On hot summer afternoons the animals often cool themselves on the snowfields and occasionally engage in ballet-like capers.

In the fall the elk congregate in the high meadowlands. This is the mating season, and the animals at this time exhibit their polygamous nature, a bull often controlling fifteen or twenty cows. He handles them with military precision, keeping the herd together, and engages in fierce combat with other bulls who challenge his authority.

When snow begins to fall in the high country in October or November, the elk descend to the river bottoms to spend the winter. The calves are born late the following spring, usually one to a cow, but sometimes two. They remain with their mothers for four or five months, then both join the bands assembling in the high meadows.

Elk live primarily on grasses and leaves, lichens, and buds and shoots of deciduous trees and shrubs. They feed early in the morning and late in the afternoon, and not just at night as is commonly supposed. Were it not for the browsing by the elk on the luxuriant undergrowth, the rain forests of the western Olympics would probably be impenetrable.

According to wildlife experts, five to seven thousand elk live on the Olympic Peninsula. The largest herds are found in the national park, where they are safe from hunters. Possibly five thousand elk roam the park during the summer, but the number remaining on these protected lands during the coldest winter weather sometimes dwindles to less than a thousand. Reduction of the park area would tend to deplete the herds, not only because of hunting but also from the invasion of roads and logging equipment into their native haunts that, at present, are no more than adequate to sustain them.

Black-Tails and Mule Deer

Deer are numerous on the peninsula, especially the Columbia black-tailed, which is common on the northern and eastern slope of the mountains. The animals are not abundant in the rugged interior, however, where habitat conditions, colder winters and natural enemies restrict their numbers. The larger Rocky Mountain mule deer was introduced into the Olympics some years ago, apparently unsuccessfully, for it appears to be gradually disappearing from the mountains.

The black-tails are about six feet long, stand slightly under three feet at the shoulder, and weigh from one hundred and eighty to two hundred and twenty pounds. Their coat is yellowish-red to reddish brown in summer, but takes on grayish tones in winter. The distinguishing feature of these animals, however, is the black and white tail. The antlers, shed in the spring, are not large. Mating occurs in the fall, and the doe often has two or three fawns at a single birth.

Where unmolested, deer become very tame and frequent campgrounds, sometimes chewing up clothing and making general nuisances of themselves because of their curiosity. The animals are semi-nocturnal in habit, and eat the twigs and leaves of evergreen plants in preference to grasses. These deer jump when startled, all four feet hitting the ground simultaneously, and the animals move across tangled windfalls with amazing speed and ease. Their migratory habits are not as clear-cut as those of the elk, but they generally winter in the lower river valleys and move higher in the summer.

Mountain Goats

Mountain goats are not native to the Olympics. Eight goats imported from British Columbia years ago were released on Mount Storm King, near Lake Crescent. The relatively dry northeastern side of the mountains has proved ideal, and they have spread across the northern and eastern sections of the park. The goat population of Olympic National Park today is estimated to be in the neighborhood of one hundred. Clues to their presence are small clumps of fur stuck to the branches of trees and shrubs, usually in groves of subalpine trees along ridges where the animals bed down at night. Mountain goats are normally timid, but they have become more or less fearless around Mount Constance, where they are most abundant. Here they often come down at night to campsites at Lake Constance.

These animals are gregarious only during the late autumn or winter mating season, but they sometimes gather in small groups in early summer. The "goat families" are not large, however, usually consisting of five to nine members. Really antelopes with goatlike qualities, the stocky animals are sturdily built, and they are very sure-footed. Their legs are short and stout. Except for black horns and hooves, the goats are white throughout the year. Mature males are about five feet long, three feet high at the withers, and weigh anywhere from one hundred and eighty to three hundred pounds.

Mountain goats are usually found in the snowy Arctic-Alpine zone, among the inaccessible cliffs and crags above timberline. During the winter the animals sometimes remain as solitary sentinels in the high country. More often, however, they descend to the lower, timbered slopes where they graze on any vegetation they can find. The scarcity of the food supply limits their numbers, as do the trophy hunters in regions where the goats are not protected. Other than man their chief enemy is the cougar, which preys on the kids.

The Black Bear

The black bear ranges over most of North America and has several color phases—black, cinnamon, "blue," and nearly white. This species is the only member of the bear family found on the Olympic Peninsula, where only the black phase has been reported. However, the animal is well distributed throughout the Olympic Mountains.

Males and females are robust and about the same size—approximately six feet long, three feet high at the shoulders, two hundred to four hundred pounds in weight. These omnivorous animals eat berries, fruits, grass, bird eggs, and anything they can catch in the way of animal life—mice, squirrels, frogs and fish. When the blueberries and huckleberries ripen on sunny slopes in late summer, the bears feast on the luscious fruit until satiated.

Bears mate before going into hibernation. This usually begins in December, the time varying with the altitude and the weather. The animals are easily aroused from their sleep and emerge during April or May, depending on weather conditions. The cubs, one to four in a litter, are born in the den during late winter before the mother comes out. After the bears awaken, they are thin because they have used up their body fat during the winter. It takes a while for them to accustom their digestive organs to food, so they are not too inclined to eat at first.

Only in the past few years have bears prowled Olympic campgrounds, but they are becoming a problem in some areas. The animals go to great lengths to obtain foodstuffs and can be very dangerous when they have lost their fear of man. Although large and powerful, bears are good natured and harmless, as a rule. They are not gregarious and seem to fear each other as much as they fear man. Except for a mother with cubs, bears usually live a solitary existence, although several may occupy the same area, each apparently unaware of the other's presence. Normally the black bear walks lazily, plopping its feet down like someone shuffling about in house slippers or moccasins. When startled, however, a bear usually lumbers away rapidly, sometimes stopping when reaching protective cover, there to peer in timid wonderment at the intruder. Bears enjoy frolicking on snowfields and swimming in the cold alpine pools. Their most spectacular diversion is sliding down steep snowbanks, sometimes on their rumps, but more often on their bellies, facing downhill.

The Olympic Mountain Lion

Of all our national parks, Olympic has the largest population of mountain lions. The animals are seldom seen by man because of their retiring nature and secretive habits, but their presence has been detected in all watersheds. Wildlife experts believe cougars are more common in the foothills, however, where deer are plentiful, than in the high mountains. A hiker may walk many miles through the Olympics and never glimpse one of these large cats, but he may detect evidence of their presence—padded footprints in soft mud, or heaps of earth pawed up along the trails.

The mountain lion—variously known as puma, panther, painter, cougar or catamount—is second in size in the American cat family. Only the jaguar of South and Central America is larger. The Olympic mountain lion is a variant of the common species, and is somewhat larger in size and darker in color. A plain animal, it lacks manes, spots or stripes, and is a pale tawny brown, lighter underneath. The eyes are yellow. The lean, lithe body, including the long, thick tail, approaches eight feet in length and weighs up to two hundred pounds. The animal is never fat and, except for aged ones, is usually graceful and sleek. One of the cougar's notable habits is twitching its long, cylindrical tail, a reflection of the cat's nervous disposition.

The mountain lion is strictly carnivorous. Deer and elk are its natural prey, but it also feeds on smaller animals. The animal prowls chiefly at night and, although a good climber, usually hunts on the ground, where it creeps upon its victim as a housecat stalks a robin. When pursued, it runs in long cat leaps.

A male cougar may have several females under his jurisdiction, each with her own lair. The spotted kittens are born at three year intervals. The male will kill the kittens whenever he can, but the mother guards her offspring jealously and will attack any creature attempting to molest them. Except for this defense of the young, the cougar usually retreats in the face of danger.

The mountain lion is a crafty and cunning predator, but hikers need have no fear, for the animal is afraid of man and attacks on human beings are extremely rare. Sometimes, however, a lion will follow a lone traveler for miles, usually remaining hidden though making no attempt to conceal itself. Apparently it has no intention of attacking, but follows merely out of curiosity.

Outside the national parks and monuments the mountain lion has been severely persecuted, primarily because it competes with hunters for deer and elk. Unlike man, however, the cougar removes diseased and old or weakened animals from the herds, leaving the healthier animals to reproduce. It also helps keep elk and deer populations in check, preventing their multiplying to the point where they overtax their food supplies.

The cougar is tenacious and adaptable. Despite the fact that it has been persistently hunted, with a view toward extermination, the animal has survived. In national parks and wilderness areas, where the preservation of a natural biotic balance is desirable, protecting the mountain lion is a wise policy.

Wildcats, Wolves and Coyotes

Northwestern wildcats live throughout the Olympic Mountains. These variants of the common wildcat or bobcat have very full, soft fur, reddish chestnut brown in color, paler on the sides, with the ends of their short bushy tails black; the under parts are white, with grayish to black spots or stripes. The animals attain lengths of three feet or better and weights of twenty pounds or more.

Wildcats prey mostly on small mammals and birds, devouring snakes, mice, squirrels, rabbits and grouse. They hunt mostly in the evening or early morning, thus are seldom observed by outdoorsmen, but their screams or caterwauls are often heard at night. These animals stalk their victims in the same manner as does the domestic cat and, when cornered, hiss and spit in typical cat fashion. When they, themselves, are the hunted, bobcats usually do not climb trees but elude the dogs on the ground. Wildcats spend the daylight hours in their dens, which they build in hollow logs or trees.

Coyotes are not common in the Olympic Mountains but they are found in some numbers. Most likely they are not native to the peninsula but have invaded the area since the coming of civilization. They prefer remote, inaccessible parts of the wilderness, such as the Bailey Range, since they prefer seclusion and avoid man whenever possible. Occasionally they are heard in choruses of barking, but not often, for they are not as noisy here as they are on the plains.

The coyote belongs to the dog family and is peculiarly dog-like in appearance. Generally it is near four feet in length and weighs twenty to forty pounds. The thick, coarse fur is grizzled grayish or tawny with the underparts tending toward white. The coyote resembles the domestic collie, but is smaller overall.

These animals prowl chiefly at night and prey on anything they can catch, mostly birds and small animals. Because of their craft, cunning and adaptability, coyotes have survived in regions where their larger cousin, the wolf, has disappeared.

The Olympic wolf is believed to be extinct, but occasionally someone reports sighting one. However, wolves are easily confused with coyotes. If, indeed, wolves are present in the Olympic Mountains today, most likely they have migrated from the Cascades and are not survivors of the original Olympic strain. The last known kill of an Olympic wolf was more than forty years ago.

The timber wolf, of which the Olympic variety was a subspecies, is a large gray animal weighing from seventy-five to one hundred pounds, with a typical doglike appearance. The wolf is strictly carnivorous and feeds on animals varying in size from mice to elk. A swift runner, this predator hunts both day and night, and can overcome animals such as deer, a favorite prey.

Wolves mate in late winter, and the whelps, born in the spring, usually number about a half-dozen.

The Olympic Marmot

The Olympic marmot, a squirrel-like rodent related to the eastern woodchuck, is outstanding among the smaller mammals of the mountains. This species is unique to the Olympics but is very similar in size and appearance to the hoary marmot of the Rockies and Cascades. The animals are fat and robust, larger than a big housecat, and reach lengths of thirty inches and weights of ten pounds. Their color ranges from light rusty or reddish brown, buff or yellow ochreous on their upper parts, with a dark bar across the face, and creamy or gray below. In the fall they tend to become darker, usually a deep brown but sometimes almost black.

Marmots are most abundant above the timberline where they inhabit the high meadows in colonies and often live on the tops of mountain peaks. They sun themselves near the entrances to their burrows and on warm summer days the young marmots play together like puppies, tumbling and falling over each other. These rodents appear to be partially migratory, appearing and disappearing in a manner not completely understood, but possibly related to the drying up of alpine pastures during arid summer weather.

The marmot has a clear, piercing and unmistakable whistle that breaks the mountain solitude and serves not only as a means of communication with other marmots but also as a signal of impending danger to all wild creatures. What Olympic hiker has not heard this shrill warning emanating from a rock slide or jumble of boulders near a high country trail? In former days, when hunting was permitted in the mountains, hundreds of these inoffensive creatures were shot because their whistling warned elk and deer of the presence of hunters.

During the short summer and autumn in the mountains the marmots fatten themselves on small plants, roots and seeds. When the first snows whiten the peaks they hibernate, beginning their long sleep of seven months that ends early in May with the advent of spring in the high country.

Squirrels and Chipmunks

Douglas squirrels, also known as chickarees, live in the conifer forests of the Olympics, usually in hollows in old Douglas firs. They subsist primarily on the seeds of fir, spruce, pine and hemlock, and also eat roots, berries and buds.

These rodents are slightly larger than their cousins in the eastern states, but at best their total length, including the big bushy tail, does not exceed fifteen inches. They are dark reddish olive, gray in winter, with orange underparts.

The animals are frisky, and commence a noisy chatter when alarmed, flipping their bushy tails and scampering up the nearest tree from where they pour forth a volume of "squirrel profanity" that brightens up the somber mood of the forest.

Olympic flying squirrels are found only in the Olympic Mountains. They are the largest of the flying squirrels, attaining a total length of fourteen inches, and are dark in color, with softer fur than the Douglas squirrel. Their mode of aerial travel is gliding from tree to tree by means of a membrane of skin on their sides which can be extended outward.

Flying squirrels are gentle, graceful animals, nocturnal in habit. They live in arboreal communities, sometimes a dozen or more occupying a hollow tree and eating from the storehouse of seeds gathered for the winter, or foraging for buds and fruits.

The species of chipmunk so commonly found in the Olympic Mountains is Townsend's, the largest of all, about nine or ten inches long. This animal's coloration is very dark brown, a response to the heavy rainfall and lack of sunshine of its habitat. On its back it has full length alternating light and dark stripes. Its hair is very soft.

Chipmunks feed on seeds, insects and bird eggs. Like the squirrels, they store food and hibernate through the snowy winter months.

These little rodents are saucy, impertinent and inveterate snoopers about campgrounds. When frightened or aroused they squeak and point their tails straight up, meanwhile darting about in a most engaging if confused fashion. Sometimes they take refuge under rocks or logs, from where they chipper rapidly in indignant, high-pitched tones.

The Washington Varying Hare

Washington varying hares, better known as snowshoe rabbits, are very common in the high country of the Olympic Mountains, where they lead a precarious existence. They are food for birds of prey and minks, weasels, coyotes and mountain lions. In spite of having so many natural enemies, they seem to have no difficulty surviving and are fairly abundant over most of their range.

These gentle, inoffensive hares are small, about eighteen inches long, and weigh up to three pounds. They are reddish in color, with little or no white. Unlike other varying hares, they do not turn white in winter.

Although often called snowshoe rabbit because its tracks in the snow resemble snowshoe prints, the varying hare is not a rabbit.

Skunks and Raccoons

Spotted skunks and Puget Sound skunks are both common in the Olympic region. Puget Sound skunks inhabit the coastal forests of Washington and northern Oregon, and are a variant of the common skunk. They prefer settled rural areas where fewer natural enemies exist, thus are more abundant on farmlands than in the mountains. These robust animals weigh up to eight pounds, and feed on insects, small mammals, birds, frogs and snakes. They are nocturnal in habit, but occasionally prowl about on cloudy days, and sometimes hibernate during severe winter weather. Their homes are burrows often marked by prodigious quantities of earth thrown out around the entrances.

Western spotted skunks are slightly smaller than the Puget Sound skunk and are also found in considerable numbers. Their coats are prettier, mottled all over with black and white. These skunks can easily be tamed and make excellent pets.

Raccoons also live in the Olympic Mountains but, like the skunks, they concentrate in settled districts in preference to the primitive conifer forests with their harder living conditions. These valuable furbearers have been widely trapped, thus deserve the protection they receive on national park lands.

During severe winter weather raccoons hibernate, and their dens are usually hollows high up in old trees. The animals are nocturnal, and eat crayfish, worms, grubs, mussels, fruits, and almost any edible meat or vegetable. In the coastal strip of Olympic National Park raccoons commonly visit the beaches at night, where they dine on crabs, oysters and other forms of marine life.

The raccoon ranges up to three feet in length, and weighs from ten to twenty-five pounds. The animal is easily identified because of the black mask over the eyes and the alternate light and dark bands on the tail.

Mountain Beaver

The sewellel or aplodontia is an oddity of the Pacific Northwest known to the layman as the mountain beaver. Actually it is not a beaver at all but a strange looking tailless rodent found only west of the Cascades from lower British Columbia as far south as northern California. Anatomically, the sewellel is among the most primitive of existing animals.

The Olympic showt'l is a variant of the common sewellel, and is confined to the Olympic Peninsula, principally on the eastern side of the mountains where it sometimes does extensive damage to the trails. These animals are found from sea level up to approximately three thousand feet.

Larger and darker than the common sewellel, the showt'l has a short, stout body reaching a foot in length. The animal is characterized by a musky odor and has a rather surly disposition.

Sewellels are nocturnal in habit and retiring in nature. Their extensive runways and burrows may extend more than a hundred feet and are marked by numerous large holes ringed by heaps of dirt. Despite the large amounts of earth disturbed, a burrow usually contains only one family.

These rodents feed on tender vegetation, the leaves of green plants and shrubs. Fern shoots are a special delicacy on their menu.

The Furbearers

Otters are rare in the Olympics, but inhabit the shores of lakes, rivers and creeks in the national park, having been reported near Lake Crescent and along the western streams. These aquatic animals subsist mainly on fish, shellfish and frogs, but occasionally they dine on birds and small mammals. Otters do not hibernate, but remain active throughout the winter. Sometimes they are observed sliding or glissading down steep snowbanks.

Now that the wildest part of the peninsula's Pacific coast has been brought under the protection of the National Park Service it is hoped the big sea otter will return. The rocky, isolated coast is an ideal habitat for this animal, which reproduces slowly and has been unable to survive where the marks of civilization are strong. Unfortunately, the sea otter has been hunted to near extinction, and a single pelt has brought as much as fifteen hundred dollars in the fur market.

Beavers are rare in the Olympic Mountains but have

been observed in the Quinault and Queets watersheds and in the Skokomish valley above Lake Cushman. This variety is the Pacific beaver, largest of all beavers, and hence the largest North American rodent. Sometimes it attains a weight of fifty or sixty pounds. Their color is a reddish chestnut. These animals eat the bark of deciduous trees, and in the springtime fell small cottonwoods or alders along creeks by gnawing at the trunks until the trees topple.

The Cascade weasel lives throughout the Olympic Mountains and is occasionally observed along roads and trails. Dark brown in color and slightly more than a foot long, the weasel is bold, courageous, and often kills more than it can eat. Sometimes it attacks animals much larger than itself. Generally, however, it preys on mice, birds and hares, and does its hunting mainly at night.

The western mink is somewhat larger and darker than the common mink and resembles the smaller weasel. The animal is not numerous in the Olympics, but has been observed along the western streams. The mink is a strong swimmer, semi-aquatic in habit, and preys on small mammals, including meadow mice and rats, marsh birds and their eggs, fish, freshwater shellfish and frogs. The mink lives in a hole in a stream or lake bank. Mating occurs in late winter, and the young are born in the spring.

The Pacific marten or sable—larger and darker than the common American marten—is by no means abundant, since it has been persistently hunted, but it is found in all sections of the park. A close relative of the weasel, this slender furbearer is shy and retiring, and seldom lives below the Canadian life zone. The marten is arboreal, living among the conifers and preying on birds and small animals such as mice and squirrels. Occasionally it dines on insects.

Also a member of the weasel family, the Pacific fisher is a rare animal in the Olympics, but it has been reported near Lake Crescent and Barnes Creek. Brownish-black and darker than the common fisher, at maturity it may reach a length of three feet and weigh from ten to eighteen pounds. The fisher nests high in hollow trees, is nocturnal in its habits, preys chiefly on small animals and has an unpleasant disposition. Intensive hunting in past years has greatly reduced its numbers.

Other Wildlife

A myriad of lesser life forms is found in the Olympic Mountains, inhabiting the forests, meadows, streams, and lakes. The deer mouse is especially abundant in the forests. These rodents are commonly found living in the trailside shelters, and are often so tame they will take food from a person's hand while allowing their backs to be stroked. Several kinds of shrews and toads are also common in the mountain forests, and snails and slugs creep about on the ground. Frogs live on the marshy margins of high country lakes, along with the orange-bellied newt, a type of salamander. The only serpent found in the Olympic Mountains is the harmless garter snake.

Significant because of their absence in the Olympics are several species of animals native to the Pacific Northwest. When the continental glacier invaded western Washington during the Ice Age, the wildlife was, of course, forced to migrate southward ahead of the advancing ice. After the ice sheet receded, the animals gradually returned. Some species, however, did not survive the cold period and are now extinct; others still exist, but have never made their way back to the peninsula. Still missing, probably because the Olympics are isolated from other mountains, are such typical animals of the Pacific Northwest as the red fox, wolverine, pika, and ground squirrel. Until recently the porcupine was also on the missing list, but it now appears to be extending its range to include the peninsula. The coyote is believed to have migrated into the area since the coming of the white man, and in a sense now takes the place of the missing Olympic wolf in the biotic balance.

Fish

Fish are not commonly thought of in the same sense as wildlife which moves about on the land, but they are an important element in the zoology of the wilderness. The lakes and streams of the peninsula, and the surrounding seas, contain many fish, and therefore attract anglers from all parts of the nation. Salmon swim up the larger rivers to spawn in the fall, and several species of trout are common in the rivers and lakes.

Among these are cutthroat, rainbow, Eastern brook, Dolly Varden and steelhead. The latter is sometimes called an "ocean-going trout" because it spends most of its life in the sea, but returns periodically to the rivers to spawn.

Birds of the Olympics

According to the naturalist E. A. Kitchin, two hundred and sixty-one species of birds have been noted on the peninsula, and twenty-four others probably are casual visitors although no specimens have been taken. This variety of avian life is due in large measure to the different habitats present. On three sides of the peninsula rich coastal zones provide sustenance for millions of marine birds. Other species live inland—along the rivers, on logged-off lowlands, in the dense mountain forests, or the high meadowlands. All but very few of these species are found within the boundaries of Olympic National Park.

The Pacific coast of North America is a major flyway for migratory birds, and many species of sea and shore birds frequent the shores of the peninsula. Some are resident the year round; others are present only at certain seasons, especially during the migratory periods.

Diving birds such as grebes, loons, auks and puffins are principally winter migrants, but the murres and auklets live on the peninsula throughout the year and nest in colonies on offshore islands. The tube-nosed fulmars, shearwaters and petrels are commonly seen on the ocean beaches. Other swimming birds found in abundance include cormorants and mergansers, the whistling swan, seven kinds of geese and twenty-six species of ducks.

Long-winged swimming birds are numerous. Eleven species of gulls, three terns and the jaegers are spring and fall wanderers along the coast, but some of the gulls live on the peninsula throughout the winter. Most common are the glaucous-winged and herring gulls. Skuas live on the peninsula during the summer.

In the swamps, sloughs and marshes, where cattails and rushes provide protective cover, dwell bitterns, cranes, rails and coots. Blue herons frequent the tideflats where they procure food, and build their nests in the tops of tall nearby trees. Following the nesting season, the old birds sometimes fly alone upstream to the alpine lakes in the high mountain meadows.

Many species of shore birds frequent the mud flats. Most of these are migrants that nest in the far north. The killdeer is the most common, but the group also includes plovers, snipes, curlews, dowitchers, oyster-catchers, surf-birds, turn-stones, greater and lesser yellow-legs, red and northern phalaropes, and eleven species of sandpipers.

Inland from the sea the bird population varies greatly, depending upon the habitat. In the lowland forests, especially along or near streams, bird life is varied, and includes wrens, swallows, sparrows, thrushes, crows and eight species of woodpeckers. Most conspicuous is the pileated woodpecker, a splash of black and red flashing through the forest. Often observed along streams are the western belted kingfisher and the water ouzel or dipper.

In the forests of the lower mountain slopes live grouse, owls, swifts, warblers and jays. Sometimes the hiker will hear the band-tailed pigeon calling from a secluded spot; more often he will be startled by the guttural croak of the raven.

Higher up, in relatively open meadow country near timberline, sparrows, finches, horned larks, mountain bluebirds and ravens are numerous. Clark's nutcrackers caw, often continuously, from perches in the subalpine firs, and rufous hummingbirds dart from flower to flower. Hawks soar over the meadows, searching for rodents or other prey, easier to find here than in the dense forests of lower elevations. A few birds inhabit the barren land of snow and ice at the highest altitudes. Most notable are the pipit and Hepburn's rosy finch.

Five "upland game birds" live on the peninsula, but only two are native, the sooty grouse and the Oregon ruffed grouse. Introduced species are the ring-necked pheasant, California quail and mountain quail. The sooty grouse lives from the coast to the high mountain country, and in the fall feeds on wild buckwheat in the meadows. The ruffed grouse has a more restricted range and is seldom found above the lower altitudes.

Birds of prey are common in the Olympics. Bald eagles haunt the ocean beaches, and often sit for hours in the tops of dead snags overlooking the sea. In the fall the eagles gather on the rivers to dine on spawning salmon. Falcons engage in aerial gymnastics along the coast, the black pigeon hawk is a fall and winter migrant, and occasionally an osprey is seen during the summer. Several species of hawks live in the forests and on logged-off lands. Most numerous are the western goshawk, Cooper's hawk and the western red-tailed hawk. Owls inhabiting the dense, shaded forests include Kennicott's screech owl, dusky horned owl, coast pygmy owl, northern spotted owl, short-eared owl and the saw-whet owl. The latter is found at higher altitudes, primarily the Hudsonian zone. Rare winter visitors to the peninsula are the snowy owl, great gray owl, and Richardson's owl.

Perching birds live in great variety on the Olympic Peninsula. Among them will be found flycatchers, kinglets, waxwings, vireos, chickadees, blackbirds, robins, grosbeaks, juncos and nighthawks. Friendliest of all is the Oregon jay or camp robber, a charming thief well known to every mountaineer.

Chapter IV

Man in the Olympics

The First Inhabitants

The first men who lived on the Olympic Peninsula were Indians whose ancestors migrated from Asia by way of Alaska and western Canada. The date of their arrival on the peninsula is not known, but extensive kitchen middens found along the shores indicate the Indians were present many centuries before the white man came.

Indian settlements were limited to the coastal perimeter, but warriors occasionally ventured into the interior on hunting trips, tribal traditions telling of expeditions to the "land of snow and ice" in quest of elk, deer and bear. The Indians relied chiefly on the beaches and ocean for their food supply, however, and used their dugout canoes on the rivers and lakes, as well as the sea, in their constant search for food and the simple raw materials needed for fuel, shelter and clothing.

The Indians of the northwest coast were squat and chunky, lacking the tall, slender physique common to the plains Indians. Their way of life was more sedentary, but they did excel in water crafts and by occupation were primarily fishermen. Several tribes lived on the Olympic Peninsula. The Makahs occupied the northwestern corner, around Cape Flattery and Neah Bay. The Klallams made their homes farther east, along the Strait of Juan de Fuca, and the Skokomish tribe resided on the shores of Hood Canal. On the Pacific coast lived the Quileute, the Quinault, the Hoh (Ohalet), the Queets (Quaitso) and the now extinct Ozette tribe. Today most of these Indians are found on a few reservations along the coast, chiefly the Quinault and the Makah. The Quileute have the distinction of being the last remaining tribe of sealing Indians in North America.

On occasion the tribes would travel beyond their regular territories to fish, hunt, pick huckleberries, make war or visit the hot springs in the mountains. Whale hunting was one of their more spectacular activities. The Makahs ventured onto the open sea in large dugout canoes, and they used bone-tipped lances tied to ropes of cedar bark, with sealskin floats attached to prevent the whale from diving. When subdued, the huge mammal was towed in with the tide and beached, and after the tide receded the villagers would strip the blubber from the carcass and cut up the meat. The Makahs no longer hunt whales, but now confine their seagoing activities to halibut fishing.

The Indians fished the coastal waters and streams, using hooks, lines, traps, harpoons, and spears. Salmon and candlefish provided the staple diet, and the latter was also a source of oil. Halibut, cod and shellfish were important in the Indians' diet, as were the delicious smelt taken in the summer as they swam onto the beaches to spawn. Activity during these fish runs was feverish, as the Indians prepared the fish for later use. The men also hunted elk, deer, bear, and fowl in the woods, and the women gathered berries, nuts, roots, herbs and bulbs to supplement the basic fish and game diet. Agriculture was unknown.

During mild weather the Indians wore breech-cloths or robes. In the colder weather the men's clothing consisted of buckskin shirts and moccasins made from hides tanned without removing the hair. The women dressed in petticoat style affairs woven from twisted strands of cedar bark or dried grasses. Sometimes these garments were colored with vegetable dyes. The Indians living along the strait were known for their blankets made of dog hair.

In the summer the Indians lived in temporary bark or rush shelters. For the colder, rainy winter months they built permanent houses along the coast, usually near the mouths of rivers. Constructed of cedar planks or logs, thèse "longhouses"—rectangular buildings providing shelter for several families—occasionally reached a hundred feet in length.

Using crude tools made from stones and elk antlers, the expert woodworkers of the tribes carved canoes from giant cedar trees. These were hollowed out with hot rocks, and rubbed with dogfish liver oil to prevent warping and checking. However, the most highly developed art of these people was basket weaving. The women wove colorful watertight baskets of unique design from the stringy bark of cedars or the roots of spruce and cedar. The Indians boiled the roots in water to remove the bark, split them with their teeth, and wove baskets of all sizes which were used in their daily activities.

The Pacific Northwest is one of the few areas in the world where primitive people developed a complex social system based solely on fishing, hunting and gathering. Warfare and slavery were not uncommon, and the tribes were ruled by chiefs and tribal councils. Social classes existed, with the women, who did most of the drudgery, occupying a position of inferiority. The chief social events were the potlatches or ceremonial feasts. The Indians placed great value on displays of wealth, and in order to impress the guests at potlatches, valuable items were destroyed or given away. However, friends and neighboring tribesmen were obliged to respond in a like manner at a future potlatch.

These primitive people were highly superstitious and believed in personal guardian spirits. These varied with the person's occupation. Each village had at least one medicine man or shaman who treated the sick and conducted mysterious rites. Often he was as powerful as the tribal chief. There was also some development of secret societies, but since the imprint of civilization has touched these people most of their picturesque rites and customs have disappeared. However, a few have been preserved for ceremonial occasions.

Although the Indians had no written language, they developed a complex lore to explain natural phenomena. They had none of our concepts of natural forces. Instead, they believed their gods had the power to control the forces of nature, and the talent of prophecy, as well as being diviners of thought.

The Indian myths, traditions and legends were mainly stories of the performances of their ancient gods, and usually related to animals of land and sea, and to the sun, moon and stars. The mountains also appear in some of the stories. Because the myths were unrecorded and had been passed down for centuries by word of mouth, the legends varied from tribe to tribe and sometimes even within a tribe. They were told around tribal campfires, and one can easily imagine their impact on the primitive mind.

Like most North American Indians, they were animists. They believed that at one time gods existed in the form of a race of giant "animal people." All living things were dual in nature, having both physical bodies and a supernatural existence complete with "souls." Some of the deities were good; more often they were evil. They could change form at will and travel great distances almost simultaneously.

These ancient gods were believed to be still living in the form of the present race of animals, but the supernatural part of magic power and great intelligence existed elsewhere as a spirit. This spirit was revered as a god and appealed to for aid. Even inanimate objects like mountains and rocks were considered to have once been living beings, later transformed into stone because of some sin or transgression, but still possessing the qualities of living beings with intelligence. The wildlife observed in the forests and seas were successors, on a smaller scale, of these ancient people. All animals and birds, particularly owls, were considered personifications of the gods and were supposed to be invested with vast power and influence. Sometimes in the stories a small or weak animal would triumph over a greater, thus symbolizing the victory of good over evil.

Indian tradition held that the high peaks of the interior were the home of the Twana Thunderbird, an immense creature responsible for lightning and thunder. According to the Makah tribe the Thunderbird was a gigantic Indian who dressed as a bird when he left his high mountain abode to seek food. He clothed himself in raiment consisting of a bird's head, a pair of large wings, and a feather covering for his body. Around his waist he tied the "lightning fish." Thus arrayed, he was thought to resemble a raven or eagle, and to be of a size capable of darkening the heavens. His body was the thunder cloud, the flapping of his wings produced the earth-shaking thunder, and lightning resulted from the flashing of his eyes or bolts of fire expelled from his tongue. Occasionally the Thunderbird would strike a tree; less often a man.

The Indians regarded the Thunderbird with great awe. His image often appeared on their weapons, and a man who possessed one of his feathers or a bone from the lightning fish was believed to be endowed with supernatural powers. The Thunderbird lived on whale meat and occasionally battled one of the large mammals, killing the whale with the lightning fish or by firebolts from his mouth. Seizing his prey, he then carried it to his home among the glaciers of Mount Olympus.

In the Indian religious ceremonies the Thunderbird performance was the most savage and bloody of all. The performers painted their bodies black, especially their faces, and scarified themselves in order to bleed profusely. They whistled sharply in imitation of the wind, and hooted like owls or howled like wolves. Pitchwood torches were flashed to represent lightning; thunder was simulated by pounding on drums and, following the introduction of firearms, by the firing of guns.

The European Seafarers

Today the Olympic Peninsula is still sparsely populated, but its wilderness core is circled by settlement and development. Yet it was one of the areas of the Pacific Northwest with which white men first came in contact, partly because it stood between Puget Sound and the sea and could not be completely ignored. The acquaintance was casual, however, and for years the peninsula was virtually inaccessible except from the surrounding seas. The dense forests, incessant rains and lack of readily navigable steams closed the region to all but an occasional hunter, trapper or prospector. Not until trails and roads were built, well into the twentieth century, did the interior become accessible.

As early as 1543, Bartolomeo Ferrelo, under orders from the Viceroy of Mexico, sailed along the Pacific coast of North

America. Thirty-six years later Sir Francis Drake followed essentially the same course in the *Golden Hind.* Historians believe that neither explorer went north of latitude 43°, near Cape Blanco, Oregon, and the reputed discovery of the Strait of Juan de Fuca by a Greek sailor in 1592 is believed to be merely a legend. In fact, another two hundred years passed before any genuine exploration of the northwest coast was made.

The earliest recorded notice of the Olympic Mountains is that of Juan Perez, a Spaniard who was cruising along the coast in search of new lands for Spain. On August 10, 1774, Perez sighted the trident-like summit of Mount Olympus and called it *El Cerro de la Santa Rosalia.* This was apparently the first time that a white man had viewed the peak, and the first place-naming by a European of a geographic feature in what is now Washington State.

The following year two other Spanish explorers, Bruno Heceta and Juan de la Bodega y Quadra, landed parties near Point Grenville, about thirty miles north of Grays Harbor. On July 14, 1775, Captain Heceta anchored his schooner, the *Santiago,* then went ashore and took formal possession of the land in the name of the Spanish king. Records were sealed in a bottle and placed at the foot of a white cross. This was evidently the first actual contact western civilization had with the soil of the Olympic Peninsula. On the same day, Quadra's sister ship, the *Sonora,* lay at anchor to the lee of an island off the mouth of the Hoh River, a few miles to the north. Quadra was visited by Indians in canoes who held up pieces of metal, indicating they wished to barter. Because he needed fuel and water, Quadra sent several men ashore, but the Indians promptly killed them and destroyed their boat for the iron and copper it contained. Saddened by the incident, Quadra then left, calling the island *Isla de Dolores.*

Twelve years later Captain Charles William Barkley (sometimes spelled Berkeley), commanding an East India Company ship, anchored near the same spot and sent a boat with five men ashore for fresh water. They met a similar fate. Barkley called the stream Destruction River, but later this designation was given to the island, and the river was called the Hoh, after the Indians.

In 1778 Captain James Cook, an English seafarer, sailed

by the peninsula while searching for the Northwest Passage. "It is in this very latitude where we now were," Cook recorded in his log, "that geographers have placed the pretended Strait of Juan de Fuca. But we saw nothing like it; nor is there the least probability that ever any such thing existed." Cook named the northwestern corner of the peninsula Cape Flattery, but he somehow missed the strait and continued northward to Nootka Sound on the west side of Vancouver Island. There he obtained a valuable cargo of furs from the Indians for practically nothing. Cook then sailed on to China with the furs, and the following year he was killed by Hawaiians during a fight over a boat.

Less than a decade later, in 1787, Captain Barkley again explored along the Pacific coast and this time found the strait and named it after the legendary Greek discoverer. The next summer John Meares, a British sea captain flying under the Portuguese flag to avoid paying license fees to the East India Company, entered the fur trade at Nootka. He reconnoitered the strait and was welcomed by an Indian chief fishing with a band of his people at a little island near Cape Flattery. Meares called it Tatoosh Island in honor of the chief. On the fourth of July, Meares sighted the high, snowy peak in the interior of the peninsula and called it Mount Olympus after the Greek mountain supposedly the home of the gods. In 1792 Captain George Vancouver adapted the name to the whole cluster of peaks, listing them in his records as the Olympic Mountains, and gradually the designation was extended to the entire peninsula.

Another Spaniard, Manuel Quimper, sailed into the strait in 1790 and explored the San Juan Islands and the coast around present day Port Townsend. The following year Captain Francisco de Eliza, on a discovery mission for Mexico, entered the harbor of what is now Port Angeles. On the bay, protected by a sandspit known today as Ediz Hook, he found an Indian village and named it *Puerto de Nuestra Señora de los Angeles* (Port of Our Lady of the Angels). The name was gradually contracted to Port Angeles, and today a modern city stands on the site. Ediz Hook protects the harbor during storms and has a Coast Guard station on its tip.

In 1791 Francisco de Eliza established a base at Discovery Bay and Lieutenant Salvador Fidalgo, a subordinate of Bodega y Quadra, set up a short-lived colony at Neah Bay.

Although soon abandoned, this post had the distinction of being the first settlement of the white man in what is now Washington State.

Two important events occurred in 1792, the three hundredth anniversary of Columbus' discovery of the New World. Captain George Vancouver explored Puget Sound and, impressed by its beauty and recognizing the economic value of the sheltered waterway, claimed it for England; and Captain Robert Gray, representing the United States of America, discovered what is now known as Grays Harbor, and entered the mouth of the Columbia River after many others had failed.

With the advent of the Americans, the Spaniards withdrew to California, leaving the English to contend with the Americans for the "Oregon country." Gray's discovery of the Columbia closed the book on the discoveries by sea. After that the explorers came by land—a vanguard that later expanded into the migration of covered wagons, the settlers who trekked westward over the Oregon Trail.

Explorers by Land

Adventurers by-passed the coastal Pacific Northwest for almost half a century following the explorations by sea late in the eighteenth century. The Lewis and Clark expedition, a notable exception, ended its long continental journey at the mouth of the Columbia, but the Olympic Peninsula remained wild and untraveled, though not unclaimed.

The United States negotiated a treaty with Spain in 1819 and another with Russia in 1824 which removed these countries from imperial contention in the Oregon country, leaving the United States and England to quarrel over the area north of the Columbia and south of latitude 54° 40′ N. The English coveted the Puget Sound region and at one point offered the United States the whole of the Olympic Peninsula north of a line from Grays Harbor to Hood Canal if the boundary between the nations would be drawn along the Columbia River. This offer was refused, and after much wrangling the boundary was fixed in 1846 at the 49th parallel. In 1841, before the controversy was settled, the United States commissioned the Wilkes expedition to survey Puget Sound. Twelve years later hunters from the Hudson's Bay Company at Victoria entered the northern Olympics, becoming the first white men to penetrate these mountains to any distance.

Washington Territory was established in 1853 and Isaac I. Stevens, its governor, negotiated three treaties with the Indians in 1855–56, in which the Indians ceded the Olympic Peninsula to the United States except for some portions set aside as reservations.

Other than Mount Olympus, none of the mountain peaks on the peninsula had been distinguished with a name. In 1856, however, a surveyor named George Davidson was impressed by the peaks visible from Puget Sound. He named Mount Constance for Constance Fauntleroy, sister of his sweetheart, Ellinor, whose name he gave to a lesser summit near Lake Cushman. He also called a conspicuous, double-peaked mountain The Brothers, in honor of Edward and Arthur Fauntleroy.

For the most part, however, the Olympics remained unknown territory right up to the end of the nineteenth century, more than a hundred years after the first seafarers sailed along the shores. Although settlement had taken place along the Strait of Juan de Fuca and Puget Sound, no one except an occasional hunter, trapper or prospector ranged through the densely forested foothills surrounding the mountains. These men left no records or trails, and the mountainous interior was still mysterious and unexplored.

The First O'Neil Expedition

In 1882 Lieutenant Colonel Alexander Chambers, Twenty-First Infantry, United States Army, stationed at Fort Townsend, endeavored to penetrate the mountains behind the fort and construct a trail. After six months of difficult labor his party abandoned the project while still in the foothills. Three years later, however, Lieutenant Joseph P. O'Neil was attracted "by the grand noble front of the Jupiter Hills, rising with their boldness and abruptness, presenting a seemingly impenetrable barrier to the farther advance of man and civilization." His exploratory instincts aroused, the young officer made inquiries and received conflicting reports on the nature of the country, among them that the mountains enclosed extensive prairies, and that one could pole a canoe up one of the rivers to its source, cross over the divide and float down another stream to the Pacific. O'Neil persuaded the commanding general, Nelson Miles, to organize a reconnaissance party. On July 16, 1885, a detail of eight men under command of O'Neil started from Port Angeles "because of its seeming nearness to the mountains" and entered the northern Olympics. The pack train consisted of four mules, later increased to eight. From Port Angeles the explorers, guided by an Indian, followed an old, ill-defined trail toward the foothills. The Indian deserted them when he realized where they were going, and neither promises of wealth nor threats of death induced him to remain. With reluctance he camped with the party at the base of the mountains, but slipped away quietly during the night.

Undeterred by the Indian legend of the Thunderbird who would inflict terrible punishment on transgressors of his sanctum, the party followed the course of Yennis Creek and hacked a path through dense forests, choking underbrush, and around windfalls, precipices and canyons. The men struggled slowly through the foothills and up the northern slopes to the high country overlooking the Strait of Juan de Fuca. Excursions were made from here in various directions, the main exploration being to the south and east along the crests of the higher ridges.

Wildlife was abundant in the mountains. From the beginning panthers prowled about the expedition's camps, frightening both men and mules, and great herds of elk, almost as tame as cattle, roamed the mountain meadows. The explorers also encountered an occasional black bear, one lone wolf which they shot in the leg, and numerous marmots whose whistling confused the men.

Lieutenant O'Neil was impressed by the view from a high gap above Port Angeles. Snow-covered mountains, extending well above the timberline, rose in "wild, broken confusion" to the east, west and south. O'Neil picked out what he thought was Olympus, the highest point in a cluster of snowy peaks to the south, a mountain range that apparently circled on itself. "There is no regularity about their formation," he wrote of the Olympics in general, "but jumbled up in the utmost confusion, and the only regularity which does exist is that the ranges nearest the Strait and Sound seem to run parallel to those bodies of water, and with all their irregularity, ruggedness and at present difficult of access, the day will come when the State of Washington will glory in their wealth and beauty."

In the high country the party divided into two groups. One, under a man named Hawgood, left to explore toward the Elwha, but lost some provisions in crossing a stream and had to return. The other, led by O'Neil, proceeded southeasterly to the divide separating streams flowing north to the strait and east to Hood Canal. The men then explored the headwaters of the "East Fork of the Elwha" (probably the Lillian, but possibly the Hayes) and got far enough south to see the source "and the field of ice from which it started." In this remote area one member of the party lost his way and was never found.

Although O'Neil's expedition did not cross the mountains, it aroused speculation as to what the interior contained and kindled interest in various plans for further expeditions which came to nought. But O'Neil's party made a beginning and was to be followed within five years by a more ambitious operation, the Press Exploring Expedition.

The Press Expedition

"Washington has her great unknown land like the interior of Africa." Thus did Elisha P. Ferry, governor of the newly created state, preface his remarks when he declared, in 1889, the "advisability of having the area between the Olympic mountains and the Pacific ocean explored." The mysterious interior of the Olympic Peninsula, untrodden by the foot of civilized man, afforded a fine opportunity for someone "to acquire fame by unveiling the mystery which wraps the land encircled by the snow capped Olympic range."

Because the mountains presented rampart-like walls on all seaward sides, men believed the streams draining them rose only on the outward slopes, none originating in the area enclosed by the mountains. Supposedly a great central basin contained a large lake that drained, via a subterranean outlet, to the sea. The unexplored region was also rumored to consist of "rolling prairies on a huge plateau." Game was abundant, as were minerals, and the whole paradise was guarded by fierce, hostile Indians.

Such tales aroused interest in exploratory missions and several groups planned to enter the Olympics in the summer of 1890. However, the party organized by the *Seattle Press* stole a march and to them went the glory of the first crossing of the mountains, during the winter and spring of 1889–90.

The party of six men and four dogs left Seattle in early December, 1889, for Port Angeles, "to ascend the mountains by way of the Elwha pass." They expected to live largely off game, but packed 1500 pounds of provisions with the help of two mules acquired at the last minute.

By Christmas the expedition was camped in a canyon along the Elwha River west of Port Angeles. After a great snowstorm the weather turned cold and the men kept a monster fire going day and night while they built a crude flatboat from frozen green lumber. When launched on New Year's eve, the boat promptly sank, but the explorers hauled the vessel out and recaulked it. This time it floated.

In freezing weather, the men towed the boat, laden with their supplies, up the icy Elwha. After twelve days, however, they reached the end of what they believed to be navigable water. Here the boat was abandoned. The explorers now built various types of sledges, none of which worked, and they were forced to backpack their supplies, with the assistance of the mules. However, while the expedition was crossing the face of a mountain spur known as the Devil's Backbone, one of the mules fell over a cliff and was killed.

In late February the expedition reached "The Forks," then the limit of exploration. The men pushed slowly ahead, plagued by incessant rain and snow. When spring came the party was camped in a little mountain valley. Here the explorers lived mainly on fresh meat and fish, but as they moved deeper into the mountains the country became rougher, the snow deeper and game scarcer. Their remaining mule, exhausted from the ordeal, finally gave up, unable to go further. The men and dogs, also near exhaustion, pushed on.

The explorers left the Elwha, which appeared to trend in the wrong direction, and labored up the canyon of the Goldie

River. Their packs, stripped down to sixty pounds each, contained only essentials, and their clothes were rags, but hope was in their hearts that they would soon reach the Quinault and a path back to civilization. Their provisions were getting low, their starving dogs stole the last of their bacon, and the canyon became increasingly precipitous. Their progress slowed to a crawl, and in an effort to cross the mountains quickly they threw away a lot of useless equipment.

The expedition arrived in the heart of the mountains at the peak of the avalanche season. In constant fear of slides, the men climbed steep, snow-covered slopes, and upon reaching a high vantage point were "almost stunned by the sea of mountains across the path" to their journey's end. Eventually they reached the top of a high divide, only to discover they were within the confines of a vast curve of the Elwha. Obviously a descent of several thousand feet to the river was necessary before an ascent could be made to the true watershed. James H. Christie, the expedition leader, reported this disagreeable discovery gave rise to "sundry hard expressions not usually found in Webster, but quite excusable under the circumstances."

From the Elwha valley, using ropes, the explorers climbed rock cliffs to the Low Divide. Their food supply, now reduced to nothing but flour, was nearly gone and time was running out on them. At the divide they found two small lakes, and near them a stream flowing south. Almost immediately the dogs flushed a dehibernating bear. The men shot the bear, then fried bear grease all day, and drank it as fast as it was ready, ravenous as they were for fat. While camped in the mountain pass they killed two more bears in the next few days, and thus saved themselves from starvation.

Anxious to get out of the wilderness, the men hurried down the Quinault valley, and fought their way through endless thickets of brush in dense rain forests. Ragged, battered, half-starved and nearly barefoot, they stopped long enough to build a raft that would, they hoped, float them down the river. The raft struck a log jam, however, and was swamped. Miraculously, all survived the incident, but most of their equipment was lost. Somehow they managed to save their diaries and films and the invaluable topographical map their historian, Captain Charles Barnes, had made of the mountains.

On May 19 a white man and two Indians canoeing up the Quinault picked them up and carried them downriver to the lake, then to the ocean where they hired a team to take them to Grays Harbor and civilization. It had been nearly six months since they had disappeared in the wilderness on the lower Elwha. Shortly afterward the men returned to Seattle and the *Press* published a detailed account of the expedition. The first crossing of the Olympic Mountains was history.

Later Expeditions

The Press party was followed in the summer of 1890 by a second expedition under Lieutenant O'Neil. This group, composed of soldiers from the Fourteenth Infantry and members of the Oregon Alpine Club, crossed the southern part of the Olympics from Lake Cushman to Lake Quinault, and explored the mountains on all sides. The lieutenant reported that one party led by B. J. Bretherton, the expedition naturalist, succeeded in climbing Mount Olympus and noted that its immensity made the surrounding mountains appear insignificant although they were only about a thousand feet lower.

In the next few years other groups explored segments of the Olympics. C. A. Gilman and his son ranged the length of the peninsula for the National Geographic Society, Judge James Wickersham and his family explored the eastern Olympics, and at the turn of the century a government party spent three years in the mountains surveying a new forest reserve. Thus within a decade the veil of mystery was lifted from the white peaks, although untrodden spots remain in the Olympics to this day.

The various exploratory parties named many geographic features of the Olympic Mountains and some of their nomenclature has survived the passage of time. Their chief contribution, however, was disproving the rumors. The Olympics did not contain a central valley or a plateau of rolling prairies covered with lush grasses. Nor was there a great lake with a subterranean outlet. The mountains were lacking in important mineral deposits, and no fierce Indians guarded the mythical paradise of rich lands awaiting settlement. Furthermore, the rivers were found to originate in the interior, not on the outer slopes of the mountains as had been supposed. The greatest surprise, however, was the discovery that the Olympic Mountains were not a range but a jumbled cluster of precipitous, snow-burdened peaks.

Early Mountaineering

Despite the information gathered by the pioneer explorations and the government survey party, the Olympic Mountains remained unnecessarily shrouded in mystery and were virtually unvisited right up to the beginning of the twentieth century. Gradually, however, hunters, campers and mountain climbers began to filter into the rugged interior.

Mount Olympus was the lodestone drawing the early climbers and several doubtful claims of a first ascent have been recorded. In 1854 two white men, B. F. Shaw and H. G. Cook, accompanied by two Makah Indians, supposedly canoed up the Hoh and climbed the peak, but mountaineers seriously question the authenticity of this claim. Equally doubtful is the claim that Michael Simmons ascended the mountain in the same year. Far more credible, however, is the report by Lieutenant O'Neil that a group from his second expedition reached the summit on September 22, 1890, where they left a copper box containing the record book of the Oregon Alpine Club, together with other items. The party had left the headwaters of the Quinault's east fork nine days before and approached the mountain via an "oval glacier supplying the Queets." This was probably the Humes Glacier.* The copper box has never been found, however, and no one knows the specific peak of the many in the area this group climbed. Their aneroid barometer indicated the mountain's elevation to be 7875 feet, very close to the established altitude of Mount Olympus.

In late August, 1905, Grant Humes, who lived on the lower Elwha, attempted with two companions to scale Olympus, "this little-known but much talked of peak." As the men

---

* In a report of his attempted climb in 1905, Grant Humes refers to Olympus' eastern slope as being "for the most part occupied by the Queets Glacier." Later the glacier was named after him and his brother, Will, and the original name given to a glacier on Mount Queets.

approached the mountain huge blocks of ice broke from the glaciers at intervals and crashed into canyons, the rumbling echoing among the peaks. The climbers reached a point they thought was less than a mile from the summit, but turned back when heavy fog closed around the peak. In returning to their camp of the previous night they discovered a shortcut "by following the tracks of a bear in the snow through a narrow pass, which saved about two miles of difficult going." Thus did Bear Pass receive its name.

The first authenticated ascent of Olympus' main peak occurred in the summer of 1907 when the newly organized Mountaineers club held its first annual outing in the remote central part of the mountains. Months of preparation, including the building of thirty-five miles of trail, enabled the party of sixty-five men and women to make the long trek in to the Elwha Basin, near the source of the Elwha. The main objective of the outing was to climb Mount Olympus, hopefully for a first ascent. Just before the outing began, however, word came that three members of the Explorers Club—H. C. Parker, Belmore Browne and Walter G. Clark—had quietly gone into the Olympics and climbed the mountain. Insult was added to injury, for the Parker party had used the new trail built for The Mountaineers, and had even engaged as their guide Will Humes, whom The Mountaineers had previously employed as their leader. Hastily published accounts of "the first ascent of Olympus" appeared soon afterward. The Parker party described, photographed, and gave names to the highest peaks of Olympus and called the gap in the ridge between the Humes and Hoh glaciers Explorers' Pass.

Members of The Mountaineers' outing made several first ascents in the central Olympics. Then, on August 10, a large party attempted Olympus, but a furious storm that dumped a foot of fresh snow on the upper levels of the mountain forced the party to turn back. When the climbers emerged from the protection of a stone ridge and stepped into Explorers' Pass they were met by fierce winds whirling the snow along as it fell. The summit peaks were lost to view, and the climbing party "appeared suspended in the heavens on the edge of some great cloud, with a white desolate world forming out of the chaos." Not knowing the gap had been previously named, they promptly christened it Blizzard Pass and hastily retreated down the mountain.

Their troubles were not over. Below the moraine of the Humes Glacier one of the women slipped on wet heather and slid over a hundred feet on rocks and snow, thus becoming the first mountaineering casualty on Mount Olympus. First-aid was rendered and the injured girl carried to a quickly improvised hospital camp in the rain-drenched Queets Basin. Most of the party then returned to the outing's base camp in the Elwha Basin, and as they crossed over Dodwell-Rixon Pass, "the vast bulk of Mt. Olympus, shrouded in clouds, refused even to bid them farewell."

Two days later, however, three of the climbers returned and ascended the East Peak, where they found a cairn containing an old scrap of newspaper, believed to have been from Shelton, Washington, from extracts contained therein, and bearing a date in August, 1899. The Mountaineers recorded their own ascent, and added: "We salute the brave pioneers who climbed in 1899." Later they learned that Jack McGlone, a cook for the government survey party, had made a lone ascent from the Elwha Basin on August 12, 1899.

On August 13, 1907, clouds shrouded Olympus and rain seemed likely. Nevertheless, eleven members of the outing, ten men and one woman, started for the main summit. This party reached the upper snowfields under cloudless skies and ascended Middle Peak, by-passing the lower East Peak, "with its clear-cut profile of a sphinx head." On the summit of Middle Peak the climbers found a tin can containing the names of the four men who claimed the first ascent of Olympus—the three from the Explorers Club, and W. E. Humes, the guide. The Parker party had left a note stating that, while climbing, they believed Middle Peak was the highest point, but after having gained its summit they were in doubt and thought possibly the West Peak was higher.

The Mountaineers recorded their ascent of Middle Peak, then descended its western side and crossed snowfields toward West Peak. Clouds closed in, however, obscuring the view. After climbing a false summit, they saw West Peak close at hand through the parting fog and hurriedly made the ascent. After a thorough search for traces of other climbers they concluded that theirs was the first ascent of the highest peak in the Olympic Mountains.

On July 7, 1908, four mountain climbers from Bremerton, Washington, ascended "Five Fingers Peak," a collection of false summits adjacent to West Peak. They then climbed West, Middle and East Peaks. This was the first time that all three summits were climbed in one day. The climbers called the notch between West Peak and the false summits Crevasse Pass.

The Mountaineers held further summer outings in the Olympics in 1913, 1920, 1926 and 1933. During this period small groups of independent climbers also made trips into the region. One by one the higher, more attractive peaks were conquered by the alpinists. In 1912 climbers reached the top of The Brothers, and in 1920 Mount Anderson yielded. Then, on June 26, 1922, two young men climbed Mount Constance after many others had failed, and the ascents of the major peaks had been completed. A few unclimbed peaks remain, however, and first ascents are still being registered.

The early mountaineering exploits brought to a focus the need for a national park on the Olympic Peninsula. Although most northwesterners by-passed the mountains until the opening of the Olympic Highway in 1930, it soon became obvious that the splendid scenic resources of these mountains needed permanent protection.

Chapter V

Storm over the Olympics

The National Park Idea

The year 1890, which marked the closing of the American frontier and the beginning of the automobile era, was significant in the history of the Olympic Peninsula. Not only did the Press Expedition accomplish the first crossing of the Olympic Mountains during that year, but also the first recommendations were made to establish a national park in the mountains. The long centuries of isolation had ended, and the peninsula was soon to be washed by stormy waves of controversy.

Judge James Wickersham, who explored the eastern Olympics during the summer months of 1889 and 1890, and Lieutenant Joseph P. O'Neil, who had commanded military expeditions into the mountains in 1885 and 1890, met on the upper Skokomish in July, 1890. They exchanged ideas and information, and in November both men recommended that the interior of the Olympic Peninsula be set aside as a national park. They may have arrived at their idea independently, or perhaps while together, sitting beside a campfire in the mountains.

Wickersham was the first to put the suggestion in

writing. His conception was that the park "should be 30 miles wide, north and south, and 40 miles, east and west, containing 1,200 square miles or 768,000 acres, which is about one-third the size of Yellowstone Park."

Lieutenant O'Neil's report on his second expedition in the Olympics appeared shortly afterward. In it, O'Neil declared: "While the country on the outer slopes of these mountains is very valuable, the interior is useless for all practicable purposes. It would, however, serve admirably for a national park. There are numerous elk—that noble animal so fast disappearing from this country—that should be protected. The scenery, which often made us hungry, weary, and over-packed explorers forget for the moment our troubles, to pause and admire, would surely please people traveling with comfort and for pleasure."

These proposals fell on unsympathetic ears. The Pacific Northwest was still a virgin land. The problem, as the settlers saw it, was how to clear the forests to make way for agriculture, not how to preserve them. It probably never occurred to these people that in the not too distant future the wilderness, then widespread, would become scarce.

The Olympic Forest Reserve

By executive order on February 22, 1897, President Cleveland created the Olympic Forest Reserve, thus withdrawing more than two million acres from settlement and entry. The reserve included the Olympic Mountains in their entirety, plus extensive lowlands lying between the mountains and the Pacific. The purpose of the reserve was to protect the forests from wasteful destruction, but almost before the ink from the president's pen had time to dry local commercial interests began attempts to have the reserve abolished or reduced in size.

Henry Gannett, chief geographer of the United States Geological Survey, organized a survey of the new forest reserve. The actual field work was done by two young surveyors, Arthur Dodwell and Theodore F. Rixon, aided by several assistants. The men worked long hours running compass lines, triangulating, checking altitudes, and photographing the forests and mountains. Three years—1898, 1899 and 1900—were required to complete the survey, the men working the lowlands in the winter and moving into the high country with the coming of summer.

The Dodwell-Rixon report, published in 1902, described all the area originally included within the reserve, although most of the lowlands were eliminated while the survey was proceeding. The same local interests who had opposed the reserve from the beginning succeeded in getting more than seven hundred thousand acres covered with prime timber removed, mostly in the southern and northwestern parts of the reserve. The deleted timberland soon passed into private ownership.

The surveyors reported that the Olympic Forest Reserve contained almost sixty-one billion board feet of timber, enough to supply the entire demand of the United States for two years. The reserve was one of the most heavily forested regions in the country. Thus the economic stakes were enormous.

In 1907 the name of the reserve was changed to Olympic National Forest. The forest's supervisor, R. L. Fromme, stated in 1913 that the region's value for recreational purposes was entirely beyond calculation, especially in view of its easy access from Puget Sound, Grays Harbor and Vancouver Island.

The Mount Olympus National Monument

As the new century began, the pace stepped up, settlement and development were rapid, and opportunists scrambled madly for timber claims. Unrestrained exploitation of the enormous forest on the peninsula became the order of the day and, crude as their equipment was, the loggers cut wide swaths of destruction.

The establishment of the forest reserve was a forward step, but it did not assure permanent preservation of the mountain wilderness, only some control over its exploitation. At best, it meant a few decades of delay before the forest giants fell under the impact of the loggers' axes.

Obviously, better protection was needed, and various

groups began to press for establishment of a national park or game refuge in the Olympics. Several bills were introduced in Congress, but commercial interests prevented their passage. In spite of determined resistance, however, Congressman William Humphrey persuaded President Theodore Roosevelt to establish the heart of the peninsula as the Mount Olympus National Monument. This was done in March, 1909, under the authority of the Act for the Preservation of American Antiquities. The Forest Service administered the monument until 1933, when all national monuments were transferred to the jurisdiction of the National Park Service.

The monument covered six hundred and twenty thousand acres, or a little less than one thousand square miles. Protection of the Olympic elk was the primary reason for establishment of the monument, but it also served to preserve the high alpine country, the glaciers, and some of the surrounding virgin forest. Unfortunately, between 1912 and 1929, three presidential proclamations reduced the size of the monument until it contained less than three hundred thousand acres. The largest withdrawal was during World War I when timber and mining interests, under the pretense of military necessity, induced President Wilson to withdraw almost half the monument. Following this reduction only a few of the big trees in the lowlands remained within the monument boundaries.

In October, 1927, the Mount Olympus National Monument was closed to trapping and hunting in perpetuity in an effort to conserve the wildlife of the mountains. Biologists thought that a surplus of animals would develop, with a consequent overflow into districts more easily accessible to hunters. However, supervised killing of the so-called predatory species was allowed.

Revival of the Park Movement

The park movement became quiescent with the establishment of the monument, but each year more people came to this strange land of white peaks and green forests, and the feeling gradually grew that this country deserved to be protected permanently in its natural state.

As interest in a national park grew among outdoorsmen and conservationists, the logging was accelerated. The stands of towering virgin timber that had reached to the edge of the sea were disappearing with amazing rapidity. During the 1920's the Grays Harbor mills alone cut nearly a billion board feet a year. Bleak, ugly stumplands gradually replaced the forest as the loggers cut their way ever closer to the foothills and the still inviolate high peaks.

The national park movement that had begun in the first decade of the century was revived in the thirties. Many scientists and naturalists who felt that the area should be preserved joined conservationists in a drive which culminated in the introduction of bills by Representative Mon Wallgren of Washington to create a national park in the Olympic Mountains.

The first bill, introduced in 1935, provided for a park of approximately seven hundred and thirty thousand acres, but it failed to pass. A second bill was introduced in 1937. In deference to timbermen more than one hundred thousand acres in the Bogachiel and Quinault valleys were excluded, and in lieu thereof fifty thousand acres of commercially useless alpine country on the eastern edge of the mountains was substituted.

This second bill, conciliatory as it was, met opposition from lumbermen who maintained that the park should not be larger than three hundred square miles, or less than two hundred thousand acres. Such a park would have been roughly contiguous with the high country above timberline and actually smaller than the existing national monument.

Franklin D. Roosevelt visited the peninsula in 1937. The President's enthusiasm over the region revived hope and interest in the idea of park protection for the Olympic rain forests.

The Olympic Primitive Area

Meanwhile, in 1936, the United States Forest Service established the Olympic Primitive Area adjacent to the Mount Olympus National Monument. Those who opposed creation of a national park claimed that existence of the monument and primitive area made a national park unnecessary. However, both the monument and primitive area occupied primarily country lying at high altitudes. The primitive area was essentially a series of ridge-top projections extending outward from the monument like the arms of an octopus. The prime forest areas were still largely unprotected.

Moreover, the primitive area had been established by the Secretary of Agriculture and, according to the law, he could reduce its size or abolish it at any time. But a national park could be altered only by an act of Congress.

Thus, the primitive area really lacked protection. At one time its boundaries were modified to permit the construction of an aerial tramway near Lake Quinault, but the structure was never built.

When the national park was finally established, the Forest Service abolished what remained of the Olympic Primitive Area on the illogical theory that since the greater part of it was incorporated within the park, what remained had little value as wilderness.

The Battle in Congress

When the park bills came up in Congress, proponents and opponents appeared at hearings held by the Committee on Public Lands of the House of Representatives. Those who favored a national park stressed the values of wilderness preservation and the immeasurable benefits to be gained by future generations. Emphasis was placed on the necessity of protecting some of the best of the Pacific Northwest's virgin forests, as well as the wintering grounds of the Olympic elk. Scientists also pointed out the great value of an area relatively untouched by man, one that could be studied in its natural state. Leading the battle against the proposed park were the timber companies, who stressed the usual economic motives. They were strongly backed by hunters, advocates of organized winter sports, and by hydroelectric interests who wished to construct dams on the rivers. Anti-park sentiment was also expressed by local chambers of commerce who failed to appreciate the future harvests their communities would reap from the tourists. The Forest Service, reluctant to give up its own plans for the area, also expressed opposition to the park idea. However, the Forest Service plan would have permitted heavy logging in the choice timber areas, as it called for the retention of only narrow strips of virgin forest along the trails and larger streams.

Those who opposed inclusion of the west side rain forests painted a forbidding picture of that region. This was a dark, gloomy place where the sun never shone, lashed by relentless wind and rain from ocean gales. No one, they declared, dared venture into this forest unless clad in mackinaw and hip boots, for seldom could a man travel through the western Olympics "without going through a terrible deluge of rain." Moreover, to go more than thirty feet from road or trail was dangerous, for one would likely become hopelessly lost in the dismal jungle. The region would never attract visitors like national parks located in arid lands, for the fog, rain and dense forest growth would repel visitors. "To what purpose," one man eloquently proclaimed, "do we ask that this land of heavy rainfall, fog flying in from the ocean, and subject to these heavy winds be preserved, when it cannot be seen by any human being?" But these park opponents conveniently forgot to mention that during the summer months, the season of tourist travel, rainfall on the peninsula decreases drastically, sometimes to the point where lawns and gardens must be irrigated.

As Congress began to move toward establishing a park, the opposition became increasingly desperate, and wild, unfounded charges were bandied about. Conservationists were even accused of attempting to destroy the lumber industry by reserving the entire peninsula as a national park. Fortunately, Congress ignored these absurdities, and on June 29, 1938, established Olympic National Park.

Olympic National Park

After years of bitter struggle between conservationists and commercial interests, the park was in being. It consisted of 648,000 acres of primitive mountain land, of which 645,700 acres were owned by the federal government. Included within the new park was all of the national monument, much of the primitive area, and other lands taken from the Olympic National Forest. Only 2,300 acres of privately owned land were involved. Thus it was truly a great bargain for the taxpayer.

A provision in the law empowered the president to add to the park, by proclamation, up to 250,292 acres. This was to be done after studies were made by the Forest Service and after due consideration had been given to the effect on commercial interests. On three different occasions land was added to the park. The additions consisted of a large area of high mountainous country in the north and southeast, plus lowland extensions down the western river valleys to provide protection for the best of the rain forests and the winter range of the elk. Land was also acquired fronting the Pacific Ocean, together with a corridor along the Queets River. This assured preservation of a representative portion of the primitive ocean beaches, and one river from the mountains to the sea.

Olympic National Park was dedicated on June 15, 1946, and at present it contains 896,599 acres, of which 888,557 are federally owned. Fifth in size among the national parks, it extends roughly forty miles in each direction. At least ninety-five per cent of the park remains in its natural, primitive condition, unmodified by man. No commercial activity is allowed except on privately owned lands or valid existing claims. Otherwise, lumbering, grazing, prospecting and mining are prohibited.

Thus the park preserves a wilderness landscape of mountain peaks, glaciers, lakes, rivers, canyons and valleys. Included is a spacious sample of virgin forest, plus a large variety of wildlife, and various geologic features. Primarily, however, the park protects the lowland virgin forest, the finest remnant of the original Pacific Northwest forests that once extended from the Cascades to the sea.

The Continuing Controversy

The controversy over the forests of the Olympic Mountains did not end with establishment of the national park. The battle has been a continuing one, times of turmoil alternating with periods of calm. This conflict over use of the forest will probably never end as long as valuable trees remain within the reservation.

The debate has revolved around a basically simple question: shall the virgin forests within the park be preserved as an exhibit of the forest primeval, or shall they be cut to benefit the peninsula's lumber industry? In other words, shall the national park be held inviolate, or shall it be subject to the depredations of short-sighted commercialism?

Over the past few years the tide has turned toward conservation, but the battle gains in bitterness as it rages. The timber companies would like to plunder the park for personal profit, leaving unspoiled only the higher mountain regions that have no commercial value. Thus they keep alive an active program calling for the removal from the park of approximately three hundred thousand acres, more than one-third of its area. This would mean elimination of most of the impressive stands of virgin forest now preserved. Yet the acreage of park land desired by industry is equivalent to only ten per cent of the timberland on the Olympic Peninsula presently available for logging. Nevertheless, the plywood and sawmill operators, widely aided by the local press, clamor for the park resources and exert continuous pressure to have large areas returned to the Olympic National Forest, where logging is permitted.

Olympic National Park is fortunate, however, in having many defenders willing to fight for its protection. The battle has been long and hard fought, and is far from over. Conservationists cannot relax, but must remain alert and ready to defend, else watch their heritage ruthlessly destroyed.

Arguments against the Park

The timbermen have a number of arguments filed away to use against the park, and these are pulled out as the occasion affords an opportunity. Many are deliberate fabrications and distortions. The simple basis of these efforts is economic greed which looks to enrichment of a few at the expense of many, and indifference to the will of the public as manifested in the legislation that created the park.

The arguments are varied generalizations and include

assertions that the park is too large, the forest is locked up, a boundary problem exists, the local mills need the park trees to sustain their operations, the forests are "over ripe" and therefore going to waste, the forests could be selectively logged without injury to the park landscape, and the old growth forests constitute a fire hazard and are also highly susceptible to destruction from insect infestations and storm winds. In the park's early days the claim was also made that few people went into the region, and those who did could not see the forest because of the fog and jungle-like growth. This argument is seldom heard today, obviously because of the tremendous number of park visitors.

Certain types of arguments are reserved for special occasions, like the one made during World War II that the spruce trees in the rain forests were needed for airplane construction. Harold Ickes, Secretary of the Interior, effectively pointed out, however, that adequate supplies of spruce were available elsewhere, and the park trees were saved. Not long afterward came the post-war assertion that the park forests were needed to provide lumber for the veterans' housing program, despite the fact that enough standing sawtimber existed in the Douglas fir belt alone to build two houses for every family in the United States.

Too Large a Park?

How large is "too large"? Considerable emphasis has been placed on the size of Olympic National Park, the claim being that too much land has been protected. Invariably, however, those who base their attack on this ground fail to mention that most of the park land is rugged mountain country having little economic value. In fact, the opposite is usually implied, the park being described as "nearly a million acres of virgin timber."

As the years pass by, however, it becomes increasingly apparent that more, not less, land is needed for recreation. For several hundred years the American wilderness has retreated before the encroachment of civilization, and we cannot afford to lose what little remains. Today's civilization provides us with mobility and increased leisure time. These factors, coupled with rapid population growth, particularly in the Pacific Northwest, foretell continuously increasing use of the mountain lands in this region. Clearly, the area reserved must be spacious in order that people can disperse, without crowding, and experience the feeling of isolation and solitude.

The "Over ripe" Forest

The contention that the Olympic rain forests should be "harvested" because they are "over ripe" or "over mature" is meaningless. These are silvicultural terms, applicable only to lands managed for timber production, not those dedicated to recreation and esthetic enjoyment. The terms merely mean that the trees are too old to make the best lumber, an immaterial consideration on park land. The park is a museum of old growth forest, not a timber reservoir. This primeval forest presents essentially the same appearance today as it did a century ago or will a century hence. It has survived a good many centuries without the help of man and, except for protection from his own depredations, does not need the interference of man to maintain itself. The forest is not rotting away, but is very much alive and growing, and contains trees of all sizes and stages of growth. In its natural cycle of perpetuation, the trees mature, grow old, fall to earth during winter storms, and are replaced by young trees. Growth and depletion are continuous processes, and in a relatively large undisturbed area such as this, they tend to balance each other. The balance is delicate, however, and can be easily upset by the activities of man.

Selective Logging

The suggestion has also been made that the rain forests could be logged selectively, but this contention lacks merit. Such logging would result in destruction of the unique characteristics of the park. Selective logging means the removal of mature trees without cutting the entire stand, as contrasted to clear cutting, where solid blocks of forest are cut and nothing is left standing. Clear cutting is the only practical harvesting method in this region. In either case, however, the forest is destroyed for esthetic enjoyment, therefore logging would negate the purpose of the park—the preservation of virgin forest in a natural, unmodified state. If logging were permitted on park lands, the forest giants, once cut, would be lost forever, their place taken by a dismal array of gigantic stumps and logging debris, and the visitor passing through such a mutilated forest would be shocked and disillusioned.

Needs of the Local Mills

The claim has often been made that the local mills need the park timber to sustain their operations. However, testimony given at congressional hearings has proved, time and again, that this contention is untrue.

Actually, the quantity of available timber on the peninsula is increasing rapidly. Outside the park are three million acres of top-quality timber growing land primarily suitable for the growing of forest products. This is all available to industry.

Washington's two national parks, Olympic and Mount Rainier, contain less than two per cent of the land in the state classified by foresters as "commercial timberland." Our entire national park system, in fact, contains only 1.4 per cent of the total forested area of the nation. Obviously, logging national parks will not sustain the timber industry. Attempts to grab park lands are merely examples of the greed and cynicism that must be fought at every turn by the informed citizen determined to protect his rights and his heritage.

The Boundary Problem

The most recent attack on Olympic National Park has been on the basis that its boundaries are illogical because they do not always follow natural topographic lines—that is, the ridges defining watersheds—therefore causing "administrative problems." It is suggested that the boundaries be redrawn, in such a manner as to exclude several heavily forested areas. In this connection the contention has also been made that land "not suitable" for park purposes has been included within the park.

In many instances, of course, a topographic boundary is the most desirable, but not necessarily essential. For example, very few of our states and counties have topographic boundary lines, but this fact has not prevented their governments from administering them effectively. Moreover, the boundaries of Olympic National Park follow topographic lines more closely than do the boundaries of most national parks, so it makes little sense to attack this particular park on that ground.

The boundaries of Olympic National Park have been the subject of controversy for years. In 1947 a bill to create a commission to "study" the park boundaries was introduced in Congress. The purpose was really to release forest land from the park. The National Park Service, fearful that the attempted raid would be successful, offered to relinquish fifty-six thousand acres, of which thirty-three thousand acres were in the superb Bogachiel wilderness. In response to this open invitation, the lumbermen moved in for the kill, but they were defeated by the determined resistance of conservationists.

Boundaries are, of course, man-made lines. They are not sacred, and can always be changed. In fact, the park itself could be abolished at some future time, but this is unlikely. Obviously a given boundary will not satisfy everyone, but Olympic National Park has probably received more attention with regard to boundaries than has any other national park. Generally speaking, the lines were well drawn, and they have withstood the test of time because the park has met the public need. If any changes are to be made, conservationists feel the boundaries should be extended outward to include additional land of park quality rather than deleting any areas presently within the park.

Salvage Logging

In the 1950's the National Park Service itself conducted "salvage logging" operations within Olympic National Park, contracting with timber companies for the removal of fallen trees. The funds thus obtained were used to purchase privately owned lands within the national park. The acquisition of in-holdings was a worthy motive, but unfortunately the salvage operations were, by their nature, inconsistent with the purpose of a national park, where it is desired to preserve a natural landscape. Furthermore, considerable destruction attended the use of logging equipment removing the fallen trees, thus dis-rupting the natural scene. Conservationists voiced objection to the salvage operations, and eventually the park service, respond-ing to the public outcry, abolished the salvage program.

Park Visitors

At the time the park was established the most reliable estimates indicated that about five thousand people entered the Mount Olympus National Monument each year. Thus the claim was made that not enough people used the area to justify a national park. Ten years later, however, nearly two hundred thousand persons visited the park, and the figure doubled the following year. Twenty years after park establishment the num-ber of annual visitors surpassed the million mark. In 1962, for the first time, more than two million people entered Olympic National Park. This annual influx of visitors brings an immense economic bounty to the Olympic Peninsula.

Although many people are attracted to the meadows, flowers and snowfields of the high country, most park visitors stay in the river valleys, the natural entrances to this mountain land. Here, in surroundings of great natural beauty, unspoiled by man's pathetic attempts at development, they camp and fish, walk beneath towering trees, and breathe smog-free mountain air. Unfortunately, commercial interests seek to destroy these natural entrances, and if they had their way visitors would encounter a desolation of slash and stumps, polluted water and silted streams.

The Roadbuilding Threat

Loss of its virgin forests is not the only danger that threatens the superb wilderness contained within Olympic National Park. Pressure is also exerted, from time to time, to build roads across the park, and to extend the trail system into the remotest parts of the interior. Man is an inveterate road builder and, since the advent of motor cars, not many areas have escaped. Roads, of course, make areas more accessible, but they have no place in a wilderness. Indeed, the quickest way to destroy the outstanding wilderness character of Olympic National Park would be to construct roads, because the chief attraction of the park's interior lies in its wild and rugged beauty, beyond the reach of the automobile. Extension of roads across the park would destroy the aura of enchantment that still pervades the Olympics. The solitude of the wild, lonely recesses of the mountains, unbroken by the sound of motor vehicles and unmarred by the works of man, appeals to persons sensitive to the lure of primitive country. The region seems to have been unaltered since time began, not only in the depths of the mysterious rain forests but also on the windswept, rain-drenched slopes and snow-filled basins above timberline.

This roadless interior of the park should remain isolated from mechanized travel, for nothing destroys wilderness more effectively or permanently than invasion by motor vehicles. It would be wise to keep this one park, at least, primarily an area for the horseback rider or the backpacker. We do not need to make all our scenic areas accessible to the motorist. Olympic National Park has several unique features, and most of these—the rain forests, the elk herds, the mountain-and-sea vista from Hurricane Ridge—are presently accessible to visitors who travel solely by car. However, the park's wilderness character cannot be appreciated from a highway. In order to savor wilderness, one must lose himself in the lands beyond the highways.

The existing road pattern in Olympic National Park is adequate with the possible exception of one or two additional loop roads near the perimeter. The spur roads that now enter the park from all sides provide convenient access to the park's extensive trail system.

At the present time the park exhibits, more by accident than plan, a natural zoning. The wild core of the park is not only roadless but also free of trails, inviting the traveler who wishes to traverse country that is truly primeval. Surrounding this undeveloped core are two belts, like concentric circles. The inner, broader belt contains most of the park's vast trail system of nearly six hundred miles. The outer band also contains trails, plus the spur roads that extend into the perimeter of the park. This natural zoning should be retained for the future, for it is both logical and desirable.

Two-thirds of the Olympic Ocean Strip is also roadless, the last significant primeval coastline on the Pacific between Canada and Mexico. This wilderness coast should be protected from encroachments of civilization. The area is not inaccessible, for several roads leading to the beaches provide starting and terminal points for hikes along the beach. The proposed highway paralleling the coast would add little in the way of benefits, but would irreparably harm the remnant of coastal wilderness. This wild coast at present complements the mountain wilderness. It should be remembered that the various parts of the park are interdependent. One is a necessary element to the enjoyment and appreciation of the other. Any devastation or diminution in one area diminishes the whole.

Under the "Mission 66" program considerable work was done to make the park accessible to the casual visitor. A few additional developments of a limited nature are probably needed, but they should be undertaken in such a manner as not to impair the park's wilderness character. The lodge at Big Meadow on Hurricane Ridge, with the all-weather access road, is an excellent example of what has been done in good taste to open vistas to people who are unable to hike. But most of the park should remain roadless. The very essence of the Olympic wilderness is its natural landscape, unmarred by the works of man.

Wilderness Values of the Park

Olympic is a relatively new member of the national park system and, like all our nature reservations, has many values which cannot be measured by a money standard. This outdoor museum and nature sanctuary has a varied array of exhibits that are not "locked up" from use. They have been denied to commercial utilization and made available for esthetic and scientific purposes, just as minerals on display in museums are exhibited for inspiration and study.

The park provides us the opportunity to return to the well-springs of nature, to renew and replenish our spiritual energies. Olympic is also an outdoor laboratory for students and scientists who are drawn by its primitive features, now so hard to find in our mechanized, transistorized world. In a real sense, the park provides benefits of inestimable value to each of its visitors.

Above all, perhaps, Olympic National Park is a testimonial to the judgment and foresight of the people who fought so hard to make it a reality, and who are dedicated to the park's continued preservation. Thus, in a sense, it is a tribute to the character and values of the people of the United States.

Olympic's virgin forests are unique. These forests are valuable today, but they will have still greater value in the future when all virgin growth outside of parks and memorial forests has been cut, the victim of the chain saw and the bulldozer.

Not only are the virgin forests a prelude to the mountains, they are one of the park's outstanding attractions, and the most accessible. The forest and high country complement each other. Without the forests, Olympic National Park would be like a mansion standing on barren ground, devoid of lawn, trees and flowering shrubs. The unbroken forests that clothe the valleys and lower slopes provide the framing for the meadows, snowfields and rocky peaks that rise above the timberline. Thus the forest offers a gradual transition into the inner wilderness, a transition necessary for true appreciation of this primitive land.

The trees protected in Olympic are only remnants of the virgin forests that once blanketed the Pacific slope. These forest remnants should remain intact, and the trees permitted to live their lives to completion in natural surroundings. Somewhere we must draw a line beyond which logging is forbidden, for the virgin forest is vulnerable. In the Olympics, aged trees that have withstood the storms of centuries can be sent crashing earthward in a few minutes with modern logging equipment.

In our national economy the park trees, as merchantable timber, are insignificant. As a superlative example of the original forests of the Pacific Northwest, they are priceless and irreplaceable. Obviously no comparable area will ever again be left undisturbed for the many centuries required to produce such a forest. We are not yet so poor in resources that we cannot spare a few examples of outstanding virgin forest, untouched by the savage destruction of civilized man. Somewhere there must be a sanctuary from axe, saw and bulldozer.

In Olympic we have such a sanctuary—a living wilderness where all plant and animal forms live their lives without interference. Here, where man is merely an observer, tiny treelets may grow to be towering giants, themselves to fall back to the nurturing earth to provide sustenance for those that follow.

Years ago we exterminated the passenger pigeon, the great auk and the Olympic wolf, and we nearly destroyed the buffalo and the whooping crane. We have polluted rivers and lakes, inundated canyons, demolished and burned our primeval forests, and plowed up the prairies. But man, the despoiler of his earth, has also tried to protect and conserve.

Here and there, as in Olympic National Park, we have managed to preserve relatively pristine samples of the good, green earth as a gift to future generations. We give them this in the hope that they, too, will have the land, and the time to see and enjoy the living wilderness.

Book II

In the Mountains

The impact of civilization on the Olympic Peninsula has produced a land of strange contrasts. Despite the fact that the State of Washington proudly advertises the region as "the unspoiled last frontier," the country has been greatly altered. Vast areas have been devastated by fire and lumbering operations. Bleak lands, denuded and ugly, stretch for miles, with blackened stumps and logging debris left to greet the eyes of the visitor. Most of the giant trees that once stood in unbroken stands from the seashore to the mountain snows are gone—cut to supply voracious sawmills in a rapid exploitation of what must have seemed an inexhaustible resource.

The interior landscape of the peninsula retains its wild and primitive loveliness, however, and the person who prefers to haunt remote regions can still find some of the nation's finest remaining stands of virgin timber, principally in the lower river valleys of the Olympic Mountains. These dark forests of aged trees tower nearly three hundred feet high, almost as high as the famed redwoods, and, second only to those redwoods, they are the forests of broadest girth and greatest height in North America.

Winding through the forests are moss-carpeted trails that follow the river valleys to the back country, the remote mountain interior where elk, deer and bear roam unmolested. Cold, swift rivers cleave the forests as they flow through the narrow canyons and valleys. These streams descend rapidly as they progress from the mountains to the sea. Near the timberline a multitude of deep blue lakes lie cupped among heather-covered mountainsides. Above them, subalpine meadows and barren ridges are splotched with snowfields and glaciers.

In summer melting snowbanks on the meadowlands are bordered by colorful wildflowers. Later, blueberries and huckleberries ripen on the high slopes, and black bears dine on the luscious fruit. This is the season, too, when herds of elk wander over the high country before descending to winter in the lowland valleys, where they often congregate on gravel bars bordering the rivers.

The heart of the peninsula—the wilderness enclosed within Olympic National Park—is largely "undeveloped" road-less country that retains the charm of landscape unmodified by the technology of man. This is wilderness where the backpacker can lose himself in a return to the primitive with a realization that civilization is actually a superimposed state on the earth; that wilderness landscapes dominated the planet for millions of years, and that civilization is unlikely to survive when man fails to live in harmony with nature.

Chapter VI

Tramping Olympic Trails

The Pulse of the Seasons

Because the Olympic Peninsula lies at high latitude, closer to the North Pole than the Equator, the summer days are long, up to sixteen hours intervening between sunrise and sunset. During the warm months, from May through September, the trails become worn by the footfalls of the backpacker and the trailrider's horses. But to really know the Olympic Mountains one must visit them at all seasons because they have variable moods and present different faces as the seasons change with the turning of the earth. To see their sharp outlines softened by summer haze is not enough, for the peaks are equally interesting when shrouded in autumn's fogbanks and winter's mists, or in the spring, when they lurk behind dark clouds in an elusive game of hide-and-seek.

Snow usually begins to fall in the high country in October. The first autumn storm drenches the lowlands and whitens the higher summits and ridges left barren by the summer sun. This frosting of the mountaintops signals the approach of winter and indicates that hibernation time has arrived for the animals that sleep through the cold months, and that migration

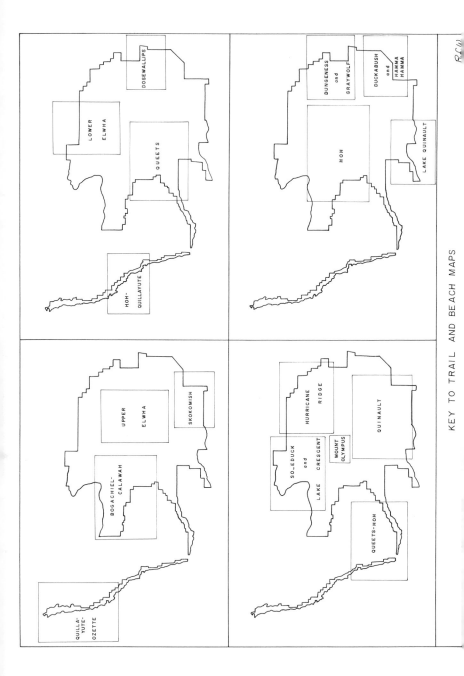

KEY TO TRAIL AND BEACH MAPS

DOSEWALLIPS

LOWER
ELWHA

QUEETS

HOH-
QUILLAYUTE

UPPER
ELWHA

SKOKOMISH

BOGACHIEL-
CALAWAH

QUILLA-
YUTE-
OZETTE

DUNGENESS
and
GRAYWOLF

DUCKABUSH
and
HAMMA
HAMMA

HOH

LAKE QUINAULT

HURRICANE
RIDGE

SO-EDUCK
and
LAKE
CRESCENT

MOUNT
OLYMPUS

QUINAULT

QUEETS-HOH

RCW

time down to lower elevations has come for those who must face the winter awake. During this seasonal transition the weather pattern is variable and quick-changing. One day the skies are sunny, the air redolent with the mesmeric charm of Indian summer; the next, the sun has disappeared and ragged nimbus clouds scud across the skies, trailing rain as they move inland.

The dark days of November bring a chill to the land that replaces the transitory warmth of Indian summer. Gray clouds roll in relentlessly from the Pacific, releasing heavy rain on the lowlands. Higher up snow falls steadily and the snow line descends lower and lower on the mountainsides as the weather becomes colder. By the end of December the high country above four thousand feet lies deeply buried, and on clear days the mountains, snow-covered from base to summit, appear to have been chiseled from pure white marble. Now the peaks stand aloof, undisturbed by man except for a few hardy mountaineers.

Spring comes early to the lowlands, arriving in April when the dogwoods splash white against the conifers' somber greens, and climbs the mountainsides as the snowline recedes, to culminate at higher elevations when the rhododendron buds open in early July. Spring is uncertain and tentative in the Olympics, with damp, chilly weather, and fog lingering in the deep canyons. A noisy season, it contrasts vividly with the white silence of winter. The squawking of the ravens and the jays, and the booming of streams carrying the melting snow to the sea are punctuated by the rumble of avalanches as tons of snow thunder down the mountainsides. On the lowlands the forest floor comes alive, exhibiting many shades of green, and the rain forests display their own special splendor.

In the high country spring fades almost imperceptibly into the brief but lovely summer. From early July until October the days are cool and sunny, warming in the afternoons. The morning skies are generally clear, but clouds often gather in the afternoon, when cumulus masses float around the higher peaks. Occasionally these develop into thunderheads accompanied by lightning and heavy showers, but this is rare. As night approaches the clouds dissipate, the air chills and the stars appear, incredibly bright in the blackness of the night sky.

Indian summer adds a delightful touch to the close of summer. The days are warm and pleasant, deceptive in that they give no hint of the approach of winter. Traveling is easiest then, for the high country trails are free of snow. In the lowland forests the maples turn scarlet and gold, accenting the dark green of the conifers, and the slim trunks of the alders stand starkly white beside the swift-flowing rivers. On high, exposed meadows above timberline huckleberry bushes glow like red and purple beacons, and the hiker is likely to see bears gorging on the berries to store fat for the coming winter hibernation. Nights become longer and crisper, frost comes to the higher elevations, and the stage is set for snowfall when autumn storms arrive. Once again ragged clouds move, wraithlike, across the timbered mountainsides and winter establishes itself among the high peaks, its cold, brooding stillness quietly and inexorably completing the majestic turn of the seasons.

Access Roads

For decades the mountainous interior of the Olympic Peninsula was largely ignored by travelers because, lacking roads and trails, exploration was difficult. The land is still wild, but no longer unknown, and is easily reached from a dozen spur roads penetrating inward up the river valleys from the encircling highway like broken spokes of a wheel. Except for two routes which ascend to the high country, these roads follow rivers and end at low elevations while still in the foothills.

Although Olympic National Park is essentially roadless, unmarred by a network of highways, these spur roads permit the automobile traveler to see representative portions of all the major park features except the glaciers. Several roads on the western side provide access to the rain forests, where deer and elk are often observed. From the Hurricane Ridge and Blue Mountain roads, which climb above five thousand feet, a succession of snowfields and meadows parades before the traveler.

The National Park Service maintains free public campgrounds at most of the roadheads. These have piped water, comfort stations and individual camping units with cooking facilities and picnic tables.

The Central Olympics: Mount Olympus Range, right and center background; Bailey Range, foreground, left background.

Photograph by Asahel Curtis, courtesy Washington State Historical Society.

Photograph by Robert L. Wood.

View down the Hoh Valley from near the summit of Mount Carrie.

Hoh Lake, with Mount Olympus (left) and Mount Tom (right) in the background.

Photograph by Charles L. Allyn.

Photograph by Charles L. Allyn.

View south from Mount Stone, on the national park boundary. Sawtooth Range (capped by Mount Cruiser) on left; Mount Skokomish to the right.

Photograph by Charles L. Allyn.

Mount Olympus; East Peak (center) and Middle Peak (right), Blue Glacier in foreground.

Photograph by Charles L. Allyn.

Photograph by Charles L. Allyn.

Mountain goat on Mount Angeles.

Lake Crescent, looking west.

Traversing on Mount Constance; the climbers are on the "Terrible Traverse," the "Fingertip Traverse" is almost directly above them.

Photograph by Charles L. Allyn.

Mount Olympus, its summits lost in cloud, from an alpine lake in the Queets Basin. Humes Glacier

Photograph by Bob and Ira Spring.

Mount Pershing from Mount Washington, southeastern Olympics.

Photograph by Bob and Ira Spring.

Upper Lena Lake, with Mount Bretherton in the background.

Photograph by Bob and Ira Spring.

A climber explores the Upper Cirque of Mount Olympus in the winter.
West Peak, covered with snow, rises in the background.

Photograph by Bob and Ira Spring.

Mount Steel in early summer, from above Home Sweet Home.

Photograph by Bob and Ira Spring.

Winter scene, Hurricane Ridge.

Offshore seastacks along the Olympic coastal strip.

Photograph by Bob and Ira Spring.

The "Hall of Mosses," near the Hoh Ranger Station, Hoh Valley. This luxuriance is a characteristic feature of the Olympic Rain Forest.

Photograph by Bob and Ira Spring.

A north wilderness coast beach, Cake Island offshore.

Photograph by Bob and Ira Spring.

Marymere Falls, near Lake Crescent.

The "Pony Bridge" across the East Fork Quinault, on the trail to Enchanted Valley.

Photograph by Robert L. Wood.

Climbers, ascending steep snow below West Peak, Mount Olympus.

The Trail System

The man reluctant to leave his automobile will miss the primitive interior of Olympic National Park, but the backpacker or trailrider may easily enjoy this wilderness via the nearly six hundred miles of trails lacing the region. Beginning at the spur roads, these pathways follow the valleys through virgin forests, criss-cross the foothills and ridges, then climb through meadowlands toward the barren rock, snow and ice that crest the higher peaks and ridges.

Many trails, worn deep through centuries of use, were created by the elk in their wanderings. Man has extended and improved this complex network, linking the elk paths with his own trails for continuity. Elk, deer and bear still use the trails but are sometimes frightened away by approaching travelers. The trails are safe, and most have easy gradients, but they are narrow, few being more than eighteen inches wide. Usually they follow the sides of ridges and valleys having sun exposure, thus are free of snow relatively early in the year.

Shelters are located along the trails at intervals of eight to ten miles, in both the low and high country. These lean-tos were built for trail maintenance crews, but are open to the public. Most are built of logs and cedar shakes, with crude rock fireplaces, thus harmonize with their primitive surroundings.

The trails are heavily used by backpackers and those who prefer to go by horse or who have their supplies packed in. Although some trails are steep, and dangerous places do exist, most healthy persons experience no difficulty. Because the Olympics do not rise to lofty elevation, the effects of altitude are negligible and hikers are quickly conditioned. However, the quiet face of the wilderness is deceptive, and the imprudent or inexperienced hiker who exercises poor judgment may suffer injury or death. Carelessness sometimes spells doom to the seasoned outdoorsman, and lack of knowledge is often responsible for the neophyte wandering into terrain avoided by the sophisticated wilderness traveler.

Probably the greatest hazard in the Olympics is the unpredictable weather. Fogs move in rapidly to confuse one's sense of direction, and sudden storms may bring snow and freezing temperatures at higher altitudes even in the middle of summer. The rivers are also hazardous. Flowing swift and cold over boulder strewn beds, their powerful currents are traps for the unwary. Utmost caution should be exercised when crossing on logs, or when wading.

In the higher Olympics the glaciers, streams of ice in motion, are broken by deep crevasses hidden beneath a deceptive covering of snow. Only experienced mountaineers properly equipped with ropes, ice axes and other climbing gear should venture forth upon them. Many snowfields are also dangerous because they are undermined by streams, or lie in avalanche paths. Other potential dangers are the dense forests, impassable canyons, and steep, heather-covered mountainsides.

Valley Hiking

The lowland trails begin in the river bottomlands and extend for miles up the valleys to join other paths which culminate in the high country forming the wilderness core. They are the most accessible routes in the park, and in their early stages are often used by casual hikers and those who lack the stamina for backpacking or trailriding.

These low elevation trails direct the visitor through a luxuriant green realm shaded by ancient conifers. Occasionally detouring around enormous fallen trees, the paths meander across the bottomlands, and alongside the streams. The terrain of the lowlands is sometimes smooth and level, but more often the surface is uneven and the trail climbs over low spurs only to dip down again. Although undergrowth is luxuriant, it tends to be clustered, even in the rain forests, and many places have a minimum of low-growing plants. In contrast with the much denser second growth forests, the primitive stands are comparatively free from brush, thus are easily traveled. The alert hiker, especially he who travels alone, will see many species of wildlife, large and small, including elk, deer, bear, chipmunks, squirrels and marmots.

The spirit of the lowlands is determined by the forest. On the calmest summer days mountain breezes riffle the treetops two hundred feet above the ground, creating mysterious rustling sounds. The crowns of the trees sway gently and rhythmically, and describe circles or ellipses against the background of the sky. Almost always a subdued murmur is present, often the prelude to an approaching storm. This murmur, an integral component of the primeval forest, may increase to symphonic volume as the canopy of trees is lashed by a passing gale.

Of special interest among the lowland trails are those traversing the west side rain forests. Here is a landscape that cannot be appreciated at a glance. One must linger awhile and walk among the trees—alone, if possible. Shafts of subdued green-gold sunlight piercing the treetops create a twilight effect, with dapples of sun and shadow. Cushions of moss, illuminated by vagrant rays of light, glow among the ferns on tree limbs roofing the trail, adding a mystic, eerie touch. One seems transported to an unreal, magical realm—the imaginative world of childhood where elves and goblins lurked in the shadows of secret hiding places. The visitor may walk for hours here, enchanted and humbled by giant plant forms that rise silently toward the sky.

The rain forest moods are as variable as those of the elusive, ice-clad peaks towering nearby. Most people see this forest in the dry season, when the weather is pleasant and the skies are sunny. To capture the mood of the region, however, one should come during the winter rainy season. Then clouds cling to the timbered mountainsides, and when it rains, which is often, the incessant dripping from fog-shrouded spruce and fir adds still another dimension to this brooding forest. Sound is deadened by the thick foliage, and the primitive silence is broken only by the deep, surging murmur of the west wind whispering in ancient, storm-torn trees.

The timelessness that pervades the Olympic rain forests is enhanced by their remoteness from civilization. To be alone in these forests, to walk among the huge boles and the sprawling vine maple, to hear no sounds save those made by the rain and the wind, and perhaps the call of a lone bird, is the essence of the wilderness experience.

The Long Climb

The canyonlike valleys in the Olympics seldom offer views of the peaks, and the hiker who wishes to see the mountains must climb upward to the high country. He does so via the steep, transitional trails that switchback up the forested mountainsides to connect the low and high routes. These paths ascend from the lowland forests through less spectacular mountainside stands and up to the land of scattered subalpine groves and meadows.

The traveler who hikes these trails, carrying his supplies on his back, quickly comes to realize the steepness and magnitude of the Olympics. He feels he has earned the right to enjoy the commanding views spread before him, and his emotional response is a deep one that eludes persons who gaze at the mountains from airplanes or ride to high points on ski lifts or in automobiles.

These ascending trails pass through forests of hemlock, Douglas fir, silver fir, western white pine and Alaska cedar. Beneath the thickset conifers fallen cones and needlelike leaves cover the forest floor, and gentle breezes keep a fresh supply showering down from above. Patches of snow last into summer in the deep shade. Invariably these are covered with both living and dead leaves of fir and hemlock, thus creating patterns of mingled green and brown on a white background. Avalanche and glacier lilies, nodding in the vagrant breezes, grow alongside the shaded snowbanks. Sometimes the trails cross ravines or avalanche paths where hardened snow, mixed with rocks and the debris of crushed trees, competes with rank growths of slide alder, vine maple or Devil's-club.

Fleeting views through the trees of distant, snowy peaks hint at what lies ahead and spur the tired hiker. Shafts of sunlight pierce the forest canopy, warming the brisk air which becomes cooler as the altitude increases. The wilderness silence is unbroken save for the constant murmur of soft breezes, the chattering of distant creeks, or the deep-throated call of a grouse.

Fortunately for the backpacker, most of the "climbing trails" are shaded from the sun by tall conifers. Switchback follows switchback, the trail progressing upward through forests which thin almost imperceptibly as the trees gradually become smaller.

The meadowlands appear suddenly, when least expected. The floral landscape changes from forests to open, grassy country, the terrain flattens, and the long climb is almost over.

Sweeping views prevail in many directions. Often the valleys below are swathed in fog, the mountain summits lost in the clouds. Mists rise and fall, or part, like draperies, to give glimpses of glacier and snowfield. But on other occasions the skies are cloudless and the distant, clear-cut peaks shimmer in the sunshine and deceive the uninitiated by their apparent nearness.

It is a beautiful world, almost unreal; one that repays the backpacker for his sweat and aching muscles.

On Snowfields and Meadows

Hikers who visit the Olympic high country in early summer are amazed at the enormous quantities of snow still covering the mountain basins. Massive drifts sweep upward to form wave-like cornices on the leeward sides of sharp ridges, and blanket northern exposures untouched by the sun. It looks like winter, and the air is cool when breezes blow across the snowfields, or clouds cover the sky. The sun is brilliant and warm, however, melting the snow with astounding speed to turn brooks which are dry in the morning into raging torrents by late afternoon. The melting, intensified by the warm wind, reaches its peak at this season and the water produced thereby must leave the mountains in a hurry. On hot days the booming and thundering of the creeks echoes through the canyons and valleys.

The snow disappears first from steep, exposed slopes where the depth is less than in the flatter basins, and where the sun's rays strike more directly. Often the northern sides of ridges are still covered when southern slopes are bare. In early morning the snow is hard and icy, and the hiker has little trouble finding firm footing. After the sun comes up, however, the snow softens, becoming mushy in the afternoons. Then it is tiring to hike across the snowfields. Close-set hollows known as "sun cups" cover the expanses of snow that remain in late summer. No water is visible upon the surface, the reduction of the snow mass resulting from evaporation, and seepage of the meltwater through the snow, where it travels beneath the snow or percolates into the ground.

In most years the snow on the high meadows is gone by

late July or early August, although deep banks may linger on
shaded slopes near ice-filled mountain lakes. Now the trails are
lined by masses of colorful wildflowers, among them lupine,
paintbrush and showy bear grass. Wild animals roam the uplands. Herds of elk cool themselves on snowfields; bears forage
for food.

When the mountaineer camps for the night in these
high altitude meadows, he finds the heavens afire with stars
shining through a limpid atmosphere. Tired from the day's
activities, he quickly falls to sleep and fails to notice the friendly
mountain mice that crawl into his sleeping bag to share its
warmth. Refreshed by the crisp night air, he awakens early, in
time to see red streaks gleaming over the eastern horizon as the
stars fade from an opaquely velvet western sky.

Across the Wilderness

The backpacker may traverse the Olympic Mountains
entirely by trail or by a combination of trail and cross-country
hiking. In either case the hiker should be experienced in mountain travel, and in top physical condition. He should also carry
the proper equipment (including maps and compass), be cau-
tious, and not travel alone. This is not a trip for the novice,
because it requires stamina, endurance, and knowledge of the
outdoors.

The hiker planning to walk across the mountains will
commence his trip in the lowland forest, then climb the timbered slopes over the steep switchbacks, and continue up to the
meadows and snowfields. The mountaineer who goes early in
the year meets fewer people, but the trip is likely to be more
strenuous because of snow in the high country. During the
summer, when many people travel through the mountains,
leaving the trails is a good way to escape crowds. Often the
cross-country hiker can go for days beyond the well-traveled
paths and not see anyone outside his own party.

The most popular and easiest traverse of the Olympics,
but not the most spectacular, takes one up the Elwha and across
Low Divide to the headwaters of the Quinault's north fork,
then follows that stream to Lake Quinault. This trip, most of
which coincides with the route of the 1890 Press Expedition,

follows trails all the way. More rugged trips are possible. In fact, the opportunities are almost unlimited for plan-it-yourself-trips beginning at the ends of the spur roads and traversing the mountains to emerge on the opposite side. These trips require at least a week, but an allowance of ten or twelve days is preferable.

Excellent areas for cross-country travel include the Bailey and Burke ranges, Del Monte Ridge, the Mount Stone traverse from Lena Lake to Mount Hopper, the upper Queets valley, and the high route from Anderson Pass to Hayden Pass.

Mountains to Climb

Although the mountain climber enjoys the forests, lakes, meadows, and ridges, the lodestone that calls him is the summit. He therefore willingly trudges from the high meadows to the narrow, wind-swept passes, his eyes focused on the lonely rock peaks streaked with snow.

Regular mountaineering equipment is necessary for climbing most Olympic peaks, especially the higher ones. Proper footgear for rock or ice is vital. So also is sunburn cream, because at the higher altitudes the heat of the sun is intense and the rays burn deeply and quickly.

The Pacific Northwest has many mountaineer clubs that offer climbing classes to their members. Most of the regional colleges and universities also have courses in mountain climbing. Usually these are part of the physical education curriculum. Under the supervision of experienced climbers, the students learn proper techniques in the field after they have attended lectures. The climbing season in the Olympics is limited by uncertain winter weather and spring avalanches, but usually extends from May to November. The climbs vary in difficulty, and include rock, snow and ice. The rock climbing is inferior, however, to that of many other mountains, as most of the rock is rotten or broken.

The National Park Service requires that climbers planning to ascend Mount Olympus register at the nearest ranger station. This is a wise precaution to take before climbing any major peak in this region.

The lure of the high peaks is a potent one. From a

wind-swept ridge at twilight the mountaineer watches the sun set beyond the western sea. The snowfields gleam among the peaks, reflecting reds, pinks and golds; the valleys slumber in deep purples. The moon tops the eastern horizon, illuminating the night sky; in the shadowy depths, the creaking of glaciers provides a background of sound that meshes with the sweep of the wind.

Chapter VII

The Elwha

The Elwha Valley

The Olympic Mountains were first viewed by Europeans from the sea when mariners sailing north along the coast and eastward through the Strait of Juan de Fuca caught glimpses of snow-covered peaks looming through the fog. The northern slopes facing the strait were also the first part of the Olympics penetrated by white men. The valley of the Elwha provided a natural pathway into the interior and is historically interesting as the original route of entry into the mountains. Up this valley the men of the Press Exploring Expedition plodded their way during the cold winter of 1889–90, and their route, where it followed the river, became approximately the much used Elwha trail of later years.

The Elwha valley comprises the heart of Olympic National Park. The largest watershed, it covers approximately one hundred and seventy-five thousand acres of the central and northern portions of the park. The valley is flanked on the west by the precipitous Bailey Range and, along the Elwha's lower course, by Cat Creek, Happy Lake and Boulder ridges. Eastward are the Elwha River Range, Hurricane Ridge, and the high peaks

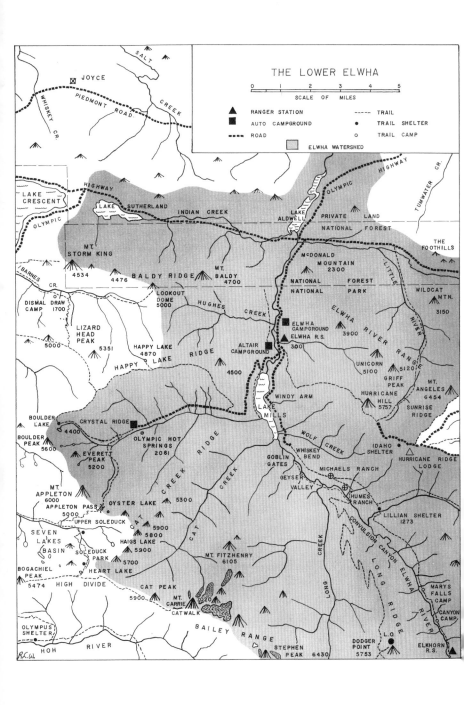

THE LOWER ELWHA

SCALE OF MILES
0 1 2 3 4 5

▲ RANGER STATION   ----- TRAIL
■ AUTO CAMPGROUND   • TRAIL SHELTER
▬▬▬ ROAD   o TRAIL CAMP

        ELWHA WATERSHED

⊠ JOYCE

SALT CREEK

WHISKEY CR.
PIEDMONT ROAD

HIGHWAY

LAKE CRESCENT

OLYMPIC

TUMWATER CR.

OLYMPIC HIGHWAY

LAKE SUTHERLAND   INDIAN CREEK

LAKE ALDWELL
PRIVATE   LAND
NATIONAL   FOREST

THE FOOTHILLS

MT. STORM KING
4534   4476

BALDY RIDGE

MT. BALDY 4700

McDONALD MOUNTAIN 2300

NATIONAL   FOREST
NATIONAL   PARK

WILDCAT MTN.
3150

BARNES CR.

DISMAL CAMP 1700

LOOKOUT DOME 5000

HUGHES   CREEK

ELWHA CAMPGROUND
▲ ELWHA R.S. 300

3900

ELWHA RIVER RANGE

LITTLE   RIVER

LIZARD HEAD PEAK
5000   5351

HAPPY LAKE 4870

ALTAIR CAMPGROUND

UNICORN 5100   5120

HAPPY   LAKE   RIDGE
4500

WINDY ARM

GRIFF PEAK

MT. ANGELES 6454

HURRICANE HILL 5757

SUNRISE RIDGE

BOULDER LAKE
4400

CRYSTAL RIDGE

LAKE MILLS

WOLF   CREEK

IDAHO SHELTER

BOULDER PEAK 5600

OLYMPIC HOT SPRINGS 2061

CAT   CREEK   RIDGE

GOBLIN GATES

WHISKEY BEND

HURRICANE RIDGE LODGE

EVERETT PEAK 5200

MICHAELS RANCH

GEYSER VALLEY

HUMES RANCH

MT. APPLETON 6000
APPLETON PASS 5000

OYSTER LAKE   5300

LILLIAN SHELTER 1273

UPPER SOLEDUCK

CAT   CREEK

CONVULSION CANYON   ELWHA   RIDGE

SEVEN LAKES BASIN

5900
5800

SOLEDUCK PARK
HAIGS LAKE 5900

MT. FITZHENRY 6105

LONG   CREEK

BOGACHIEL PEAK 5474

5700
HEART LAKE

HIGH DIVIDE

CAT PEAK 5900

MT. CARRIE 7020
CATWALK

BAILEY   RANGE

MARYS FALLS CAMP

CANYON CAMP

OLYMPUS SHELTER

HOH   RIVER

STEPHEN PEAK 6430

DODGER POINT 5753

L.O.

ELKHORN R.S. ▲

R.L.W.

and ridges from Obstruction Point southward to Mount Anderson. To the south, between Mount Seattle and Mount Christie, is Low Divide (3662 ft.), lowest trans-Olympic pass, guarded by two lovely subalpine lakes, Mary and Margaret. Beyond lies the Quinault.

In cutting through rocks of unequal resistance, the Elwha has eroded a narrow valley of variable width, one that is deeply v-shaped, indicating less glaciation than on the western slope of the mountains. Steep, forested mountainsides border the bottomlands. The latter are relatively broad near the river's headwaters, but the valley floor soon narrows to deep gorges, only to widen again downstream.

Near the center of the mountains, where the Bailey Range, the Mount Olympus Range and the glaciated peaks surrounding Elwha Basin are knotted together, a snowfinger extends down from Dodwell-Rixon Pass, the low point between Mount Queets and Mount Barnes. This snowfinger is the source of the Elwha. The river flows southeasterly through the subalpine Elwha Basin, then gradually curves to the east and northeast and finally flows northerly. The "singing Elwha" is a swift stream, often deceptively smooth, but sometimes it plunges through wild gorges, booming and thundering, with a show of white rapids, then quietly flows into deep green pools. After emerging from the mountains the river passes through broken country a few miles, then discharges into the Strait of Juan de Fuca.

The river is renowned for its excellent fishing and particularly for its rainbow trout. Before dams were built on the river's lower course, the Elwha was an outstanding salmon stream. Fishermen frequent the river banks, and often hike for miles up the valley, attracted to the isolated country above the Hayes River.

The principal tributaries are Lillian, Lost, Goldie and Hayes rivers. Creeks are numerous. The largest are Delabarre, Buckinghorse, Boulder, Long, Cat and Godkin. Hayes River was named for a member of the Press Expedition.

Access to the Elwha valley is via a mountain road that leaves the Olympic Highway at the river crossing near the national forest boundary. The road extends several miles up the valley, past old ranches, to a campground and the Elwha Ranger

Station (4.0 mi.; 300 ft.), then crosses the Elwha and ascends forested foothills to Olympic Hot Springs (11.8 mi.; 2061 ft.).

Just beyond the Elwha Ranger Station, a spur road— narrow, winding and unpaved—climbs left to Whiskey Bend (5.0 mi.; 1198 ft.), starting point of the Elwha trail. This spur was part of the original Hurricane Ridge road, but the portion above Whiskey Bend is now closed.

Elwha Trail

The Elwha trail follows the river nearly thirty miles to the Elwha Basin, deep within the mountains. The well kept trail, one of the most used park routes, is the main travel artery from the north into the heart of the park.

0.0   Much of the lower Elwha valley was burned years ago. The fires ran uncontrolled up the mountainsides, and for several miles beyond Whiskey Bend the trail passes alternately through virgin forest and stands of second-growth Douglas fir growing on the burned areas. The light green of the young trees contrasts noticeably with the darker green of the virgin forest.

As the trail approaches Geyser Valley, named by the Press Expedition in 1890, it skirts the edge of a clearing, the abandoned Michael's Ranch. Formerly a forlorn, odd-looking structure known as Geyser House stood here, a relic of the inroads of civilization. Unfortunately, the National Park Service destroyed it several years ago. Still standing, however, is the old Ludden cabin. On the clearing are remnants of an ancient orchard, strangely out of place in this silent wilderness. Near

1.8   the Ludden cabin (1.8 mi.) is a junction with the Long Ridge trail, which climbs to Dodger Point.

Geyser Valley (2.0 mi.; 750 ft.) is a stretch of

2.0   bottomland bordering the Elwha several miles between Goblin and Convulsion canyons, and surrounded by densely forested mountains. In March, 1890, members of the Press Expedition heard sounds here which they believed were made by geysers, hence the name. The general belief today, however, is that the men were deceived by the drumming of grouse. At the lower end of the valley, where the Elwha enters a deep, narrow canyon, is the phenomenon known as the Goblin Gates. At this point the river, flowing alongside a steep cliff, makes an abrupt, right angle turn and plunges through a break in the rock wall. Curiously eroded rocks, resembling faces with tortured expressions, line the dark walls of the canyon and gave rise to the name. The Goblin Gates may be reached by following an old, unmaintained path that leaves the Elwha trail at the first benchmark south of Whiskey Bend and descends to the head of Rica (Goblin) Canyon. A better but longer route is via the Long Ridge trail to the Elwha, then following the west river bank downstream to the deserted Anderson Ranch, opposite Goblin Gates.

Beyond the Ludden cabin the Elwha trail climbs a bench above Geyser Valley and contours toward the Lillian River. Between Antelope and Idaho creeks several trees beside the trail bear the Press Expedition blaze—three axe cuts, one above another—but the marks are inconspicuous and easily overlooked. Beyond Idaho Creek the trail bears left through stands of broomstick size Douglas fir. The trees, growing on burned over land, are not tall enough to shade the trail.

4.1   On the brink of the Lillian River Canyon (4.1 mi.; 1600 ft.) is a junction point with the Lillian River trail, then the route descends to the turbulent

4.6   Lillian River, where a shelter (4.6 mi.; 1273 ft.) stands beside the river in a setting of tall Douglas fir.

The Elwha trail climbs out of Lillian Canyon, then for several miles contours the mountainside at an elevation of 2000 feet, high above the Elwha's "Grand Canyon," and skirts above a large landslide. The Press Expedition called this gorge Convulsion Canyon because of Indian legends that told of a great catastrophe having occurred in the mountains, opening up chasms. Beyond the landslide the trail gradually descends, dropping eight hundred feet to the bottomlands along the river at Camp Baltimore.

Here the trail winds through lowland virgin forest, at times following the banks of the river, and crossing many creeks. Campsites are numerous, including those at Marys Falls, Canyon Camp, Little Elkhorn and Stony Point. The river follows a serpentine course at Thunder Canyon, where it is confined by vertically stratified, wavelike formations of slate, and makes a heavy booming

11.5 sound. Elkhorn Shelter (11.5 mi.; 1450 ft.), located above Thunder Canyon on the banks of the glittering river, is a favorite campsite of many hikers.

As it continues up the valley, making numerous ascents and descents, the trail slowly gains altitude. Beyond Lost River the path enters Press Valley

14.0 (14.0 mi.; 1600 ft.), named by the Press Expedition for its sponsoring newspaper. Here the Elwha's narrow bottomlands broaden perceptibly to a relatively flat expanse. Today's maps indicate Press Valley as constituting only the bottomlands along the Elwha immediately above the mouth of the Goldie. However, the name was originally applied by the expedition to the entire valley from the Goldie to the Elwha Basin.

17.0 At the Hayes River Ranger Station (17.0 mi.; 1650 ft.), the Hayes River trail climbs up the east side of the valley to Hayden Pass.

Above Hayes River the Elwha trail penetrates wild, isolated country. At irregular intervals the booming of the river resounds through the forest. Blue sky and white cloud, framed by the crowns of tall firs, contrast with dense growths of vanillaleaf mingling with masses of feather moss on the forest floor. Lupine grows abundantly in small openings. The trail climbs a mountainside and contours high above the rushing Elwha. Because this river is not a glacial stream, its waters are clear and the bottom is often visible. Then the path drops to flats along the river and meanders among giant firs. Cool breezes sweep down the valley from the snowfields above, and the thunderous roar of the river is ever present.

21.5 Camp Wilder (21.5 mi.; 1885 ft.) is situated among soaring conifers near the river. The trail now trends westward and drops to Godkin Creek, spanned by a high wooden footbridge. Between Godkin and Buckinghorse creeks the route traverses dense stands of Douglas fir. The largest trees are eight to ten feet in diameter, more than 250 feet tall. Silver fir and western hemlock are also present. The path crosses the Elwha over a picturesque bridge, then enters forests of silver fir and western hemlock.

25.0   Chicago Camp (25.0 mi.; 2185 ft.), the "crossroads of the Olympics," lies deep within the primitive wilderness of the central part of the park. A large, barnlike shelter stands by the trail, several hundred feet from the river, in the depths of a dense, damp forest. Chicago Camp is located about as far in the mountains as is possible from a road. Nearby is a junction with the Low Divide trail, which climbs to Low Divide and the head of the Quinault.

The Elwha trail continues upstream beyond Chicago Camp, passing through hemlock and cedar forest, then into the subalpine meadows of the Elwha

28.0   Basin (28.0 mi.; 2700 ft.). This deep cleft is closely hemmed by rugged, snow-clad peaks, their steep lower flanks covered with conifers, slide alder and meadows. Elk often graze in the basin. To the southwest stand Mount Noyes and Mount Meany, with their snowfields, cliffs and cascades; to the west, Mount Queets, grim as a medieval fortress, its scarred walls draped with waterfalls and thick masses of snow. Near the lower end of the basin a cave-like recess beneath an overhanging rock wall has provided shelter for more than one traveler during the storms which often rake this region.

The trail vanishes in the basin, but elk paths provide a way to the snowfinger at the upper end. This snowfinger was a glacier sixty years ago, and early accounts tell of potholes in the blue ice. A long, gradual climb up the snowfinger leads to historic Dodwell-

30.0   Rixon Pass (4750 ft.), used by the original surveyors of the Olympics. On hot days hikers welcome the cool breezes that descend the defile. Numerous cascades decorate the mountainsides enclosing the narrow trough. Near the

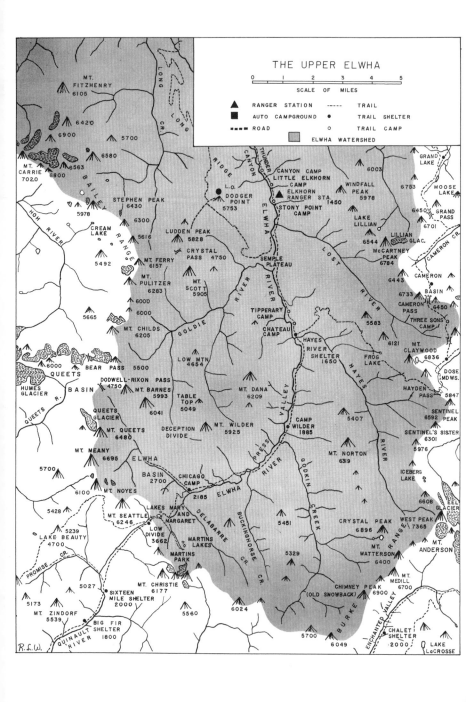

pass the snowfields become steeper and the wind blows continuously. Elk tracks, made by the animals in their migrations back and forth between the Elwha and Queets basins, often churn up the snow. Sometimes hikers are fortunate and see a herd on the broad snowfields of the upper Queets Basin.

Dodwell-Rixon Pass stands on the watershed between the headwaters of the Queets and Elwha rivers, and offers a varied panorama. The view to the southeast encompasses the Elwha Basin, ringed by rugged peaks, and to the west the Queets Basin unfolds. Here the winter snowfall is so heavy cornices often remain until midsummer. Directly across the basin stands Mount Olympus, wreathed in cloud and fog, its dull-colored peaks rising above the Humes Glacier. This glacier formerly extended over a cliff, thus forming an ice cascade, but the snout has receded. The glacier is growing again, however, as evidenced by thickening of the ice on the edge of the precipice. Sharp-pointed cliffs to the right of the glacier stretch toward Bear Pass (5400 ft.), and wall in the Queets Basin on the north.

Masses of brownish bedrock, vertically stratified, project through the snowfields at Dodwell-Rixon Pass. This region was once overwhelmed by the Olympic icecap, and this rock was shaved flat during the Ice Age by the rasping action of rocks frozen in the bottom of the glacier.

The pass is an excellent place to pause for lunch or picture-taking before dropping into the Queets Basin, the approach route to ascend Mount Olympus from the east. Climbers establish their base camp on meadowland by one of the small lakes in the basin, or on the moraine of the Humes Glacier below the terminal icewall. This cliff of blue ice, about one hundred feet high, is marked by shear lines, and cones of blue ice fifteen to thirty feet high stand at its base. The moraine is rather cold, an inhospitable place to camp, but the view is superb, overlooking the basin to Mount Queets and the sprawling Queets Glacier.

Olympus is climbed by first ascending the Humes Glacier to Blizzard Pass (6100 ft.), then descending steep snowfields about six hundred feet to the heavily crevassed Hoh Glacier. This ice stream provides a direct route to the neve fields and the final rock peaks.

Krause Bottom Trail

0.0 The Krause Bottom trail begins 1.5 miles south of
    Whiskey Bend on the Elwha trail, and provides
    an alternate route across the floor of historic Geyser
1.0 Valley. The abandoned Humes Ranch (1.0 mi.)
was homesteaded by two brothers, Grant and Will
Humes, about the turn of the century. The Humes brothers
often served as guides for mountaineers and hunters in the early
1900's. In later years the ranch was occupied by Herb and Lois
Crisler, wildlife photographers, while they made the motion
picture, "The Olympic Elk." Decaying buildings and gnarled
fruit trees accent the isolation, and a rusting cider press adds a
touch of nostalgia. The old barn, destroyed coincidentally with
Geyser House, contained antiquated farm machinery that had
been packed in from Whiskey Bend.

    The trail continues past the ranch to a junction
1.3 point with the Long Ridge trail (1.3 mi.).

Long Ridge Trail

    The Long Ridge trail extends southward from
Geyser Valley to Ludden Peak, thirteen miles distant.
Most of the way the route gradually ascends aptly named
Long Ridge, a spur extending north from Dodger Point.
Contouring below the ridgecrest, the path switchbacks
through forests on the Elwha side, then crosses over and the
last few miles traverses above Long Creek. This is a dry
    trail and during late summer water is not available.

0.0 Near the trail's point of origin at Michael's Ranch,
    two miles south of Whiskey Bend, is a junction
with the Krause Bottom trail, then the path crosses the
    clear waters of Idaho Creek and descends to the
1.3 Elwha (1.3 mi.; 900 ft.), where the river, spanned
    by a wooden footbridge, emerges from Convulsion
Canyon. Below the bridge the river broadens and flows quietly
through the bottomlands in Geyser Valley. On the west side of
the river another spur trail leads downstream to the old Anderson Ranch, opposite Goblin Gates.

After crossing the Elwha the route climbs sharply toward the northern end of Long Ridge, passing through dense stands of tall, second growth fir. The original forest was burned years ago, but a few large trees that escaped the holocaust attest to the majesty of the virgin forest that once covered these slopes. Beneath the trees the ground is padded with feather moss. Winter wrens flit through the bushes, and peer with curious, friendly eyes at the intruder.

In a dense stand of broomstick size trees the trail gains the ridge, then begins a direct ascent southward and enters forests of old Douglas fir festooned with lichen. Dense thickets of salal carpet the forest floor. In late summer the bushes are covered with flavorful, dark-colored fruits.

The trail drops below the ridgecrest and traverses Long Ridge on the Elwha side, with views of the Elwha valley and across to Hurricane Ridge. Again the trial climbs toward the ridgecrest. The ascent, via thirteen sweeping switchbacks, is so gradual the sensation of gaining altitude is almost absent. The length of the trip to Dodger Point makes it a tiring climb, however.

Crossing over the ridge to the western slope, the route follows the nearly level top of the mountain spur. The Bailey Range stands to the west, and Mount Carrie and Stephen Peak, covered with gleaming snowfields, dominate the view. The trail traverses an old burn, where fire-killed trees contrast sharply with green timber nearby, then enters subalpine forest and shortly breaks out into meadows dotted with mountain hemlocks. Timbered ridges fade away to the horizon, and part of Lake Mills is visible through a gap formed by the Elwha. Directly north is Hurricane Hill.

As the trail contours the west side of the ridge below Dodger Point, Mount Olympus rises partially into view, beyond the Bailey Range. Mount Carrie and Stephen Peak still dominate the scene, however, but to their south a massive dome of dark rock comes into view. This is Ludden Peak, originally named Mount Squire. Behind it rises the bulk of Mount Ferry.

The trail crosses rockslides, then edges a meadow containing two alpine pools. Beyond this point the country opens into a broad, grassy basin swept by cool breezes from the mountain snowfields. Camp robbers protest the intrusion of hikers, and the wind murmurs softly in the mountain hemlocks on the bordering ridges. Otherwise silence prevails, accenting the feeling of solitude, for this is getting into the remote interior of the Olympics.

11.0   At the base of Dodger Point (11.0 mi.) the trail crosses a boulder-strewn basin, snow covered in early summer, to a low, forested ridge where a spur trail climbs to the lookout. The cabin sits atop a rounded, grassy knoll 11.3   (11.3 mi.; 5759 ft.), and is anchored by cables for protection against winter storms. Because of its central location, this lookout is one of the superlative viewpoints in the Olympic Mountains, and the vista is outstanding. Many of the major peaks are visible, in addition to the long chain comprising the Bailey Range. Olympus dominates, however, looming high above the other mountains. Southward is the Elwha valley, with snow covered peaks standing in the distance. To their left, beyond the Elwha, the precipitous cliffs of Mount Anderson rise above the dark, shadowy canyon of the Hayes. Northward and eastward are meadow-crested ridges that are almost barren in late summer. Beyond them is the Strait of Juan de Fuca.

The main trail traverses slopes covered with mountain hemlock and subalpine fir and descends gradually to the low point between Dodger Point and Ludden Peak 11.4   (11.4 mi.; 4900 ft.), where the Dodger Point trail drops to the Elwha River at Semple Plateau, five miles distant. The path now contours a slope overlooking an unnamed tributary of the Goldie, then rounds a bend, bringing Mount Scott into full view. As the route crosses the face of Ludden Peak, the terrain becomes increasingly precipitous, the trail having been blasted from a shale cliff. Here the route has not been maintained and rock debris lies in the path. The trail ends abruptly at the 5000-foot level on the east face of Ludden 13.4   Peak (13.4 mi.).

The untrained hiker should stop here, but the experienced mountaineer can work his way, across precipitous mountainsides matted with junglelike growth, to Crystal Pass (4750 ft.), between Ludden Peak and Mount Scott, or climb over Ludden Peak itself, then continue cross-country to the Bailey Range.

Lillian River Trail

0.0 This unmaintained spur trail leaves the Elwha trail a half mile north of Lillian River and leads easterly through the forest. It contours the mountainside above the lower Lillian Canyon, then descends to the river

3.5 bottoms, and terminates (3.5 mi.; 2300 ft.) near where the river emerges from the upper Lillian Canyon.

Hayes River Trail

0.0 The Hayes River trail is an important connecting route linking the Elwha and Dosewallips valleys. The trail begins at the Hayes River Ranger Station (1650 ft.) on the Elwha and ascends the long spur between the

8.8 Hayes and Lost rivers to Hayden Pass (8.8 mi.; 5847 ft.). Near the pass the midsummer view southward, across fields of nodding avalanche lilies and receding snowdrifts, is particularly attractive. On the skyline the rugged north face of Mount Anderson rises above the snow-covered Eel Glacier.

This trail is a long climb, used chiefly on trans-Olympic trips by hikers crossing Hayden Pass from one valley to the other. The climb up this route from the Elwha valley should be avoided after July, because few sources of drinking water are available in late summer. From several points on the trail the peaks at the head of the Elwha are visible, also the Bailey Range and Mount Olympus.

The route continues past Hayden Pass, where it becomes the Dosewallips trail.

Appleton Pass Trail

The Appleton Pass trail connects Olympic Hot Springs with the Soleduck River trail several miles above Sol Duc Hot Springs.

0.0 Commencing at the Olympic Hot Springs campground (2200 ft.), the route meanders through dense stands of

1.0 fir and hemlock to a junction (1.0 mi.; 2350 ft.) with the Boulder Lake trail. Beyond this point the trail continues up the valley and crosses Boulder Creek twice over footlogs. The chattering sound of tributary creeks is frequently heard just around bends in the path.

Beyond the second creek crossing the trail ascends through subalpine forests along slopes lush with huckleberry and other shrubs. Above the forests it crosses meadows and climbs sharply via switchbacks to Appleton Pass (6.0
6.0   mi.; 5000 ft.).

On the north side of the pass looms craggy Mount Appleton; on the south a spur path follows the ridge to nearby Oyster Lake. This small pool, shaped like an oyster shell, is nestled in meadows on top of the narrow ridge. The wind whips across this exposed ridge, sometimes blowing fiercely throughout the night, even in summer. The lone camper who spends a night here, warm and snug in his sleeping bag beneath thick-spangled subalpine firs, may listen for hours to the alternate roaring and whispering, with the realization that the still primeval wind is one of the few phenomena on earth that man has not been able to alter or conquer.

Beyond the lake a short walk along the ridge leads to a promontory (5500 ft.), an excellent place to view the sunset. Oyster Lake glimmers on the ridgetop like a pool of molten silver, and beyond rises the bulk of Mount Appleton, dark and mysterious, overlooking the Soleduck and Boulder Creek valleys. The Strait of Juan de Fuca and the San Juan Islands are visible to the northeast. Ten miles away, directly south, the crest of Olympus rises over the sharp peaks of Cat Creek Ridge and the meadows of Soleduck Park and the High Divide.

From Appleton Pass the trail descends rapidly to the Soleduck River, dropping two thousand feet in two miles, occasionally passing through dense thickets of vine maple. The trail ends in a forest of tall conifers at a junction with
8.0   the Soleduck River trail (8.0 mi.; 3100 ft.).

Boulder Lake Trail

0.0   The Boulder Lake trail splits away from the Appleton Pass route one mile west of the campground at Olympic Hot Springs and follows Boulder Creek to the lake.

The path climbs steadily through dense Douglas fir

forest alongside Boulder Creek canyon. The creek is hidden from view in the depths of the forest, but its roar breaks the mountain stillness. Higher up the forest is less dense and bear grass makes showy displays in small openings. The trail flattens when the canyon head is reached. Here it crosses well-watered meadow and subalpine forest. Marshmarigolds add a touch of color in early summer.

3.0   Topping a small rise, the trail ends abruptly at a shelter on the north shore of Boulder Lake (3.0 mi.; 4350 ft.), but the western terminus of the Happy Lake Ridge trail can be picked up nearby. Boulder Lake, cupped in a recess on the north side of Boulder Peak, is almost encircled by a forested ridge with cliffs to the southwest.

Snow-mantled Boulder Peak (5600 ft.) stands above the ridge. The walk to the summit is steep but easy, and rewards the hiker with commanding views in all directions. Immediately south is Mount Appleton and, in the distance, the northern spurs of the Bailey and Mount Olympus ranges, topped by Mount Carrie and Mount Olympus. Far to the east, beyond timbered ridges, are snow-flecked peaks of the eastern Olympics. Forested ridges and valleys extend west, and northward to the Strait of Juan de Fuca. Directly below are several mountain tarns—Boulder Lake and the two Three Horse Lakes—nurtured by perpetual snowfields.

Happy Lake Ridge Trail

The Happy Lake Ridge trail begins nine miles from U. S. 101 on the road to Olympic Hot Springs. This route climbs gradually but steadily to the crest of Happy Lake Ridge, then follows the ridge (4500–5200 ft.) westward to Boulder Lake (10.0 mi.).

0.0   The trail begins (1750 ft.) in an open stand of Douglas fir. Near the ground the trees have been blackened by fire, and the forest floor is covered by thick growths of salal. The trail contours west along a steep slope, and openings in the forest permit one to look across the Boulder Creek valley. Mount Carrie stands above timbered foothills, its glaciers shimmering in the summer sunshine. As the route steepens and turns northward, the undergrowth suddenly disappears.

2.0 The trail now traverses a badly burned area with blackened tree trunks. Higher, beyond the two-mile marker (near the only source of water on the trail), the route crosses grassy glades dotted with scattered, shaggy-barked firs. As the trail contours the southern side of the ridge, Mount Olympus and Mount Carrie appear to rise side by side across the valley. Actually they are separated by the deep Hoh canyon. To the southeast is the Elwha valley, with Mount Anderson beyond.

On the nearly flat ridgecrest the trees are small and scattered. Daisies, thistles and bear grass dot the meadows. The view to the north and east includes the Strait of Juan de Fuca and Port Angeles, with Mount Baker on the horizon.

The trail drops to the northern side of the ridge, where it penetrates dense growths of mountain hemlock and passes through a stand of fire-killed trees. Further along the ridge small meadows alternate with subalpine forest.

5.0 On the ridge is a junction (5.0 mi.) with a half-mile trail that drops rapidly through stands of mountain hemlock to small, tree-ringed Happy Lake (4870 ft.).

7.5 The ridge trail continues westward, alternately gaining and losing altitude. At 7.5 miles is a junction with the Aurora Ridge trail. Beyond this point the route traverses meadowlands, with views of the interior peaks of the Olympics, to a junction with the abandoned Crystal Ridge trail, then terminates near the Boulder Lake shelter
10.0 (10.0 mi.; 4350 ft.).

Dodger Point Trail

0.0 This old trail, which is not maintained, leaves the Elwha valley about one mile north of the mouth of the Goldie River, and climbs to the south end of Long Ridge.

The trail first crosses the benchland known as Semple Plateau, once thought to be the site of an old Indian village, then begins to climb the mountainside. Just above the plateau it passes a jutting rock which the 1890 Press Expedition named The Gallery, because of the view and the pictures they obtained there. From here one can look across Press Valley and up the Hayes River canyon to Mount Anderson.

       The trail climbs through dense forests to a junction with the Long Ridge trail just south of Dodger Point

5.0   (5.0 mi.).

Chapter VIII

Lake Crescent

The Lake Crescent Trough

Lake Crescent, lying five hundred and seventy-nine feet above sea level in the northwest corner of Olympic National Park, is an arc of intensely blue water about eight miles long and a mile wide. Originally called Lake Everett in honor of John Everett, a trapper who sought furs along its wooded shores, the lake was later given its present name because its form supposedly resembled a crescent. The park's largest lake, it occupies a trough or valley that was deepened during the Ice Age by the lobe of the continental glacier that moved westward down the Strait of Juan de Fuca from British Columbia. The lake is surrounded by steep, forest-clad mountains, and the overhanging slopes, snowy from late fall to early spring, create silvery reflections on the surface.

A deep lake, Crescent offers a variety of activities, among them swimming, boating and fishing. Despite roads along the shoreline, the lake has a quiet atmosphere and is actually less "developed" today than a few years ago because the National Park Service has acquired some of the bordering private lands. From its icy depths fishermen used to troll the

Beardslee trout, a variety of rainbow. This fish, named for Rear Admiral Leslie A. Beardslee, its discoverer, was declared a new species by the ichthyologist David Starr Jordan, but no longer exists in a pure state because of cross-breeding with hatchery planted fish before establishment of the national park. The lake also contained a unique variety of cutthroat trout, the Crescenti, but it, too, has been hybridized.

Lake Crescent is paralleled on the south by Aurora Ridge, and on the north by a lower ridge culminating in Pyramid Peak. To the southeast are three high ridges, Baldy, Happy Lake and Boulder (or Appleton) that extend toward the Elwha. Near the eastern end of the lake Mount Storm King rises four thousand feet above the blue water. Mountain goats are one of the attractions of this peak, and it was here the animals were originally introduced into the Olympics.

The level of Lake Crescent is kept constant by numerous creeks flowing from the surrounding ridges. The largest, Barnes Creek, has deposited silt at its mouth, thus forming a small delta. The lake's outlet is the Lyre River. This stream flows from the lake's northernmost point to the Strait of Juan de Fuca, a few miles distant.

The Lake Crescent region, together with Hurricane Ridge east of the Elwha, is the most accessible part of the national park. The Olympic Highway parallels the lake's south shore, and a spur road running from its western end provides access to part of the northern shoreline. The bed of the old "spruce railroad" of World War I is still extant, and the National Park Service has considered adapting it as an automobile parkway. The trails on the surrounding ridges are reached from these roads as well as from those leading to the Olympic and Sol Duc Hot Springs.

The first settlers on Lake Crescent were Sarah Porter Barnes and Paul Barnes, mother and brother of Charles A. Barnes of the Press Expedition.

Aurora Ridge Trial

0.0   This ridge-running trail begins 2.5 miles south of the Olympic Highway on the Sol Duc Hot Springs road and

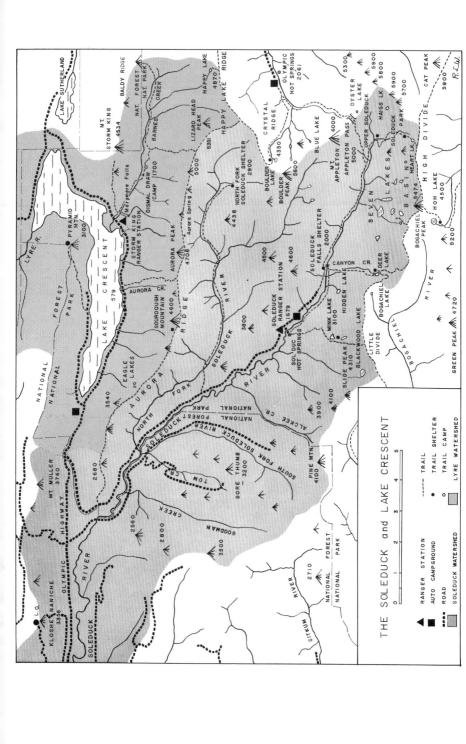

THE SOLEDUCK and LAKE CRESCENT

▲	RANGER STATION
■	AUTO CAMPGROUND
▬ ▬	ROAD
▒	SOLEDUCK WATERSHED
- - -	TRAIL
•	TRAIL SHELTER
○	TRAIL CAMP
░	LYRE WATERSHED

0 1 2 3 4 5

R.L.W.

climbs to the end of Aurora Ridge, then follows near the ridge-crest until it merges (16.0 mi.) with the Aurora Divide trail near Lizard Head Peak. Aurora Ridge is not high enough to be continuously above the timberline, but the route does cross a number of mountain meadows that provide excellent views of the surrounding country.

5.5   The three Eagle Lakes (5.5 mi., 2700–3100 ft.) at the head of Eagle Creek are small potholes below the trail on the north side of the ridge. Beyond them the route
8.5   continues along the ridge to Sourdough Shelter (8.5 mi.), located in an expansive meadow near the summit of Sourdough Mountain (4600 ft.). The wide vista here includes the Soleduck valley and Mount Olympus.

The trail continues along the ridge to a junction with
11.0   the Aurora Creek trail (11.0 mi.; 4100 ft.), in the midst of a dense forest of large silver fir, then enters a small meadow of bracken fern from where Mount Olympus is again visible. The trail reenters the forest, and Aurora Spring
12.5   (12.5 mi.), on the south slope of Aurora Peak, is the first place beyond Sourdough Shelter where water is available on this dry ridge. The spring is small, but the clear water is cool and has a delightful taste. An old shovel blade attached to a rusty file stuck in a tree trunk marks the site of the spring in a moist swale at the bottom of a boggy meadow slope partially covered with subalpine fir. Although the spring is eternal, flowing all summer and fall, there is no suitable campsite.

East of Aurora Spring the trail traverses forest for a short distance, then breaks out into a wide, grassy meadow on a steep mountainside. This meadow looks up the valley of the Soleduck's north fork and across to the surrounding ridges. Mount Olympus peeks through the trees on the right.

From here to the junction with the Aurora Divide trail a succession of meadows alternates with forests that extend to the ridgecrest. Elk use this trail and their tracks are often noted in the meadows. The views from these open areas are expansive, and include Mount Olympus, Mount Tom, some of the Bailey Range peaks, and the valley of the North Fork Soleduck and its tributaries. Most of the time the trail contours the steep slope on the south side of the ridge, but now and then follows the narrow ridgetop. Occasionally part of Lake Crescent, guarded by the vast, barren bulk of Mount Storm King, is visible. From one of the larger meadows the view down the valley of the North Fork Soleduck is particularly impressive. The river is not visible, but the line in the forest indicating its presence zigzags symmetrically because mountain spurs approaching from the north and south overlap alternately. The valley is heavily timbered, and the view of virgin forest untouched by fire, logging or roadbuilding is one of the finest in the park. Above the ridges south of the valley the ice of Mount Olympus and the Bailey Range peaks glitters in the autumn sun. The wind whispers hauntingly in the clumps of subalpine firs on the ridge, and the tall meadow grasses sway restlessly.

16.0

18.5

Beyond the last meadow the trail traverses dense forests of silver fir for a mile to a junction with the Aurora Divide trail (16.0 mi.; 4750 ft.), then contours the southwest side of Lizard Head Peak, and terminates at a merging point (18.5 mi.; 5000 ft.) with the Happy Lake Ridge trail.

Aurora Creek Trail

The Aurora Creek trail, one of the steepest in the Olympics, begins on the south shore of Lake Crescent about two miles east of Lapoel picnic ground, and climbs sharply, ascending the steep spur between Aurora and Smith creeks. Lake Crescent is glimpsed occasionally through the trees.

0.0

Near its beginning the trail switchbacks through Douglas fir forest where salal and red huckleberry are abundant. Then the path climbs directly up the narrow spine of the mountain spur. To the left of the trail the hemlocks on the mountainside stand so dense nothing grows on the shaded forest floor. The gloom is unrelieved even on the brightest days, and the forest is so dark it is depressing. On the right the forest is less dense, the trees are smaller, and enough light reaches the ground to permit a sparse undergrowth.

The upper levels of the trail pass through dense stands of mountain hemlock and silver fir. Then the trail crests the

ridgetop and drops to the south side, within a short distance
coming to a junction point with the Aurora Ridge
2.5   trail (2.5 mi.).

Mount Storm King Trail

Less than three miles long, the popular Mount Storm
King trail overlooks the blue waters of Lake Crescent, and
climbs about two-thirds the way up Mount Storm King (4534
ft.).

0.0   The trail splits away from the Barnes Creek trail south
of Storm King Ranger Station on the lake's southern
shore, and climbs steeply as it switchbacks through a forest of
tall Douglas fir. Ferns and feather moss cover the ground beneath the trees. The trail ascends to successive vantage points
providing varied views of Lake Crescent, Aurora Ridge and the
valley of Barnes Creek. Fog banks often lie over the lake in the
morning, and when the afternoon sun slants low, softening
the shadows of the tall firs, the water takes on tones of lifeless
gray. Logging trucks roar along the lake's south shore, breaking
the otherwise somber stillness. Unfortunately, an alternate commercial vehicle route bypassing the lake has not been constructed
outside the national park.

Gaining the western spurs of Mount Storm King, the
trail ascends a steep hogback ridge, switchbacking to several
turnouts or overlooks. The roar of logging trucks becomes very
pronounced, seemingly magnified by the increasing altitude.
A prominent sign at one viewpoint warns hikers that to go
further is dangerous. Only experienced climbers should proceed beyond this point.

The path becomes progressively steeper and vanishes
2.7   at a jutting promontory (2.7 mi.). Lake Crescent, completely circled by steep, forest-clad mountains, sweeps
across the line of sight. Pyramid Peak is to the west, Aurora
Ridge to the south, and immediately below lies the Barnes
Creek valley.

Beyond the promontory the ascent of Mount Storm
King becomes a combination of climbing and scrambling over

rotten rock on a narrow ridge. Across the valley of Barnes Creek the mountainside is characterized by uniform spurs between creeks flowing parallel, and at right angles to Barnes Creek, an excellent example of a trellis drainage pattern.

The southern slopes of Storm King now confront the climber. Here are steep cliffs of pillow lava and other volcanic rock. The north slopes, equally steep, are thickly covered with small trees. Mountain goats sometimes gather in small groups of five to ten on the inaccessible cliffs.

The climb is long and arduous for so low a peak. Several false summits must be climbed over or bypassed, and occasional descents are necessary along the knife-edge ridge, before the final peak is reached. The summit panorama is rewarding, however, and includes the sapphire blue expanse of the lake, the Strait of Juan de Fuca, Vancouver Island and the interior Olympics.

Barnes Creek Trail

This trail follows Barnes Creek through forests of Douglas fir, western hemlock and western red cedar, and terminates at Lookout Dome on the divide between Barnes and Hughes creeks (10.0 mi.; 5000 ft.).

0.0   The trail begins at the National Park information station on Lake Crescent, and is broad and smooth as it traverses forests of Douglas fir, hemlock, cedar and maple on the flat delta of Barnes Creek. The National Park Service has adapted this part as a self-guiding nature trail, and it becomes, during the summer, a boulevard for foot travelers. In the autumn the yellow leaves of maples and Devil's-club cover the ground and provide a colorful contrast with the bright green of the luxuriant sword ferns.

Beside a large, moss-covered rock near a stately Douglas fir ten feet in diameter, the trail divides. Here the Mount Storm King trail ascends sharply up the mountainside to the left, and the main trail continues southward. Nearby another path leads right, crosses Falls Creek, and climbs the opposite bank to Marymere Falls, named for the sister of Charles

Barnes of the Press Expedition. Handrails along the steepest part of the trail afford security to the timid. The path ends by a bowl-like basin where a cliff forms an abrupt wall. Here the small creek plunges through a notch in the cliff to form ninety-foot Marymere Falls. The water drops vertically about forty feet, then strikes a slanting ledge and ribbons down the rock face to form a small pool at the cliff's base. Ferns and mosses decorate the rock walls to either side.

Beyond the junction with the path to Marymere Falls, the trail parallels Barnes Creek through a narrow valley. The shallow stream is crystal clear, and its chatter is always present along this part of the way. Cedars overhang the creek's banks, and particularly fine displays of Devil's-club are present. The enormous leaves of this spiny plant turn golden in the autumn, rivaling those of the bigleaf maples.

The trail crosses over a footlog to the west side of Barnes Creek, then climbs high above the stream on a gradu-
3.0   ally ascending traverse through stands of hemlock and fir, and soon (3.0 mi.; 1200 ft.) begins to switchback up the mountainside. On the opposite side of the creek the slope is barren because of slides.

On the crest of a spur the trail veers away from the creek and suddenly the forest becomes very quiet, and the creek is heard no longer. The forest is thickset and further deadens
3.3   sounds. Ascending a gloomy defile, the trail crosses a small brook at Dismal Draw Camp (3.3 mi.; 1700 ft.).

The name is appropriate. Near the camp the forest is so dense that undergrowth is not present, and only moss and dead twigs cover the forest floor. Scattered among the young second growth are a few large firs, their trunks blackened near the ground from old fires. Beneath the living trees are many small, dead trees no larger than broomsticks.

The trail returns to the Barnes Creek side of the spur and the noise of the creek is heard again, but now sounds like the clatter of a distant freight train. Across the valley Mount Storm King is visible through the trees. Then the trail enters an open area. Barnes Creek flows unseen in the depths of the canyon below, and one can look up and across the valley to
3.5   Baldy Ridge. The trail again penetrates the forest, and almost immediately divides (3.5 mi.; 1500 ft.). The

left branch is a continuation of the Barnes Creek trail; the right becomes the Aurora Divide trail.

10.0   Beyond the division point, the trail continues up the valley of Barnes Creek, then climbs to the Barnes Creek-Hughes Creek divide (5000 ft.) and Lookout Dome.

Aurora Divide Trail

0.0
2.6   This short trail linking Barnes Creek valley with Aurora Ridge begins 3.5 miles from Lake Crescent on the Barnes Creek trail (1500 ft.) and climbs to Aurora Ridge (4750 ft.) near Lizard Head Peak.

The trail gradually ascends the mountain slope through stands of small hemlock. A few large firs are present, remnants of an old forest that has been largely replaced by the hemlock. Across a timber-choked ravine to the left of the trail, the hillside is covered with many fallen trees.

The climb toward Aurora Ridge is steady, by means of long switchbacks. Above twenty-five hundred feet the trail traverses almost pure stands of Douglas fir. Most of the trees are about two feet in diameter. Above three thousand feet the forest is primarily hemlock and silver fir.

Near the ridgetop the terrain eases, and undergrowth of vanillaleaf, Devil's-club and huckleberry is dense. The trail switchbacks several times across an old avalanche path overgrown with vanillaleaf, hellebore, larkspur and baneberry. The view from this avalanche path looks out the valley to Baldy Ridge.

2.6   At the top of the ridge (4750 ft.) is a junction with the Aurora Ridge trail.

Pyramid Peak Trail

0.0   This trail starts from the graveled north shore road on Lake Crescent, 3.5 miles from the Olympic Highway, and is continuously uphill, ending at the top of Pyramid Peak (3.5 mi.; 3100 ft.).

At first the trail ascends a bench covered with second growth, then contours east above the lake along a mountainside clothed with virgin forest. Through the tall, slender firs—which bear scars of some long-forgotten fire—are glimpses of the lake and the ridge beyond. Grouse live here and may be observed by the alert hiker.

Terminating its eastward contour, the trail climbs sharply to the crest of the divide west of Pyramid Peak, then drops to the north side of the ridge where it penetrates a very dense forest so darkly shaded practically nothing grows beneath the trees. Then the trail suddenly emerges from the deep shadows into the bright sunlight of the ridgetop. A large part of Lake Crescent is visible, and directly ahead is the summit cabin, used during World War II as an aircraft spotting station.

3.5

The vista from the lookout of the lake and surrounding mountain ridges is noteworthy. On sunny days the water is intensely blue. The bulk of Mount Storm King rises darkly to the southeast, dominating the scene. At its base, far below, lies the delta of Barnes Creek, protruding into the lake. Across the lake Aurora Ridge glistens blue-green, its long, withdrawing slopes heavily forested. Beyond the eastern lobe of Crescent, Lake Sutherland glimmers in the distance.

Chapter IX

Hurricane Ridge

Hurricane Ridge

Hurricane Ridge roughly parallels the Strait of Juan de Fuca in the northeastern part of the mountains and, together with Lake Crescent, is perhaps the best known part of Olympic National Park. In contrast to most of the park, the ridge is not wilderness. Access is provided by a modern highway, and developments include a day use lodge and facilities for winter skiing.

Properly, the ridge extends southeastward from Hurricane Hill (5751 ft.) to Obstruction Point (6450 ft.), but contiguous ridges of similar nature continue to the east and south. This high meadowland, flecked by clusters of subalpine firs, rises far above the saltwater of the strait, only ten to twelve miles distant, and commands a unique combination of mountain and marine scenery.

Toward the interior of the peninsula is a wilderness of rugged mountains draped with perpetual snowfields, and slashed by the deep canyons of the Elwha and Lillian rivers. Across the Elwha steep, forested slopes are capped by the snowy peaks of the Bailey Range, and Mount Olympus pokes above the highest summits. North of Hurricane Ridge the mountainsides drop abruptly to foothills and narrow coastal lowlands. Port Angeles resembles a toy town (one's outstretched hand covers it completely), and beyond Ediz Hook, the sandspit enclosing the harbor, the blue of the strait extends to Vancouver Island. Far to the northeast the sea is dotted with purple splotches, the San Juan Islands, and ships sailing the "Inside Passage" to Alaska are often visible. On the horizon are the Cascades, topped by the volcanic cone of Mount Baker. At night the lights of Port Angeles and Victoria flicker faintly, adding an aura of mystery to the loneliness and quiet charm of this high mountain ridge.

Before Olympic National Park was created, the Forest Service built a fire protection road from the Elwha to the ridge, with branches extending to a lookout atop Hurricane Hill and eastward to Obstruction Point. Because this road was steep and narrow, unsuited to today's automobiles, the National Park Service constructed a modern highway to the ridge from Heart o' the Hills on the park boundary. The new highway climbs four miles to Lookout Rock, a vantage point overlooking the strait, then traverses across the face of Burnt Mountain and Mount Angeles, and terminates at Big Meadow, where the lodge was built. The old ridge road from Big Meadow to Obstruction Point is still open, but the part between Whiskey Bend and Idaho Camp is closed, and the spur to Hurricane Hill has been converted into a footpath. The fire lookout cabin which stood on the summit of Hurricane Hill has been dismantled.

The ridge road from Big Meadow to Obstruction Point cuts across mountain meadows and through groves of subalpine firs. The trees, thick-branched to the ground, with spire tops pointing to the heavens, are most picturesque. Snow remains on the ridge well into summer, and after it melts fields of colorful wildflowers blanket the slopes, and deer and bear roam the meadows. Steeple Rock, a sharp promontory two miles east of Big Meadow, rises two hundred feet above the road, and when viewed from the west resembles a church spire. The road varies in elevation from five thousand to six thousand feet, and

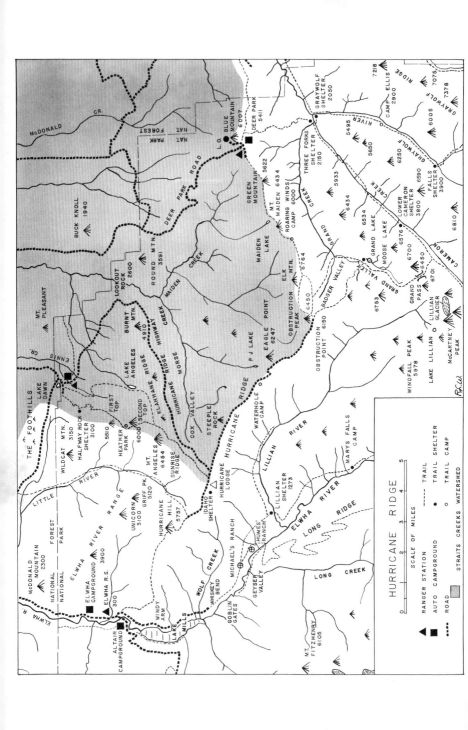

HURRICANE RIDGE

SCALE OF MILES

0   1   2   3   4   5

▲ RANGER STATION   ----- TRAIL

■ AUTO CAMPGROUND   • TRAIL SHELTER

••• ROAD   ○ TRAIL CAMP

STRAITS CREEKS WATERSHED

attains its highest altitude near Eagle Point. Trails radiate from the roadhead at Obstruction Point into the surrounding high country.

Another old fire protection road leads to the top of Blue Mountain (17 mi.; 6007 ft.). This road, also narrow, steep and winding, begins five miles east of Port Angeles. A cabin perched on the summit provides a panoramic vista. West is the timbered valley of Morse Creek, and to the south are many snow-covered mountains. Highest of all tower the jagged pinnacles of The Needles. North and east the view is essentially the same as that from Hurricane Ridge.

Deer Park (5400 ft.) is a mountain meadow and former ski area on the slopes of Blue Mountain. The weather here is favorable for winter sports because of the leeward position, but the snow cover is usually light and the wind sometimes sweeps the snow away. Since new ski facilities have been developed on Hurricane Ridge, the Blue Mountain road is no longer kept open during the winter.

Hurricane Hill Trails

Two trails lead to the crest of Hurricane Hill (5751 ft.), one from the Elwha valley, the other from the western terminus of the ridge road.

Before the old Hurricane Ridge road was constructed, the trail from the Elwha valley provided the chief access to the ridge. This trail begins near the Elwha Ranger Station
0.0 (300 ft.), and climbs the lower slopes through forests of old Douglas fir and western hemlock, then through higher altitude forests. Above the timberline the trail crosses mountain meadows, and terminates at the crest of
6.0 Hurricane Hill (6.0 mi.).

The other trail is actually the roadbed of the old spur road which climbed to the lookout cabin. The National Park Service closed the last mile of this road to automobiles, and converted the roadway into a footpath, thus providing an easy hike for persons who have driven up to the lodge at Big Meadow.

Hurricane Hill presents an outstanding vista of the interior Olympics, the Strait of Juan de Fuca and Vancouver Island.

Little River Trail

0.0 Another trail leading from the lowlands to Hurricane Ridge, this route begins outside the national park on the Little River road four miles from the Olympic Highway and Elwha River.

1.0 The trail crosses the park boundary (1.0 mi.) and follows the course of the South Branch of the Little River, which is bordered to the left by Wildcat Mountain and Mount Angeles, on the right by the Elwha River Range. The

8.4 trail gradually gains altitude, and terminates (8.4 mi.) on Hurricane Ridge at the head of the South Branch, between Hurricane Hill and Big Meadow.

Mount Angeles Trail

0.0 The Mount Angeles trail begins near Heart o' the Hills campground, climbs toward the summit of Mount Angeles, half-circles the main peak, and ends at Big Meadow on Hurricane Ridge. This route traverses an area particularly inviting to the neophyte hiker because of the views and easy access from Hurricane Ridge.

In its first few miles the trail negotiates a northern spur of Mount Angeles, ascending through second growth forests of pine, fir and hemlock. The northern slopes of the mountain were burned years ago, and blackened logs and stumps

2.0 are still present. At Halfway Rock (2.0 mi., 3000 ft.), midway to Heather Park, a shelter stands beside a large boulder. Along the way, trilliums bloom in early summer. Higher up, near timberline, the large ribbed leaves of false-hellebore are conspicuous, and violets nestle among the rocks.

The trail emerges from the forest and crosses semi-open

4.0 country to Heather Park (4.0 mi.; 5500 ft.), a meadow-land graced with subalpine firs and splashes of blue lupine. Directly above are the steep snowfields, jutting cliffs and pillow lavas of Second Peak. To the right is the lower First Peak.

4.5   The route climbs sharply to Heather Pass (4.5 mi.; 5700 ft.), a windswept gap between the two peaks, where whitened, contorted trunks of burned subalpine trees stand as grim reminders of the destructiveness of fire. A short, easy walk leads to the top of First Peak, where nature has created a flower garden in the splintered shale. Many low-growing plants live here, among them phlox, violets and lupine. On all sides are goblinlike rock outcroppings from five to thirty feet high. Hardier souls climb Second Peak, or cross over Heather Pass and make the long trek to Third Peak, the highest point of Mount Angeles.

The view from these vantage points includes the shore-line of the strait from Neah Bay to Port Townsend, with Vancouver Island lying darkly to the north. The distant San Juan Islands and Mount Baker form a scenic backdrop. To the south is the snowy wilderness of the Olympics, with Hurricane Ridge in the foreground.

For the mountaineer camped at Heather Park, the top of First Peak is an excellent place to spend an evening. As the afternoon sun sinks low, the black shadows of sharp-pointed trees cut across the snowfields like long, narrow swords, and when the sun nears the horizon it appears to flatten like a giant egg yolk. The peninsula's northern coastline quickly becomes a silhouette, the first stars twinkle dimly as the darkness deepens, and land and water turn purplish gray, then black. Later the evening chill is pronounced, the stars are brilliant, and lights appear in Port Angeles at the foot of the mountain. Often a strong, cold wind bears in from the sea, bringing with it frag-ments of gray cloud.

Heather Pass marks the ridgecrest, and the trail drops, via a shale slide, into a pocket formed by the South Branch of the Little River, then climbs the flanks of Third Peak (6400 ft.). The route traverses beneath weird pinnacles, and off to the right stands Thumb Rock, a massive, sheer-walled promontory rising above the Little River valley. Mountain goats clamber on the nearby crags.

Third Peak can be climbed by leaving the trail before

reaching the gap between it and Second Peak. The route leads directly up a snowfield on the north side. The peak is largely sedimentary rock, the strata uplifted and tilted on end, and differential erosion of alternate hard and soft layers has created stairlike chimneys and pinnacles. The shale slides below are decorated in summer with colorful displays of douglasia and erysimum.

6.5

10.0

The trail contours the east side of Third Peak to a junction with the Klahhane Ridge Way trail (6.5 mi.), then continues to Big Meadow on Hurricane Ridge (10.0 mi.), most of the distance crossing meadowland.

Klahhane Ridge Trail

0.0

3.5

5.0

This trail climbs from Heart o' the Hills to Lake Angeles (3.5 mi.), and on to Klahhane Ridge (5.0 mi.), a spur projecting eastward from Mount Angeles. As far as the lake the trail is an arterial footpath, but higher up the route becomes more or less a way trail and is unsuited to horses. The trail follows the ridgecrest, then joins the Mount Angeles trail on the slopes of Third Peak.

One of the largest Olympic tarns, Lake Angeles is picturesque because of a steep mountain headwall on one side and a small, tree-studded isle near its lower end.

Grand Ridge Trail

0.0

The Grand Ridge trail ridgeruns from Deer Park, on the slopes of Blue Mountain, to the end of the Hurricane Ridge road at Obstruction Point. The trail, an up-and-down route varying in elevation from five thousand to sixty-five hundred feet, follows the Grand Ridge westward about eight miles. Most of the way is above timberline, but subalpine trees are present at low points on the route.

Immediately west of Deer Park the trail drops to a gap in the ridge, then ascends through subalpine forest and climbs toward the summit of Green Mountain (5622 ft.). Beyond this peak the route traverses the top of a high ridge, and leaves the forest to cross open meadows on the south side of Mount Maiden (6434 ft.).

The short walk to the top of Mount Maiden is rewarding. The northeast slope drops sharply to a basin containing small Maiden Lake. Port Angeles, the Strait of Juan de Fuca, Dungeness Flats and the San Juan Islands lie to the north. Eastward is the long chain of the Cascades. Nearer at hand stands Blue Mountain, with its lookout cabin and the Deer Park road. The interior of the eastern Olympics is revealed to the south—Mount Deception, the pinnacled peaks of The Needles, and snow-clad summits between them and McCartney Peak. In the distance loom the Cameron Glaciers. Nearby is Grand Valley, sheltering Moose and Grand (Etta) lakes. Conspicuous to the northwest is Mount Angeles, the Hurricane Ridge road cutting across its face, but the view westward is blocked by the vast, arid bulk of Elk Mountain.

On the south slope of Mount Maiden the trail crosses meadows below a sharp ridge of upturned strata, then
4.0 drops to Roaring Winds Camp (4.0 mi.; 6000 ft.), located at timberline in the windy notch between Mount Maiden and Elk Mountain, which obscure much of the view. Interspersed among rock outcroppings are low, ground-hugging subalpine firs. The campsite is well named; even on warm summer days cold winds rush through this gap. Water is not available in late summer, but a perpetual snowfield lies a few hundred feet below the ridge on the north slope.

Beyond Roaring Winds Camp the trail zigzags up a sharp ridge to the plateau-like top of Elk Mountain. For two miles the path is sixty-five hundred feet high, the highest trail in the Olympic Mountains. Lying entirely above timberline, this country consists of broad, tundra-like meadows of low-growing grasses and fields of smooth stones covered by black lichen. Hawks soar overhead and twittering sparrows flit among the tufts of grass. This area, located in the dry northeastern part of the mountains, resembles the rangeland of eastern Washington.

The view from Elk Mountain is essentially the same as that from Mount Maiden, with one exception. When the hiker coming up from Roaring Winds reaches the broad, open slopes he pauses, not merely to catch his breath but also because Mount Olympus suddenly bursts into full view, surrounded by a retinue of lesser peaks. Among them are Christie, Meany, Ferry, Stephen and Carrie. Previously these peaks were hidden from view on Mount Maiden by Elk Mountain.

Crossing shale slopes, still above timberline, the trail 5.5   passes a junction with the Badger Valley trail (5.5 mi.), then drops to the low point between Elk Mountain and Obstruction Peak (6450 ft.), and contours the head of Badger Valley to Obstruction Point (6100 ft.). The trail terminates at the end of the Hurricane Ridge road on the 8.0   south side of Obstruction Peak (8.0 mi.). Barren mountains and ridges, decorated with residual snowfields even in late summer, rise beyond the green depths of Badger Valley.

At one time the National Park Service contemplated building a road along the route of the Grand Ridge trail, but because of vociferous protests by conservationists the plan was abandoned.

Grand Pass Trail

The Grand Pass trail leads southward from Obstruction Point to Grand Pass, then descends to a junction with the Cameron Creek trail, a total distance of eight miles. Most of the route lies near or above the timberline.

0.0   Leaving Obstruction Point, the trail crosses a barren, tundra-like plateau. In late summer, after the snow has disappeared, this country resembles the arid land east of the Cascades, and fogbanks often trail to the lee of ridgecrests like forest fire smoke.

4.0   The path drops to Grand and Moose lakes (4.0 mi.; 4800–5000 ft.), near the headwaters of Grand Creek. On both sides of the valley steep mountainsides sweep upward to high peaks, and scattered evergreens fringe the lakes and meadows. Close to Grand Lake is attractive Amalia Falls. Moose Lake lies cupped between rocky, forest-clad slopes.

Beyond the lakes the trail follows high, barren ridges

that lie between the upper reaches of Cameron Creek and the
valleys of Lillian and Lost rivers. The path climbs shale
6.0   slopes and crosses snowfields to Grand Pass (6.0 mi.;
6450 ft.), then descends sharply to Cameron Creek. In
the upper limits of the forest below the pass the route crosses
several small meadows covered by lush vegetation and wildflowers such as lupine, tiger lilies, erysimum, bleeding heart,
columbine, shooting stars and mertensia. Phlox is abundant on
the shale slides.

The trail ends at a junction with the Cameron Creek
8.0   trail (8.0 mi.; 4200 ft.) below Cameron Basin.

Badger Valley Trail

The old trail through Badger Valley provides an alternate route from Obstruction Point to Moose and
0.0   Grand lakes. The trail begins 2.5 miles east of Obstruction Point on the Grand Ridge trail, and descends beside the creek through Badger Valley to its confluence with
Grand Creek, then follows the latter to Grand Lake
5.0   (5.0 mi.).

Marmots, not badgers, are one of the attractions found
in the valley. Why names like Badger Valley and Moose Lake
were given to topographic features here, when neither badgers
nor moose are found in the Olympics, is a mystery.

Three Forks Trail

The Three Forks trail is a "reverse" route, beginning at
high altitude and descending thirty-three hundred feet into the
depths of the Graywolf valley at Three Forks, where Cameron
and Grand creeks merge with the Graywolf River. Water is
available at only one point between Deer Park and Three Forks,
in a gully to the right of the trail.

0.0   The trail begins at the Deer Park campground (5400
ft.), and contours a short distance to the east through

meadows colorful with lupine, thistle and bluebells. The Needles and other peaks to the south are visible.

At a junction point with the Slab Camp trail, which crosses into the Olympic National Forest, the trail enters the upper limits of the forest, here mostly silver fir and pine, and begins the descent to Three Forks. The path is not exceptionally steep, but is continuously downhill. The Graywolf valley is occasionally glimpsed through the forest.

As the trail loses altitude the forest changes to Douglas fir, and the trees are larger. Soft breezes whisper among the treetops and sometimes trees leaning against each other creak and groan as they move with the wind. Otherwise the forest is silent. The solitary hiker who listens to the creaking and moaning of the wind easily understands why primitive man ascribed spirits to trees.

4.5   The trail turns a spur and approaches Three Forks, and suddenly the pronounced roar of Grand Creek rises from the depths of the valley. Three Forks Shelter (4.5 mi.; 2150 ft.) stands on a small open spot in a deep forest setting near the confluence of Grand and Cameron creeks. Near the shelter a footlog with a wire handrail spans Grand Creek, which is clear and full of boulders, providing access to the Cameron Creek trail.

Chapter X

The Dungeness-Graywolf

The Dungeness Valley

The watershed of the Dungeness and Graywolf rivers comprises the extreme northeastern part of the Olympic Mountains. By reason of its sheltered position with respect to storms from the sea, this region has the lightest precipitation of any part of the Olympics, and in late summer is actually semi-arid.

The Dungeness valley lies almost entirely within the Olympic National Forest, except where the river flows across lowlands beyond the mountain foothills. The only parts included within the national park are Royal Basin and the river's source near Constance Pass.

A loop of lofty peaks and ridges almost encircles the upper Dungeness valley. Culminating points are Mount Deception and The Needles on the west, Mount Constance to the south, and Buckhorn Mountain and Iron Mountain on the east.

Access to the Dungeness is provided by the Louella Guard Station road.

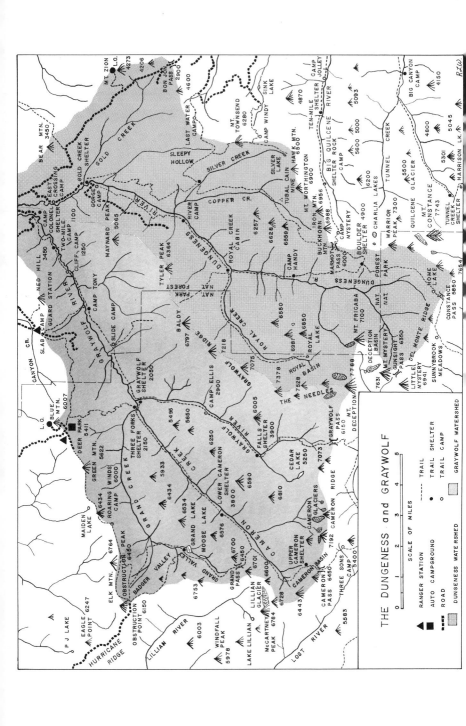

THE DUNGENESS and GRAYWOLF

SCALE OF MILES

0	1	2	3	4	5

▲ RANGER STATION   • • • TRAIL

■ AUTO CAMPGROUND   ▪ TRAIL SHELTER

▬▬ ROAD   ○ TRAIL CAMP

▒ DUNGENESS WATERSHED   ▒ GRAYWOLF WATERSHED

R.L.W.

The Graywolf Valley

The Graywolf River, largest tributary of the Dungeness, is only twenty-five miles long, but descends nearly five thousand feet from the high snowfields flanking Graywolf Pass, and thus is one of the swiftest rivers on the peninsula. The lower Graywolf flows through national forest land, but the upper Graywolf and surrounding peaks and ridges lie within Olympic National Park.

The valley is paralleled on the east by barren Graywolf Ridge, capped by Mount Graywolf (7218 ft.), and The Needles, a series of rock towers varying in elevation from seven thousand to seventy-five hundred feet. These peaks are among the highest in the Olympics, and challenge the rock climber. The high ridge dividing the Graywolf from Cameron Creek borders the valley on the west. Graywolf Pass, at the valley head, is bounded on the east by Mount Deception and on the west by Cameron Ridge.

Grand and Cameron creeks, the Graywolf's principal tributaries, are nearly as large as the upper river. All three streams merge near Three Forks Shelter to form the lower Graywolf, and this stream in turn flows into the Dungeness in the foothills of the Olympics.

Access to the Graywolf valley is by way of the Louella and Slab Camp roads in the national forest, or the Blue Mountain road in the national park. The Louella road may be taken to Dungeness Forks Camp, at the confluence of the Graywolf and Dungeness. This is as far as the road is passable for most vehicles, but it continues another mile to Camp Colonel Shelter, where the trail begins. The Slab Camp road leaves the Olympic Highway near Sequim, and climbs into the foothills. The Graywolf trail can be reached by descending the Slab Camp Creek trail from the guard station (2544 ft.) to Camp Tony (1650 ft.), on the Graywolf River. Hikers who enter the valley by this route miss the first few miles of the Graywolf trail. In the national park the upper Graywolf is reached more directly by descending the Three Forks trail from Deer Park.

Graywolf Trail

In the national forest the Graywolf trail passes through comparatively dry country covered with stands of fir and pine. Rhododendrons splash the somber forests with pink blooms in late spring; Indian paintbrush displays darker shades of red in open areas, and the showy white bunchberry is conspicuous on the forest floor.

2.0   Above Two-Mile Camp (2.0 mi.; 1100 ft.) the river emerges from a steep-walled canyon where for three miles the trail keeps near the river bank, passing Cliff

3.0   Camp (3.0 mi.; 1250 ft.). Beyond Camp Tony (5.0

5.0   mi.; 1650 ft.) the trail climbs several hundred feet above the turbulent Graywolf, and traverses talus slopes. At intervals distant snowy peaks may be seen up the

8.0   valley. Slide Camp (8.0 mi.; 2200 ft.), located near a slide area, is approached by crossing steep shale slopes. The trail then switchbacks down to Slide Creek, which flows down the north side of Mount Baldy.

8.5   Near Slide Camp the trail enters the national park (8.5 mi.) and gradually ascends as it crosses forested mountainsides. The river, roaring in its canyon far below, is lost to sight. The trail climbs over a spur and penetrates extremely dense stands of broomstick size Douglas fir. The ground beneath the trees is covered with feather moss, and so thick is the forest growth the foliage meets overhead and walking along the path is like going through a tunnel.

The trail descends gradually to the Graywolf River. The climate is wetter here than to the east, and typical trees include Douglas fir, western hemlock and western red cedar.

10.0   Graywolf Shelter (10.0 mi.; 2050 ft.), surrounded by dense forest, stands on the opposite river bank. A foot-log spans the stream. This log marks the beginning of the Cameron Creek trail. Care should be used in crossing, for the log is often wet and slippery from spray kicked up by the tumultuous current.

Above Graywolf Shelter the trail turns to the south and follows the east river bank upstream, gradually ascending through dense stands of fir, hemlock and cedar. The river is

swift, almost a continuous series of cascades, rapids and waterfalls. The Graywolf is not a glacial stream, therefore is of unsurpassed clarity. Many large boulders lie in the river bed, and
the stream is bridged every few yards by fallen trees. About a
mile above Graywolf Shelter the trail crosses to the river's west
bank via another swaybacked log.

12.7   As it approaches Camp Ellis (12.7 mi.; 2900 ft.), the
path climbs to a bench where a few old firs, remnants
of an ancient forest, are scattered among small trees. The forest
floor is largely bare of vegetation except for solid masses of
feather moss.

Beyond Camp Ellis, a rather unattractive place to stay,
the trail continues through forest, then climbs above the river
in order to cross a ravine. This defile was carved by a creek
that drops abruptly from the ridge, ribboning down in a series
of cascades. Here one can look up and down the valley, and also
across to a "silver forest" high on the opposite mountainside.
The lower slopes are heavily timbered, and the trail continues
through stands of cedar and fir. In the shadier places, protected
from the sun, patches of snow remain until late summer.

15.4   Upper Graywolf or Falls Shelter (15.4 mi.; 3900 ft.) is
located near the river, but distant enough that one can
hear the phenomenon commonly called "river voices," an illusion frequently experienced in wilderness, especially by the
solitary hiker, and may explain why primitive man ascribed
"spirits" to natural phenomena. So realistic is this illusion of
people murmuring indistinctly in the distance that the lone
camper is apt to find himself occasionally looking up, expect-
ing to see someone coming up the trail.

The shelter stands near the lower end of a meadow that
extends up the mountainside. Deer often graze in the meadow,
which is bordered by silver firs. Near its upper end, where
Cedar Creek cascades down a steep slope, Mount Deception
(7788 ft.), highest peak of the eastern Olympics, is visible to
the southeast rising above the snowfields that form the headwaters of the Graywolf.

A way trail (3.0 mi.) leads from Falls Shelter to Cedar
Lake (5250 ft.). This large subalpine lake is popular with fishermen. Several high peaks south and east form the eastern crest

of Cameron Ridge. Highest is "The Pup" (7073 ft.), directly south.

Falls Shelter marks the end of the deep, shaded forest. The trail again crosses the river, now little more than a creek, and meanders through partially open stands of lower Hudsonian zone type forest. The ground cover is luxuriant. The trail crosses back to the west side of the river, but almost immediately recrosses, then climbs through stands of Alaska cedar. Again one can hear the "river voices."

The trail turns westward and meanders through meadowlands and groves of subalpine forest, again crossing the river over a makeshift bridge of rocks and logs. Flowers are abundant: tiger lilies, daisies, lupine, heliotrope, thistles and arnica. Buttercups bloom alongside the melting snows.

The trail climbs steeply, with many switchbacks, up the west side of the valley, and breaks out into open meadows dotted with scattered subalpine firs. In early summer the trail is partially hidden by lingering snowbanks. Northward is a view down the Graywolf valley. To the east the rock pinnacles called The Needles cap the ridge extending north from Mount Deception. Southwest is a mass of rocky peaks splotched with snowfields. The meadows, cooled by breezes descending from Graywolf Pass, are colorful in late summer with lupine, mountain meadow buckwheat, daisies, gentians, pedicularis, paintbrush and red mountainheath. Seed pods of anemone sway in the wind, and small, clear brooks tumble over a series of rock ledges. Crossing snowfields that form the Graywolf's source, the trail climbs past a small, muddy lake, then leaves the meadows behind and ascends barren talus slopes.

19.5   Graywolf Pass (19.5 mi.; 6150 ft.) is a spectacular viewpoint. On warm, sunny days steady breezes from the south are invariably present. The backpacker can look north down the winding, forested valley of the Graywolf. West is the upper Dosewallips, bounded by Claywood, Fromme, Sentinel and Wellesley peaks, with Mount Anderson rising behind the latter. Part of the view is blocked, however, by mountain spurs on either side of the pass. A few minutes climb up the ridge east of the pass brings Lost Peak into view and, behind it, Olympus. In the far distance, between Olympus and Anderson, is a vast snowy area, the peaks near Elwha Basin. In the opposite direction are Mount Deception, Mount Constance, Mount Mystery and Little Mystery, with Gunsight Pass between the two Mysteries. The peaks seem to reach into the clouds, and this is often literally true. The vast sweep of the Dosewallips valley is to the south.

The pass is flat enough for camping, but cold at night because of the wind, and snow must be melted for water.

Beyond Graywolf Pass the trail descends toward the Dosewallips and loses a half mile of elevation in less than four miles as it drops rapidly in a series of switchbacks. Immediately below the pass the trail descends through open country for a considerable distance, crossing beautiful meadows naturally landscaped with clusters and solitary specimens of subalpine fir. The view of Deception and the two Mysteries, across the hanging valley of Deception Creek, is notable. Occasionally the shrill whistle of a marmot punctuates the distant roar of the Dosewallips. Surprisingly, even in late summer small streams cross the trail. This south-facing slope is well exposed to the sun, and huckleberry bushes assume vivid ruby shades and Indian paintbrush creates small red flames. Below the meadows are forests of white pine and Alaska cedar. From several points the view of Piro's Spire across the valley is noteworthy.

23.0	About two miles below Graywolf Pass the trail enters Douglas fir forest, and continues down to the Dosewallips trail (23.0 mi.) above Camp Marion.

Cameron Creek Trail

This trail follows Cameron Creek into Cameron Basin, then climbs to Cameron Pass. Beyond the pass the route continues as the Lost Peak trail, where it skirts the headwaters of Lost River and descends to Dose Meadows.

0.0	From its point of origin opposite Graywolf Shelter, the trail crosses Graywolf River via a swaying log with a wire handrail. The path then climbs a low hump, and de-
0.5	scends to the bowl (0.5 mi.) formed by the union of Cameron and Grand creeks, their combined waters

flowing through a timbered gorge to the Graywolf. The trail crosses Cameron Creek over another log, to a junction point with the Three Forks trail. This route leads to Three Forks Shelter and climbs the mountainside to Deer Park. Three Forks received its name because Grand and Cameron creeks and the upper Graywolf, all approximately the same size, combine within half a mile of each other.

For several miles the trail follows Cameron Creek, crisscrossing from one side of the stream to the other, through dense stands of large Douglas fir. Most of the trees are three to four feet in diameter, but some are five or six, and all are tall and without limbs to great heights.

4.0   The trail emerges from the forest (4.0 mi.) and enters the first of six meadows that extend from the creek up the mountainside forming the north slope of the valley. The meadow is an old avalanche path. Across the valley rises an unnamed, fortress-like peak (6590 ft.), with sheer rock walls guarding the summit. The trail again plunges into Douglas fir forest, then enters the second meadow. The Lower
4.8   Cameron Shelter (4.8 mi.; 3800 ft.) sits at the meadow's edge, and faces west, with its back to the dark forest. Here the meadow extends on both sides of the creek.

Beyond this point to the junction with the Grand Pass
7.1   trail (7.1 mi.) beetling cliffs on the valley's north side overshadow the lower mountain slopes, and the trail continues to alternate between forest and meadow until it crosses the sixth and last meadow of the series. The second and third meadows are particularly picturesque because solitary trees stand near their margins. From the fifth meadow the Cameron Glaciers are visible to the south. Beyond the last meadow the trail climbs to the junction point with the Grand Pass trail.

The path now climbs steeply, interminably it seems, through dense thickets of slide alder, salmonberry, Alaska cedar and cow parsnip. The route has been cut through, otherwise the jungle would be impenetrable. Vegetation often meets across the trail, and half the time the hiker cannot see his own feet. But eventually the trail breaks into partially open country below Lillian Divide, and one can look down the v-shaped

Cameron valley, where long sallies of trees extend up the steep withdrawing slopes on either side.

9.5   A shelter (9.5 mi.; 5400 ft.) is located near the lower end of Cameron Basin, but is sometimes difficult to find when the path is hidden by snow. This wild mountain basin occupies an old glacial cirque about one mile long by a half mile wide, varying in elevation from five to six thousand feet, and rimmed by unnamed, snow-mantled peaks. The varied terrain, including level meadows and rocky, tree-covered knolls, is quite picturesque. Moss-lined brooks meander across flats that are sometimes swampy from the melting snowbanks. In summer, wildflowers create gorgeous displays—lupine, buckwheat, asters, buttercups and elephanthead. East of the basin the sharp crags of Cameron Ridge tower more than seven thousand feet; westward is McCartney Peak. The basin is delightful, its remoteness from well-traveled paths adding to its charm.

    The trail becomes indistinct, and the route, marked by rock cairns and hardly distinguishable as a path, crosses meadowlands to the basin's head. Here the trail improves as it switchbacks across shale slopes and snowfields and

10.8   climbs a "hogback" to Cameron Pass (10.8 mi.; 6450 ft.), low point on the snow-covered ridge enclosing the basin on the south.

    The view from the pass is splendid, but still better from the peak immediately west, reached by a short walk. Here, near the center of the "high country" Olympics, one can look down into Cameron Basin, and all about are snowy peaks, including Mount Olympus in the distance. Directly east is jagged Cameron Ridge, harboring glaciers and precipitous snowfields. Far to the southwest is Low Divide.

Royal Basin Trail

0.0   The trail to Royal Basin commences in the Olympic National Forest at the confluence of Royal Creek and the Dungeness ten miles from the Gold Creek road, and fol-

lows the creek. Most of the way the trail passes through the
shadows of the deep forest. The trees are small, but set close
together. Lying as it does along the park boundary, the route
alternates between national forest and national park, but Royal
Basin itself is within the park.

The valley of Royal Creek narrows near its head, and
the trail steepens, with a strenuous uphill pull to Royal Lake.
The valley is u-shaped, showing evidence of glaciation, and
flanked on the west by barren, rocky Graywolf Ridge.

Somewhat isolated from other parts of the park, Royal
6.0   Basin (6.0 mi.; 5000–5500 ft.) is not well known to
hikers. Rock climbers favor it, however, as an ideal base
camp for excursions to The Needles, directly west. The basin
is a high country area almost encircled by lofty ridges that
form a pattern resembling an inverted question mark, with the
basin enclosed by the hook.

The upper part of the basin, bordered by barren, rocky
peaks and snowfields, consists chiefly of meadows and scattered
trees. The basin floor, especially near its lower end, is mostly
covered with subalpine forests. Moraines and other remnants of
past glacial action are found in various places, and snowfields
occupy the old glacial beds.

The last mile of the trail, which ends at Royal Lake,
crosses a boggy area with numerous small streams, and little
potholes. Royal Lake, located near the basin's lower end, is
shaped like a pork chop, and was formed by a morainal dike extending across the valley floor, thus causing the relatively level
basin to lie at a somewhat higher level than the valley of Royal
Creek. Near the upper end of Royal Lake is Big Rock, situated
in a grove of trees. The overhang of the rock provides shelter to
campers during inclement weather.

Wildlife is abundant. Deer roam the meadows in the
morning, and a few elk occasionally enter the basin. Mountain
goats clamber on the nearby cliffs.

Royal Basin is bordered to the east by the sidewall of
the ridge running north from Mount Fricaba. This ridge, composed of broken volcanic rock and talus, reaches almost seven
thousand feet, and is surmounted by pinnacles of pillow lava.
On the basin's west are the sheer cliffs of The Needles, with

many gendarmes (towering formations of rock) creating a knife-edged ridge. This area is almost completely bereft of trees and vegetation, as it is too rocky and too high for plant life.

The Needles form the high ridge north of Mount Deception, and reach heights in excess of seventy-five hundred feet. From the ridge east of the basin they appear to be a narrow ridge with precipitous towers and jagged rock fingers thrusting skyward, some with a decided lean. The pinnacles are not composed of really good climbing rock, but next to the Sawtooth Range it is the best the Olympics have to offer. Mostly the rocks are pillow-structured volcanics. The rock breaks easily, and because the cracks are all faults, pitons offer little assistance.

Access to The Needles is via a snowfield that leads from the basin's western side to snow-covered Surprise Basin and Surprise Pass. The view from this "pass," which is really only a notch in the ridge, is impressive. The Needles appear to be vertical. To the west the climber looks back into the interior of the Olympics; eastward is Royal Basin, its upper end terminating in steep headwalls. From this vantage point the basin appears to be a series of more or less level terraces. The uppermost terrace is a snowfield, and snow-clad peaks almost surround the basin. At the base of Mount Deception, at the basin's head, is a small glacier, the source of Royal Creek.

Although Surprise Pass appears from below to be a route across the ridge, it does not lead anywhere. The western slope drops vertically several thousand feet.

Chapter XI

The Dosewallips

The Dosewallips Valley

A triangular-shaped area, the Dosewallips watershed is centrally located on the east side of the park and oriented to Hood Canal. Most of the nearly fifty thousand acres of parkland drained by this river lies at high elevation, above timberline, with alpine meadows and barren land covering about half the region.

Within the park the river system forms a dendritic or treelike pattern. The upper Dosewallips and West Creek unite to form the trunk, which flows east to Hood Canal. These streams are not glacial, but an important tributary, Silt Creek, has its source in the Eel Glacier on Mount Anderson, and should be considered the principal stream by reason of its size. Numerous smaller creeks contribute to the river's volume. After heavy rains, the Dosewallips is prone to flood, and during such rampages sometimes washes out bridges and destroys portions of the road or trail along its banks.

On all sides of the valley rise lofty peaks and ridges. Between the upper reaches of West and Silt creeks, in the west, stands the massive block of Mount Anderson, decorated with glaciers and snowfields. A high ridge extends north from this mountain to Hayden Pass, beyond Silt Creek, where the upper Dosewallips is encircled by five peaks—Lost, Claywood, Fromme, Sentinel and Wellesley. These summits surround an expanse of subalpine country known as Dose Meadows.

Cameron Ridge, northeast of Lost Peak, has small glaciers on its northern slope. This lofty ridge divides the Dosewallips from Cameron Creek and the Graywolf River. The mountainsides drop steeply from the ridgecrest to the Dosewallips. The eastern terminus of Cameron Ridge is connected to the loop of high peaks surrounding the upper Dungeness. Prominent summits in this chain are Constance, Deception, Mystery and Little Mystery. The portion of the loop lying between Mystery and Constance is commonly called Del Monte Ridge.

The southern limit of the Dosewallips valley is marked by a ridge of lesser elevation isolating the lower Dosewallips and West Creek valleys from the Duckabush. This ridge is capped by White Mountain, Mount LaCrosse, Mount Elklick, and in the Olympic National Forest by Mount Jupiter.

The Dosewallips road commences near Brinnon on Hood Canal and follows the river to Camp Muscott (15.5 mi.; 1600 ft.), less than two miles inside the park. Several campsites border the river where it flows through the national forest. Within the park the road hugs the base of a cliff of pillow lava, then climbs sharply as it edges Dosewallips Falls. Here the river, confined to a narrow channel, cascades over resistant rocks. The road then drops through forests to Camp Muscott, a flat covered by large cedars and firs.

Dosewallips Trail

0.0   The Dosewallips trail begins at Camp Muscott and follows the river to its source in Dose Meadows, then climbs sharply to Hayden Pass. Beyond the pass the route is known as the Hayes River trail.

The trail gradually ascends from Camp Muscott through the forest, then drops to a campsite at Dose

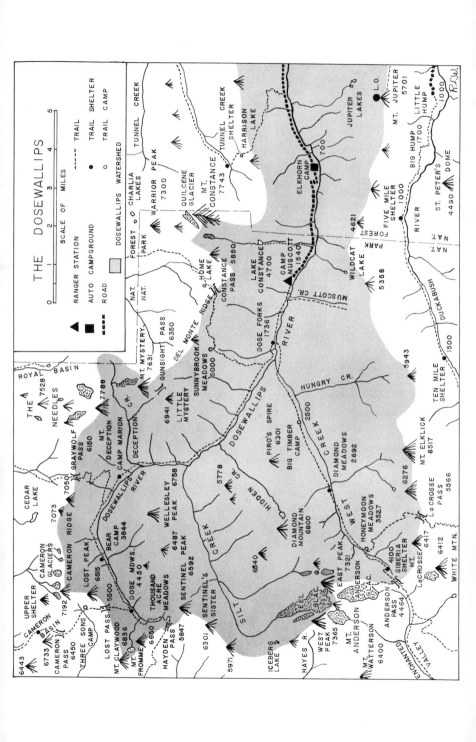

THE DOSEWALLIPS

SCALE OF MILES

0   1   2   3   4   5

ROAD

AUTO CAMPGROUND

RANGER STATION

TRAIL

TRAIL SHELTER

TRAIL CAMP

DOSEWALLIPS WATERSHED

R.J.W.

1.5   Forks (1.5 mi.; 1736 ft.), in a setting of tall firs near the confluence of the Dosewallips and West Creek. Here the trail divides. The main route continues to the right, up the river. The path to the left, known as the Anderson Pass trail, crosses the river and follows West Creek to Anderson Pass.

Two campsites are located at Dose Forks, one near the division point in the trail, the other about four hundred yards away, beside the river, on the Anderson Pass trail.

2.0   Near Dose Forks the trail passes soda springs (2.0 mi.), where wild animals are attracted by mineralized water seeping from the rocks. Footprints and game paths are numerous at this point, and this is a good place to observe deer and bear. As it winds through the forest, the trail crosses many little brooks. Salal and rhododendron cover the ground beneath the trees.

The Dosewallips trail continues up the valley, passing
2.5   the junction with the Constance Pass trail (2.5 mi.; 2182 ft.), and climbs gradually above the river. Now and then Diamond Mountain is glimpsed across the valley, and from a point about five miles beyond Muscott, Hatana Falls is visible. The path crosses a number of chattering creeks that tempt the backpacker to pause, on hot days, for a drink of cold mountain water.

8.3   Camp Marion (8.3 mi.; 3300 ft.) is located near a stand of young fir on an old burn. An ancient cabin serves as a trailside shelter. Above this campsite the trail enters a valley of great beauty, and meanders through meadows where wild flowers bloom profusely. Among the more conspicuous ones are the Columbia lily, broadleaf arnica, bear grass, cowparsnip and columbine. The meadowland vegetation is often waist-high, and on warm summer days a redolent odor is present.

9.2   Beyond the junction with the Graywolf trail (9.2 mi.; 3700 ft.), the route penetrates patches of subalpine forest, mostly silver fir. This is open country, however, and long vistas are present at almost every turn of the trail. In all directions massive peaks loom darkly above flower-covered meadows. Directly south is Wellesley Peak; north is Cameron Ridge. Upvalley are Lost Peak and Mount Fromme; downvalley, Mystery and Little Mystery.

11.0   The trail winds through the meadows to Bear Camp (11.0 mi.; 3850 ft.), located near two waterfalls about four hundred yards apart. Because of this barrier to trout moving upriver, fishing ends at this point.

12.8   Beyond Bear Camp the path penetrates dense subalpine growth, then suddenly breaks out into Dose Meadows (12.8 mi.; 4450 ft.), where a shelter cabin stands near the edge of the forest. Green-carpeted meadows, covered with lush grasses and wildflowers, sweep upward to high peaks and ridges. The naked cliffs of Mount Fromme, crowned with snow cornices, form a wall on the western margin of the meadows, and to the northeast Lost Peak pokes above forested mountainsides. The river, little more than a creek, plunges through a narrow, timberlined gorge where forest blends into meadow, and shooting stars and columbine add a touch of color to the riverbank. Near the shelter is a junction with the Lost Peak trail.

Wildlife is abundant. Marmots sun themselves by their burrows, and whistle shrilly when travelers approach. Deer are remarkably tame, and often come within a few feet of the camper, especially in early morning or evening. Bears prowl the meadows and sometimes rummage around near the shelter at night. More often heard, however, are the "river voices," occasionally accented by the scudding sound of boulders shifting position in the river.

The trail trends toward Mount Fromme, then abruptly turns south. Beyond a wooden footbridge spanning the river the path circles the basin on the north side of Sentinel Peak where the Dosewallips originates, and crosses fields of avalanche lilies massed alongside unmelted snowbanks. Pioneer violets, glacier lilies and buttercups group together to form vivid splashes of yellow. In late summer lupine laces the meadows with patches of blue.

Again the trail crosses the river, now easily waded, and begins to switchback toward Hayden Pass. The steep slope below the pass is often covered by snow, and prior to August the hiker may be confronted by a cornice overhanging the summit ridge. This sometimes makes the ascent difficult.

15.4   Hayden Pass (15.4 mi.; 5847 ft.) is merely the low point on the knife-like ridge connecting Mount Fromme and Sentinel Peak. The eastern flanks of these peaks, together with those of neighboring Mount Claywood, reveal a pronounced concavity, the result of glacial sculpturing. The western slope into the Elwha valley is less abrupt. The ridgetop, a spine of rotting shale, supports a few wildflowers and stunted subalpine trees. Beyond the pass the trail continues, as the Hayes River trail, to the Elwha valley.

Lieutenant O'Neil named Mount Claywood in 1885. Mount Fromme, first climbed by The Mountaineers in 1920, honors R. L. Fromme, supervisor of the Olympic National Forest at that time, who accompanied the climbers and obtained the assistance of the Forest Service in building a trail.

The view from Hayden Pass is excellent, with high peaks outlining the valley of the Dosewallips to the north and east. On the western skyline the Bailey Range is superimposed against Mount Olympus; on the southern the sharp peaks of glacier-clad Mount Anderson rise above those of neighboring peaks. Cross-country hikers can approach Mount Anderson from this point by following the ridge southward to Service Pass, then continuing along the divide between Silt Creek and Hayes River.

About a mile northeast of Hayden Pass, above the timbered slopes directly across the river from Dose Meadows, a large expanse of meadowland occupies an old glacial cirque varying in elevation from five thousand to six thousand feet. Two brooks fed by melting snows cross the basin, which can be reached by leaving the trail at the first sharp switchback beyond the bridge and climbing steep open mountainsides about a hundred yards, then turning left and ascending to the lower edge of the meadows.

Mount Constance Way Trail

Mount Constance way scarcely rises to the dignity of a trail, and is far too steep for horses. The path, created by the

trampling of thousands of human feet over many years, climbs
steeply northward from the Dosewallips road to Lake
0.0   Constance (2.0 mi.; 4700 ft.). To the backpacker the
distance seems much longer, for the trail ascends 3250
feet.

The route, following the course of Constance Creek,
goes straight up the forested mountainside. Half Acre
1.0   Rock (1.0 mi.), a shattered mass near the trail, apparently fell from a high cliff, and its exploration offers an
interesting side trip. The most unusual feature is a formation
resembling a guillotine.

Beyond Half Acre Rock the route becomes more difficult. In the steepest places one must often cling to small trees
or exposed roots when ascending or descending. Clambering
over fallen trees and fighting brush is common, and at one point
the only possible way necessitates walking in the edge of the
creek bed. The last half mile climbs steeply over rock ledges.
The trail is not dangerous, however, except to the careless hiker.

Near the lake the trail ascends a low precipice over
which the creek plunges, leaping free of the rock. Then the
route climbs sharply almost to the brink of Lake Constance and
suddenly flattens.

2.0   The small lake, ringed by subalpine forest and stocked
with eastern brook trout, lies cupped in a rocky bowl at
the base of Mount Constance. Surrounded by towering rock
walls, the intensely colored lake, varying from blue to emerald
green depending upon the light, mirrors the mountain ramparts.
The lake was formed by a combination of glacial action and
rock slides, and a thousand-foot-high talus cone to the northeast partially covers the base of a desolate cliff.

Mountain goats are one of the attractions of this area,
and they are more abundant here than elsewhere in the Olympics. Goat wool clings to the brush, and at night the animals
become curious and approach campsites. Marmots and birds are
also present.

Mount Constance

Mount Constance (7743 ft.) is primarily a rock climb. A mass of barren lava, the mountain rises high above talus slopes of broken rock.

In former years the mountain was approached from the east, via Tunnel Creek and the Quilcene Glacier. In 1923 Outing Magazine published a dramatic account by Henry Thompson of the second ascent. "Some of the walls," he wrote, referring to the pillow lavas, "resembled tumbled masses of hardened sacks of concrete." The peak was approached from the secluded Tubal Cain copper mine to the northeast, over a difficult route. "Like the outer battlements of medieval fortresses, sheer, rugged stone walls circled around and below us, having defeated the hopes and desires of a half century of climbers . . . at our feet extended the snow-spotted death-defying route, the valley, the Quilcene Glacier, and the pass over which we had entered into a new world."

Today the mountain is usually climbed from a base camp at Lake Constance, where the trail ends. The route is hardly definable, but continues over boulder-strewn ground up the deep gully of Constance Creek. Patches of wildflowers and scrubby subalpine trees relieve the monotony of the barren rock. Towering cliffs of pillow lava rise sheer on both sides, and look unclimbable except to experienced alpinists.

Several snow-filled chutes offer routes to the top of the main ridge, then traverses are made to the final summit. The climber has a choice of routes: the "Terrible Traverse" across a precipitous, exposed snowfield, or the equally infamous "Fingertip Traverse" where one moves crablike along a narrow rock ledge on the side of a cliff. These traverses have often caused novice climbers to turn back when almost within reach of the summit block.

The view from the top is interesting, a mixture of wilderness and civilization. On three sides a sea of peaks is dominated by the wild, snowy slopes of Olympus, but to the east are the waterways of Hood Canal and Puget Sound, bordered by lowlands dotted with cities and towns. Beyond them rise the Cascades, almost lost in summer haze and topped by volcanic cones seemingly suspended in the sky.

Anderson Pass Trail

This trail begins at Dose Forks and follows West Creek to Anderson Pass, where a spur trail climbs to the Anderson Glacier. This is the best approach to Mount Anderson.

0.0   A wooden bridge across the river at Dose Forks provides access to the river's south bank, where the trail meanders a short distance to West Creek. Rhododendrons are abundant, their pink blossoms in early summer accenting the dark greens of the conifers. Canadian dogwood and queencup beadlily carpet the forest floor. West Creek, flowing in the depths of a steep-walled canyon, is spanned by a high wooden bridge. The confluence of creek and river is visible here, the Dosewallips laden with silt from the Eel Glacier.

2.7   Big Timber Camp (2.7 mi.; 2500 ft.) is located in a stand of large Douglas fir with an understory of vine maple. The up-and-down trail continues through dense, dark forest, where moss pads the ground, to a forlorn,
5.3   weather-beaten shelter at Diamond Meadows (5.3 mi.; 2692 ft.), a small opening among the trees.

The trail then crosses the creek and steepens as it continues up the gradually narrowing valley. The creek now becomes a series of cascades as it plunges through a defile.
7.5   The terrain flattens at Honeymoon Meadows (7.5 mi.; 3527 ft.), however, an area of level, grassy country beneath the grim walls of Mount Anderson. Clumps of false-hellebore are interspersed among the lush grass. This is a junction point with the Mount LaCrosse trail, a route that crosses the ridge to the south and descends to the Duckabush River.

The trail climbs sharply from Honeymoon Meadows
8.5   through subalpine forest to Anderson Pass Shelter (8.5 mi.; 4100 ft.), commonly called "Little Siberia" because of cold winds that descend from nearby glaciers. Marshy places close to the shelter are colorful in early summer with the blooms

of shooting stars, marshmarigolds and avalanche lilies. Winter wrens flit through the bushes, and occasionally pause to trill their simple song.

9.1   An alpine pool at Anderson Pass (9.1 mi.; 4464 ft.) mirrors the surrounding crags. Here the trail merges with the route coming up from the Enchanted Valley.

Anderson Glacier Trail

0.0   A spur trail less than a mile long climbs from Anderson Pass to the moraine alongside Anderson Glacier. The path ascends through picturesque stands of mountain hemlock, then switchbacks up heather-covered slopes to the moraine.

0.75   Anderson Glacier is the second largest ice stream in the eastern Olympics, and is nearly as large as the Eel Glacier on the mountain's opposite side. The moraine consists of huge angular boulders and smaller rocks piled up in a long row. The glacier's terminus is covered by rock debris, and large chunks of ice float in a small lake impounded against the glacier's edge by the moraine.

Mount Anderson appears truly alpine from this point, its three sharp peaks overshadowing the mile-long glacier.

Mount Anderson

The ascent of Mount Anderson is usually made from Anderson Pass Shelter or a camp on the heather near the moraine. Occasionally, however, climbers backpack to Flypaper Pass (6500 ft.), the narrow gap in the stone wall between the Anderson and Eel glaciers.

Climbers should rope together to cross Anderson Glacier, although large crevasses are few in number. The glacier can be crossed at any point, but the route proceeds directly up the middle, on a beeline toward Flypaper Pass, to the headwall at the six thousand-foot level. Snow slopes are then ascended directly to the pass. These grow progressively steeper and the snowfield narrows to a chute as rock walls encroach from either side. Belaying is advisable on the upper part because of the possibility of sliding onto outcroppings of sharp rock. Climbers ascending the steep snow directly below the pass appear to be clinging to a vertical wall, and this may account for the name.

The pass, a narrow gap in the ridge connecting the East Peak with the West Peak, tops the headwall between the two glaciers. This cold, snowy place is not a good campsite because space is severely limited, water is lacking, as is protection from the wind, and even in summer it sometimes storms incessantly. Abrupt cliffs border the pass on the east and west; southward the climber looks down the steep slope he has just ascended; to the north is another, somewhat less precipitous, drop to the Eel Glacier.

The route to the East Peak (7321 ft.) descends onto the upper Eel. A bergschrund often extends from one rock wall to the other, and may be difficult to cross. The route drops slightly to bypass a rock buttress, and once this point is rounded climbers must negotiate steep glacier slope broken by large crevasses. Belaying may be necessary. After several hundred feet the gradient eases, and a traverse is made to the east, until the climbers are directly beneath the East Peak. The route follows the exposed snow ridge to rock ledges, and shortly the summit is attained. On the tip of the peak climbers have built an immense cairn more than seven feet high.

The view of snow-clad mountains in all directions is impressive. The slopes of Mount Anderson drop away sharply, and the glaciers extend down rockbound troughs to the timberline. Anderson Pass is lost in the depths of the forested lower slopes.

The route to West Peak (7365 ft.) is more difficult, and traverses northwest from Flypaper Pass beneath the peak's steep southeast ridge; then the northeast shoulder is climbed. Some very steep snow must be crossed, necessitating continual belaying, and then the route negotiates a narrow ridge of exposed, unstable rock. Several unavoidable false summits must be surmounted in order to reach the westernmost pinnacle, the highest.

Constance Pass Trail

The trail to Constance Pass splits away from the Dose-
0.0   wallips trail a mile beyond Dose Forks, and climbs over
Del Monte Ridge, the high divide at the head of the
Dungeness extending from Mount Constance to Mount Mystery. The continuously uphill trail is one of the smoothest in
the Olympics, and is neither rocky, muddy, nor eroded by
mountain streams.

The trail climbs above the Dosewallips valley via long,
sweeping switchbacks up a steep mountainside thinly covered
by small, old growth fir and a sprinkling of western white pine.
Often the forest is open underneath, but in many places the
ground is thickly clad with salal. As altitude is gained, views
unfold of the valley of West Creek, bordered by snow-covered
peaks.

Following a spur northward, the route alternately overlooks the Dosewallips valley or across mountainsides below Del
Monte Ridge to Inner Constance (7339 ft.). Above three
thousand feet the forest is denser, the trees bearded with lichen,
and rhododendron forms a dense understory. A seep
2.0   spring (2.0 mi.; 3600 ft.) near the trail is the only place
where water can be obtained between the Dosewallips
valley and Sunnybrook Meadows.

Emerging from the dense forest, the trail penetrates
subalpine growth, then breaks out into Sunnybrook
2.5   Meadows (2.5 mi.; 5000 ft.) an expanse of grassy
mountain meadow on the south slope of Del Monte
Ridge. Deer often roam the well-watered slopes luxuriant with
lupine, bear grass, parsnip and huckleberry. A picturesque touch
is added by clusters of spire-topped subalpine and silver firs.
The trail crosses several streams that collectively form the headwaters of Sunny Brook. Across the Dosewallips valley rise The
Brothers and ridges extending west of that peak.

Beyond Sunnybrook Camp, located in a stand of silver
fir and Alaska cedar by one of the streams, the trail climbs upward through meadows and reveals an ever widening panorama
of the Olympic Mountains, but the view north and east is
blocked by the barren talus slopes and jagged crest of Del

Monte Ridge. On a grassy knoll beyond a shallow tarn is another campsite that overlooks the mountains to the west. A
small brook flows nearby. Higher up, the path switchbacks
across meadowland and patches of finely broken shale. Low-
growing juniper sprawls among rocks darkened by lichen.

Where the trail crosses over, Del Monte Ridge is a
gravelly expanse covered with tufts of grass and piles of broken
rock. Marmots live among the rocks and rend the air with their
shrill whistles. A high knob (6500 ft.) to the left of the trail
marks the ridgecrest, and cross-country trips to the Mount
Mystery area begin here.

Several peaks are visible from the ridgetop, including
Mount Deception, Mount Mystery, Little Mystery and Inner
Constance. The valley of West Creek trends southwest.

The trail descends several hundred feet as it follows
the narrowing ridge eastward. Barren talus slopes and permanent snowfields, the source of the Dungeness River, lie on
the northern slope, and straight ahead are the jagged, vertical
cliffs of Mount Constance. The trail rounds a spur and overlooks another basin to the north where Home Lake occupies a
hollow in the mountainside.

5.0   Constance Pass (5.0 mi.; 5850 ft.) marks the eastern
        terminus of Del Monte Ridge, where it abuts the
abrupt cliffs of Mount Constance. Plainly visible, close at hand,
is the contact line between the volcanic rocks of the eastern
Olympics and the sediments of the western. Fog often hangs
against the mountain slopes, rolling up out of the Dosewallips
valley and through the pass into the upper Dungeness basin.

        Beyond Constance Pass the route angles left and the
        trail descends the north slope of the ridge where it
5.5   crosses shale slides and meadows. Home Lake (5.5 mi.;
        5350 ft.) has no visible outlet, but a small stream flows
into the lake's uphill side. The water level of this "bathtub
lake" fluctuates, leaving an unsightly ring around its margin in
late summer. The setting is picturesque, however, for the lake
is surrounded by slopes covered with rough boulders and scattered subalpine firs, and the clear, greenish water reflects the
rocky slopes to the west.

        Below Home Lake the trail descends five hundred feet

through subalpine fir forest where huge volcanic boulders lie scattered among the trees. Lupine is abundant, the clusters of blue flowers accenting the somber tones of the rock. The trail traverses to the left of a snowfield, then crosses a boulder-strewn basin below talus slopes lying beneath the cliffs of Mount Constance. Across the valley is the high ridge between the upper Dungeness and Heather Creek. The route now contours northward at the five thousand-foot level through subalpine forests. On the right the cliffs of Warrior Peak rise above the trail; left is a view across the upper Dungeness valley and back to Constance Pass.

7.5 Beyond the national park boundary (7.5 mi.; 5000 ft.)
      the trail continues in the Olympic National Forest to
8.5 Boulder Shelter (8.5 mi.; 4900 ft.), where the Constance Pass trail terminates. Here the route forks. To the left the Dungeness River trail descends into the valley, and the right branch climbs to Marmot Pass (6000 ft.).

The upper Dungeness valley is picturesque country, and as far north as the confluence of Royal Creek should have been included within the Olympic National Park.

Hikers can leave the Constance Pass trail where it strikes the crest of Del Monte Ridge and travel cross-country along the ridge to Gunsight Pass (6350 ft.). A hundred foot pinnacle rises from the center of this u-shaped notch between Mount Mystery and Little Mystery, giving the pass the characteristic appearance, when viewed from a distance, of a gunsight. Ascents can be made from here of Mount Mystery, Little Mystery, and other high peaks flanking the upper Graywolf and Dungeness. Of special interest is Deception Basin, an alpine area bounded by Mount Deception, Mount Mystery and Mount Fricaba. A glacier on the north slope of Mount Mystery lies adjacent to a large snowfield, and the meltwater from the two merges to form Deception Creek. One side of the stream is discolored by glacial silt; the other is clear.

Lost Pass Trail

This trail climbs from Dose Meadows over Lost Pass, then skirts the headwaters of Lost River to Cameron Pass.

Beyond this point the route continues as the Cameron Creek
    trail.

0.0   The path ascends sharply from Dose Meadows up the
0.8   north side of the valley to Lost Pass (0.8 mi.; 5500 ft.),
        low point on the ridge between Lost Peak and Mount
Claywood. In several places the trail switchbacks beneath stone
outcroppings where pentstemons brighten the somber mountainside. A wide expanse of country is visible from the pass—
Lost Peak and Mount Claywood close at hand, Mount Carrie
on the far horizon.

        Beyond the pass the trail contours around the head of
Lost River. Here are mountain meadows as beautiful as any in
the Olympics, where wild flowers bloom with lavish abandon.
In July millions of avalanche lilies wave white petals with
every passing breeze, or rub shoulders with magenta paintedcup
and mountain buckwheat. Accent is provided by fescue sand-
wort, thistle, elephanthead and arnica. The flowers grow in
such profusion the hiker cannot avoid treading upon them.
Marshmarigolds, anemones and buttercups blossom in the
wetter spots. In late summer the meadows are colorful with
        lupine, buckwheat, arnica, paintbrush and daisies.

1.7   Three Sons Camp (1.7 mi.; 5400 ft.) is situated be-
        tween two mountain brooks where a level area, pro-
tected by thick-limbed subalpine trees, provides a sleeping spot,
and a circlet of rocks serves as a fireplace. Beyond this camp-
        site the trail climbs steadily toward Cameron Pass
2.8   (2.8 mi.; 6450 ft.) through open meadowland covered
        by wildflowers—primarily asters, buckwheat and lupine
—and by low-growing blueberry bushes. When the fruit ripens
in late summer, black bears are attracted to the area.

        As the trail gains altitude, Mount Olympus pokes its
snowy crown above the meadows to the west, and Mount Anderson marks the skyline beyond Hayden Pass. Near Cameron
Pass other peaks, in the Bailey Range and surrounding Low
Divide, come into view. From the pass itself a view to the north
unfolds, and the hiker can look down into Cameron Basin.

Chapter XII

The Duckabush

The Duckabush Valley

The upper Duckabush valley lies in the southeastern part of Olympic National Park. Because the mountains here are lower than those to the north, a smaller area is included within the Arctic-Alpine zone. Meadows are extensive at the higher elevations, however, and forest growth is luxuriant on the lower slopes. Dense stands of conifers mask the rough terrain, but cliffs occasionally poke through the green cloak, and avalanche paths scar many mountainsides.

Steep ridges capped by snow-covered peaks parallel the long and narrow Duckabush valley. The ridge to the north, the divide between the Duckabush and Dosewallips, includes White Mountain, Mount LaCrosse, Mount Elklick and Mount Jupiter. A similar ridge on the south, culminating in The Brothers, Mount Lena, Mount Hopper, Mount Steel and Mount Duckabush, isolates the valley from the Hamma Hamma and the North Fork Skokomish. O'Neil Pass (4900 ft.), at the head of the Duckabush, provides access to the Quinault.

The Duckabush River is swift, and its non-glacial waters are clear. Cascades and rapids are numerous, interrupted at in-

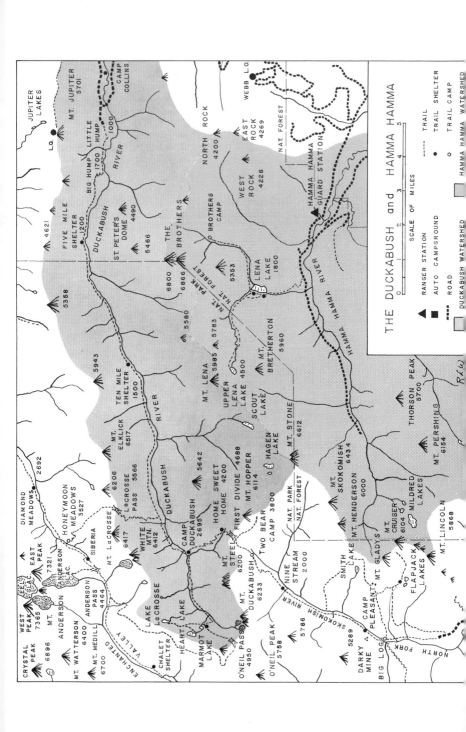

THE DUCKABUSH and HAMMA HAMMA

▲ RANGER STATION
■ AUTO CAMPGROUND
▬▬ ROAD

⋯⋯⋯ TRAIL
● TRAIL SHELTER
○ TRAIL CAMP

SCALE OF MILES
0 1 2 3 4 5

DUCKABUSH WATERSHED
HAMMA HAMMA WATERSHED

tervals by large boulders. The sparkling water, bluish-green where shaded by overhanging maples, alders and conifers, flashes white when it breaks among moss-covered rocks, and reflects innumerable glints from vagrant shafts of sunlight. Occasionally ducks are observed sitting placidly on rocks in the middle of the stream; more often, water ouzels or dippers cavort near the river's edge.

The Duckabush has many short, swift tributaries. The largest are Crazy Creek and One Too Many Creek. The latter tumbles down from small ice fields on Mount Stone. The source of the Duckabush is one of the "twin glaciers" on the north side of Mount Duckabush (6233 ft.). Next to The Brothers, this is the most prominent peak in this area. Nearby Mount Steel (6200 ft.) honors William Gladstone Steel, who fought tirelessly for many years to establish Crater Lake National Park.

The Duckabush River road spurs from the Olympic Highway near Hood Canal and penetrates wild, rugged country in the Olympic National Forest. A logging road on the south side of the Duckabush joins the river road near its end. The last mile of the old river road is rough and rocky, and motorists should use caution. The road ends on the east slope of Little Hump, at the foot of Mount Jupiter (5701 ft.).

Duckabush Trail

The trail up the Duckabush valley follows the river to beautiful subalpine meadows at the head of the valley. Here the route crosses O'Neil Pass, then contours northward to a junction near Anderson Pass with the Enchanted Valley trail.

0.0 The trail begins in the national forest. A disconcerting up-and-down route, it immediately climbs over Little Hump (1000 ft.), only to descend several hundred feet to a ledge by the river. Stands of second-growth fir nearly obscure the remnants of an old logging railroad, a reminder of forgotten activity. Then the trail abruptly begins to ascend Big Hump, a rocky buttress on the flanks of Mount Jupiter. The trail climbs alongside moss-covered rocks, and makes numerous short, steep switchbacks as it ascends a thousand feet in less than a mile.

St. Peter's Dome (4490 ft.), across the river, is visible from a
lookout point on Big Hump.

Beyond Big Hump (1700 ft.), an obstruction which
has kept civilization from the upper Duckabush valley, the trail
enters the gloom of undisturbed virgin forests of Douglas fir and
western hemlock. The tall trees are covered with lichen. The
route gradually drops to the banks of the river at Five-
5.0   Mile Shelter (5.0 mi.; 1200 ft.), a spot frequented by
fishermen during the summer. In deep forest less than
a mile beyond the shelter the path crosses the boundary of the
national park.

In the park the trail continues up the valley, gradually
gaining altitude, although making a number of minor
10.0   descents. Ten-Mile Shelter (10.0 mi.; 1500 ft.), surrounded by large firs and cedars, stands on the river
bank. Nearby, the icy waters of One Too Many Creek flow into
the Duckabush. The turbulent river, disrupted by large boulders,
makes a continuous roar, and the hiker who does not sleep
soundly will hear the booming in his dreams. This remote spot
is a favorite haunt of fishermen.

Above Ten-Mile Shelter the trail winds through dense
forest to a junction with the Mount LaCrosse trail
15.0   (15.0 mi.; 2677 ft.). Occasional breaks in the forest permit long, sweeping vistas of conifer-covered mountainsides. The trail swings back to the river opposite Camp
17.0   Duckabush (17.0 mi.; 2700 ft.), a pleasant spot noted
for its friendly mice. A large fir log spanning the Duckabush serves as a bridge. Douglas fir is still abundant, but other
forest species have appeared beyond Ten-Mile Shelter, including
Pacific silver fir and grand fir. Near Camp Duckabush is a
junction with the trail that climbs the mountainside to Home
Sweet Home Basin and crosses First Divide to the North Fork
Skokomish.

The isolation and solitude of the upper Duckabush
valley make this one of the most attractive areas in the Olympic Mountains, and a favorite wilderness region of many hikers.

The trail continues upstream along the south side of
the Duckabush, then crosses back to the river's north bank and
ascends through subalpine forest. In early summer the trail may
be partially obscured by patches of snow remaining from winter

avalanches. The snow, sprinkled with forest litter, contrasts
with the gloom of the shaded defiles. The route leads
20.2   sharply upward to Marmot Lake (20.2 mi.; 4400 ft.), a
gem-like tarn surrounded by rolling mountain meadows
dotted with clusters of Alaska cedar and mountain hemlock. A
shelter stands near the lake, and nearby is a junction with the
LaCrosse Basin trail, which climbs to Heart and LaCrosse lakes.
Across the valley, Mount Steel and Mount Duckabush,
covered with snow, soar into the sky. Far in the distance, Mount
Jupiter appears to rise directly from the valley center.

    Beyond Marmot Lake the trail climbs steadily toward
O'Neil Pass, traversing alpine meadows where, on warm summer
afternoons, marmots sun on rocks near their burrow entrances
and greet intruders with shrill whistles. These cousins of the
eastern woodchuck blend so well with the rocks they often remain unobserved.

21.7   O'Neil Pass (21.7 mi.; 4950 ft.) lies between Mount
Duckabush and a low peak to the northwest. This pass
was used by Lieutenant Joseph P. O'Neil's 1890 exploring expedition in the southern Olympics. Beyond the pass the route,
sometimes called the O'Neil Pass trail, skirts the Upper O'Neil
Creek basin and, overlooking the Enchanted Valley, traverses
northward (4800–4500 ft.) below the ridge west of LaCrosse
Basin. Because of the steepness of the mountainside, this is an
avalanche area in winter and early spring. On clear days Lake
Quinault and the Pacific Ocean glimmer in the far distance,
and Mount Anderson dominates the northern skyline. The
cliffs forming the northwest wall of Enchanted Valley, graced
by a multitude of cascades and waterfalls, stand in full view,
rising almost directly from the braided channel of the Quinault.

    The trail gradually loses altitude, and two miles west of
Anderson Pass merges with the Enchanted Valley trail
28.7   (28.7 mi.; 3200 ft.).

Mount LaCrosse Trail

    The Mount LaCrosse trail, a trans-ridge route linking
0.0   the Duckabush and Dosewallips valleys, begins fifteen
miles from the Duckabush road and climbs steeply to

LaCrosse Pass (3.0 mi.; 5566 ft.), adjacent to Mount LaCrosse, then descends to West Creek (6.0 mi.; 3627 ft.) near Honeymoon Meadows. In climbing out of the Duckabush valley the trail ascends nearly three thousand feet in three miles via a number of short, steep switchbacks.

In the high meadows near the pass, spire-topped subalpine firs stand silhouetted against cloud banks in the valley, and Mount Duckabush and Mount Steel dominate the skyline to the southwest. Snowfields streak the dark, massive bulk of Mount Steel, a rocky, six-sided peak resembling a turreted and buttressed medieval castle. Nearby Mount Duckabush outlines its jagged ridge crest and snow dome against the blue sky.

3.0   The view north from LaCrosse Pass is even more impressive. The glacier-scarred mass of Mount Anderson rises in lonely splendor above neighboring mountains. Lieutenant O'Neil named this boldly outlined peak for T. M. Anderson, an Army colonel, but on certain old maps it is designated Pyramid Mountain. Part of the Anderson Glacier is visible from the pass. Until late summer the glaciers on the peak remain snow covered, the glacial basins appearing to be large snowfields.

North of LaCrosse Pass the trail drops into luxuriant meadows bordered by clumps of subalpine firs. Buttercups, avalanche lilies and other wildflowers create colorful displays in July and August. Mount Anderson continues to dominate the northern skyline, until the trail enters the forest and
6.0   descends to West Creek.

LaCrosse Basin Trail

0.0   The LaCrosse Basin trail climbs a mountain spur above
0.5   Marmot Lake, then forks (0.5 mi.). The left branch meanders about five hundred yards to Heart Lake (4900 ft.), the right crosses meadowland to Lake La-
1.5   Crosse (1.5 mi.; 4750 ft.).

Heart Lake is the larger of the two, and cups its blue waters in a deep hollow. A small peninsula jutting into the lake contains a campsite, and from the lake's outlet the view southward overlooks Marmot Lake and the upper Duckabush valley. Mount Duckabush slashes the southern skyline.

Lush meadows surround the green water of long, slender Lake LaCrosse. Near the lake is a miniature but delicately beautiful waterfall, and from the lake the low peak northwest of O'Neil Pass resembles a massive tree stump. Nearly a mile to the east, across a low ridge, is smaller Buck Lake, sometimes mistaken for Lake LaCrosse. No trail leads to this lake.

LaCrosse Basin extends north from O'Neil Pass about three miles to the west ridge of White Mountain. Snow accumulates to great depth here during the winter and patches last until late summer. The lakes, surrounded by fields of snow, remain frozen until summer is well advanced. When bare spots appear on the mountainsides the basin's meadows become a brilliantly colored garden of wild flowers.

Chapter XIII

The Hamma Hamma

The Hamma Hamma Valley

The Hamma Hamma is a short river flowing through the eastern margin of the Olympic Mountains, and most of its watershed lies outside the national park, largely within the Olympic National Forest. The North Fork Skokomish semi-circles around the Hamma Hamma headwaters, and the peaks on the divide between the two streams—including Mount Washington, Mount Pershing, Mount Cruiser and Mount Skokomish—are as rugged as those within the park, but their lower slopes have been burned or logged. The ridges between the Hamma Hamma and the Duckabush River, to the north, are dominated by The Brothers. Lena Creek, one of the largest of the river's numerous tributaries, originates in the park. Hamma Hamma is an Indian name meaning "big stink"—a reference to the unpleasant odor left by decaying salmon that died after spawning.

The Hamma Hamma road extends about fifteen miles inland from Hood Canal, ending in primitive mountain country. Beyond the Lena Creek trail (8.5 mi.) the road is not maintained and is impassable for most vehicles.

[182]

Lena Creek Trail

0.0   The Lena Creek trail, the only route entering the na-
       tional park from the Hamma Hamma road, switchbacks
       through Douglas fir forest in the Olympic National
2.0   Forest to Lena Lake (2.0 mi.; 1800 ft.). Several shelters
       stand near the water's edge. This lake is not glacial in
origin but was formed by slides which dammed the creek. The
trail follows the west shoreline, and climbs over Chapel Rock,
a good place to view the forest-rimmed lake. Scars on the mountainsides across the lake reveal where the slides originated. On
hot days the constant booming of the East Fork of Lena Creek,
carrying meltwater from snowfields on The Brothers, sounds
like distant cannonading.

Camp Cleland, located among big Douglas firs, is often
occupied by Boy Scouts during the summer. Here a way trail to
The Brothers leads right, crosses Lena Creek and follows the
East Fork. The main route continues up the valley of Lena
Creek, and about two miles beyond the lake crosses into the
national park.

6.0   Upper Lena Lake (6.0 mi.; 4500 ft.) lies between
       Mount Lena (5995 ft.) and Mount Bretherton (5960
ft.). Mount Lena, also known as Baldy, commands a view of
surrounding peaks, particularly The Brothers, Mount Stone and
Mount Bretherton. The latter was named for a member of
O'Neil's 1890 expedition, B. J. Brotherton (or Bretherton), of
the Oregon Alpine Club. A snow chute above Milk Lake, on a
bench overlooking Upper Lena Lake, leads to the top.

The trail ends at Upper Lena Lake, but cross-country
trips are often made from this point to Scout and Hagen lakes,
on the northern slopes of Mount Stone. The route climbs to
the top of the ridge extending from Mount Lena to Mount
Stone, then follows the ridge, passing above Scout Lake, and
crosses a narrow pass called St. Peter's Gate. Hagen Lake is
located below the way trail in Crazy Creek Basin on the north
side of Mount Stone. The route now traverses the ridge between Mount Stone and Mount Hopper to the end of the
Mount Hopper spur trail.

The Brothers

The Brothers, a quadrangular, double-peaked mountain on the national park boundary, stands north of Lena Lake. One of the most conspicuous mountains visible from Puget Sound, it rises abruptly less than eight miles from Hood Canal. The south peak (6866 ft.) is the higher, but the north peak is only about fifty feet lower. A cirque on the mountain's east face is occupied by snowfields that never melt away completely from one summer to the next. This cirque, the source of Lena Creek's east fork, is bordered by two precipitous cleavers (rock walls) that extend down from the twin peaks. The cleavers are impressive viewed from the fire lookout on Mount Jupiter, in the Olympic National Forest.

Climbers often ascend The Brothers, but the route is devious and not well marked, and the climb should not be attempted without someone who knows the way. The ascent starts at Lena Lake or from a base camp near the head of the Valley of Silent Men. From the lake a way trail leads northeast through this valley, following the East Fork of Lena Creek, then the route angles northwest and ascends a precipitous snow chute. Near the top is a short rock scramble. No technical difficulties are involved, but the climb is long and strenuous.

The south peak is climbed more often, because it is the highest point, but the slightly lower north peak is a more difficult ascent. Mountaineers sometimes traverse along the jagged ridge from one peak to the other. The descent from the south peak includes, in late spring, an uninterrupted glissade down a long snowfield. Climbers should not glissade, however, in the steep snow chute.

Chapter XIV

The Skokomish

The Skokomish Valley

The Skokomish River has two main stems—the North Fork and the South Fork, which join together about seven miles from the Big Bend of Hood Canal. The upper valley of the North Fork, above Lake Cushman, lies within Olympic National Park, as does a small area constituting the headwaters of the South Fork near Sundown Pass.

Snowfields on Mount Skokomish in the Olympic National Forest are the source of the North Fork, which loops across the park's southeast corner, then reenters the national forest, where it flows into Lake Cushman. The valley of the North Fork is abutted on the east by the Sawtooth Range (extending from Mount Lincoln to Mount Cruiser), and a number of other peaks, including Mount Stone, Mount Skokomish, Mount Henderson and Copper Mountain. Beyond these peaks is the upper Hamma Hamma. To the north and west are Mount Hopper, Mount Steel, Mount Duckabush and other mountains, plus a long ridge running southwest from Mount Duckabush to Mount Olson. During the Ice Age the valley was deepened by a mountain glacier and dammed by

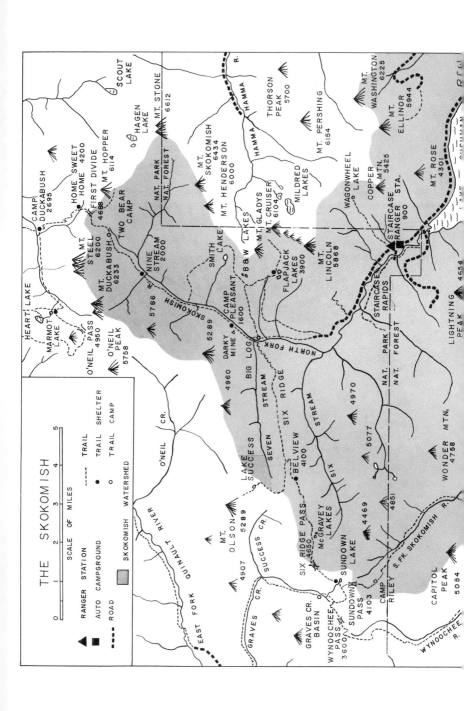

material deposited by the Puget Sound lobe of the continental glacier that came down from the north.

The watershed of the South Fork Skokomish lies almost wholly within the Olympic National Forest, and is bounded on the west by low, forested mountains across which lie the Satsop and Wynoochee watersheds; on the east by other forested peaks and ridges that separate it from the North Fork.

Where it flows through the national park, the North Fork often forms dark pools, filled with fat trout, then plunges through rock-girt channels, the water showing white as it tumbles over boulders. Occasionally, however, the river is smooth and tranquil. Tributary creeks are numerous. Those joining the river from the east are short, but those coming from the west are longer, flowing as they do between parallel ridges that lie at right angles to the river. The largest tributary is Six Stream. Several of the creeks, beginning with Four Stream and concluding with Nine Stream, were named by the 1890 O'Neil expedition.

The upper Skokomish valley within the national park is a splendid example of primeval landscape. The ever-changing vistas are always accompanied by the symphony of the Skokomish as it dashes over rocks, its waters scintillating in the sunlight breaking through the forest canopy. The forests in this valley contain some of the finest Douglas fir and western red cedar in the park. Heights of 250 feet or more and diameters of six to eight feet are common. Because of the valley's southerly orientation rainfall is heavy, resulting in a luxuriance of plant growth that rivals the rain forests of the western Olympics.

The Staircase road begins at Hoodsport on Hood Canal and climbs over low hills to Lake Cushman, then follows the north shore of the lake to the park boundary. Within the park the road follows the river, and terminates five miles above the lake. This approach to Olympic National Park gives little hint of the beauty to be found there, for the road passes through a region that has been savagely exploited, and one can only imagine the scene that greeted the eyes of Lieutenant O'Neil when he explored here in the summer of 1890.

The road forks (4.0 mi.), the left branch leading to the upper Cushman dam, the right continuing north. Originally a small lake nestled here among the foothills. B. F. Shaw, who claimed a first ascent of Mount Olympus in 1854, discovered the lake in 1852. He named it for Orrington Cushman, a lumberman commonly called "Devil Cush." When the dam was constructed the lake was inundated, and the valley flooded as far as the present national park boundary.

The main road crosses logged off land east of Lake Cushman, then enters the Olympic National Forest and merges (10.0 mi.) with a major logging road that leads across to the Hamma Hamma River, with spurs to the Mount Washington area. Beyond this junction the Staircase road twists along the north shore of Lake Cushman. On the lake's opposite side logging operations are in full swing in the national forest, and entire mountainsides have been shaved clean of trees. Young growth is beginning to cover the logged areas, however, and the scene appears less desolate than it did a few years ago.

Within the park (15.0 mi.) the scarred lands of the logger are left behind as the road plunges into a picturesque region little changed by the hand of man. Shaded by towering firs, the road follows the river to the Staircase Ranger Station (16.0 mi.; 800 ft.). The small cabin is dwarfed by the giant trees. Nearby is a public campground.

Beyond the ranger station the road climbs to a vantage point looking up and across the valley. The river meanders across bottomlands as it cuts through dense virgin forest. In early morning and late afternoon the shadows of trees form dark bars across the sunlit Skokomish.

The road gradually attains altitude as it traverses a mountainside above the river. The Mount Lincoln trail (18.4 mi.) climbs to the right above the road, which terminates at a turnaround (19.8 mi.; 1500 ft.) where the Skokomish River and Flapjack Lakes trails begin.

North Fork Skokomish Trail

The North Fork trail follows the Skokomish River to Nine Stream, climbs over First Divide into the Duckabush valley, then descends to merge with the Duckabush trail.

0.0   The trail begins where the Staircase road ends, five miles beyond the ranger station, and contours a mountainside through dense Douglas fir forest. The river, several hundred feet below, can be heard but is lost to sight. Elk roam the forests, especially during the fall when the animals retreat into the park to escape hunters.

Lined by huckleberry bushes and clumps of deer fern, the trail dips slightly to cross Madeline and Donahue

1.8   creeks. The old Black and White Lakes trail (1.8 mi.; 1500 ft.) climbs steeply up the mountainside on the right, and nearby, on the river bank, Big Log Camp nestles among large firs.

Near the river the trail crosses a small flat covered by large firs and cedars. Some of the trees are eight feet in

2.0   diameter. A wooden footbridge spans the Skokomish, here confined between rock walls about twenty feet apart, the channel overhung by the foliage of small trees. The water is deep and swift, but the clarity is such that sand patterns on the bottom are easily discernible. Across the bridge, on the west side of the river, is the junction with Six Ridge trail.

The trail continues up the valley along the west bank of the river. Dense forest alternates with lush glades overgrown by low plants and bordered by "wolf trees"—large firs, irregular in form, with gnarled limbs branching close to the ground. A sign by one of the largest trees indicates the old Darky Mine nearby, reminder of an ill-fated venture to extract manganese ore.

Occasionally the trail crosses flats covered by maples festooned with ferns and mosses in a manner similar to the rain forests of the western Olympic valleys. Not far beyond a

2.9   giant cedar leaning over the river is Camp Pleasant (2.9 mi.; 1600 ft.), a breeze-swept spot on the river bank.

North of Camp Pleasant the trail penetrates magnificent Douglas fir forests typical of those that covered the Puget Sound region in pioneer days. For several miles the path is shadowed by the giant conifers. Then the trail crosses Nine Stream, a tributary sustained by the melting snows of Mount Duckabush. On warm summer afternoons this creek becomes a brawling torrent.

5.8   Beyond Nine Stream Shelter (5.8 mi.; 2000 ft.) the route ascends toward the Skokomish-Duckabush Divide.

The large forest growth is left behind, replaced by higher altitude species. In shaded places old avalanche snow remains, covered with twigs, branches and other forest litter. Near
8.9   the divide is a junction (8.9 mi.; 4500 ft.) with the indistinct and seldom used Mount Hopper trail.

9.1   From the crest of Skokomish-Duckabush Divide (9.1
mi.; 4688 ft.), also known as First Divide, White Mountain and Mount LaCrosse stand across the Duckabush valley,
their sides scarred by numerous avalanche chutes.

The trail drops rapidly to Home Sweet Home Shelter
9.4   (9.4 mi.; 4200 ft.), near the edge of a lovely subalpine
basin through which a noisy creek races toward the
Duckabush River. This basin, recessed on the north side of
Mount Hopper, is often covered by snow until late July, but
when the snow disappears the slopes are smothered with avalanche and glacier lilies. Overlooking the meadows is the craggy
bulk of Mount Steel, particularly impressive at sunrise or sunset.
Beyond Home Sweet Home the trail descends through
heavy forest, including a stand of large Alaska cedar, to a junction with the Duckabush trail at Camp Duckabush
11.8   (11.8 mi.; 2695 ft.).

Staircase Rapids Trail

0.0   The Staircase Rapids trail begins across the Skokomish
from the ranger station and follows the west bank of
the river several miles, then climbs above Four Stream.
Near the beginning of the trail, which passes through
fir and hemlock forest, a spur trail leads to an enormous cedar
fourteen feet in diameter and more than two hundred feet tall.
Another side path descends to picturesque Red Reef Pool,
created by a barrier of red rock that nearly dams the river. Upstream is another deep pool, the Dolly Varden, bordered by
rock ledges.

Above these pools the trail winds through conifer forests
0.5   near the river, then edges Staircase Rapids (0.5 mi.),
where rock barriers form a series of low terraces or step-

like cascades in the Skokomish. Tall trees shade the river banks, and cool breezes are usually present, discouraging insects, thus making this a pleasant place to rest. The origin of the name Staircase is uncertain. The topography was probably responsible, but one story relates that the name refers to ascending steps cut around a cliff by O'Neil's expedition in order to get the pack mules around a difficult spot.

Beyond the rapids the trail veers from the river, climbs Dead Horse Hill, and continues through forests of large fir and hemlock. The route then descends onto a flat covered with cedar, fir and moss-padded alder, crosses Four Stream and climbs above the creek. The trail ends near the national park boundary (3.5 mi.; 1800 ft.).

3.5

Shady Lane Trail

0.0   The Shady Lane trail also begins across the Skokomish from the ranger station. The path follows the west side

1.0   of the river to the park boundary, about one mile south.

The trail crosses a wooden bridge spanning Elk Creek, at the south end of the picnic ground, then skirts a rock cliff jutting over a deep pool. On the opposite river bank is the public campground. Beyond this cliff, an obstruction to timid persons only, the path crosses level bottomland and traverses impressive groves of giant fir, cedar and hemlock, probably the finest stand of virgin forest on the east side of Olympic National Park. Many of the trees have diameters of six to nine feet and heights in excess of 250 feet. Beneath the conifers is an understory of bigleaf and vine maple. Deer often wander among the trees.

Unfortunately, the National Park Service permitted the building of a logging road across this corner of the park. Tons of rock, blasted from the mountainside, tumbled down, leaving an ugly scar that spoiled the beauty of the forest backdrop. Worst of all, however, was the destruction of the solitude. Cars and trucks roar up and down the road, kicking up dust and breaking the stillness. One can turn his eyes from the sight, but he cannot ignore the noise. Prior to construction of the logging road one heard only the sighing of the wind in the trees and the distant murmur of the river.

Flapjack Lakes Trail

0.0   The trail to Flapjack Lakes begins at the head of the Staircase road and climbs to Gladys Divide. Near Flapjack Lakes a spur trail branches left and connects with the Black and White Lakes trail. Huckleberry bushes line both trails.

4.1   Flapjack Lakes (4.1 mi.; 3900 ft.) are two small, round tarns surrounded by forests. Camp robbers are abundant, and quite tame. A shelter and an abandoned ski hut stand nearby. Above the lakes loom the rugged peaks of the Sawtooth Range. The rocky crags of Mount Lincoln, at the southern end of the range, appear desolate and lonely. Also visible are The Fin and Picture Pinnacle. Climbers making ascents in the Sawtooth usually camp at the lakes.

East of Flapjack Lakes the trail ascends through meadows to Gladys Divide (5.6 mi.; 5000 ft.), between
5.6   Mount Gladys and Mount Cruiser. The view overlooks the mountains at the headwaters of the Hamma Hamma, but the area directly east is hidden by the precipitous walls of Mount Cruiser.

An easy walk leads to the broad top of Mount Gladys (5600 ft.), where the view is better. Mount Anderson pokes above the ridge to the north, and Mount Olympus is visible far to the northwest. Experienced mountaineers often scale the cliffs of nearby Mount Cruiser (6104 ft.), one of the more difficult rock climbs in the Olympics.

Black and White Lakes Trail

0.0   The Black and White Lakes trail begins near Big Log Camp on the Skokomish and climbs a steep mountain
2.5   spur to Black and White Lakes (2.5 mi.), then continues north along the ridge above Smith Lake. A forest

fire once raged on the crest of the spur, and the blotched trunks
of dead trees stand stark, bleached white from weathering and
blackened by fire. The dead timber contrasts sharply with neighboring areas still clothed with green forest. The name "Black
and White Lakes" refers, however, to the mottled manganese
ore once taken from a nearby mine, marked by a dilapidated log
cabin.

The lakes are little more than potholes. Beyond them
the trail contours along the north side of Mount Gladys to the
saddle between that peak and Mount Henderson, and
4.5   overlooks Smith Lake, near the head of Hammer Creek,
and the Murdock Lakes, source of the Hamma Hamma
River. Beyond Smith Lake the trail, dim and hard to follow,
contours the west slope of Mount Henderson, then
7.0   descends to the Skokomish River opposite Eight Stream.

A short connecting trail links the Black and White
Lakes trail with the route to Flapjack Lakes.

Wagonwheel Lake Trail

0.0   The steep trail to Wagonwheel Lake begins at the
Staircase Ranger Station, and climbs through forests on
the lower mountain slopes. Crossing the national park
1.5   boundary (1.5 mi.), the trail enters the Olympic Na-
3.0   tional Forest. Wagonwheel Lake (3.0 mi.; 4150 ft.) is a
small mountain tarn cupped in a hollow on the north
side of Copper Mountain.

Mount Lincoln Trail

0.0   The Mount Lincoln trail climbs from the Staircase road
about half way up the southwestern side of Mount
2.6   Lincoln (5868 ft.), and ends in an old burn (2.6 mi.).
Brush and logs on the slopes above where the trail
terminates make the climb strenuous, and inexperienced hikers
should avoid going higher.

Mount Hopper Trail

0.0   The Mount Hopper trail begins near First Divide, on
       the North Fork Skokomish trail, and contours around
Mount Hopper to the divide above Crazy Creek. This path of-
       fers views across the Skokomish valley of Mount Sko-
2.0   komish and Mount Henderson. The trail ends (2.0 mi.)
       on the east side of Mount Hopper, but cross-country
travelers can follow a way path on the ridge to Mount Stone
and continue to Upper Lena Lake.

Six Ridge Trail

       This trail, one of the most strenuous in the Olympics,
begins where the North Fork route crosses the Skokomish
above Big Log Camp, follows the river's west bank south to
Seven Stream, then climbs to the east end of Six Ridge. After
gaining the ridge, the trail follows along or close to the crest
about seven miles to Six Ridge Pass. Many ups and downs on
       the ridge test the mettle of the veteran hiker.

0.0   Between the Skokomish bridge (1500 ft.) and Seven
       Stream the path lies close to the river's edge, and is
shaded by moss-padded maples and alders. The trail crosses
Seven Stream where the creek emerges from a cleft canyon,
then shortly begins to switchback up a forested mountain spur
to the east end of Six Ridge.
       The trees are not large except for a few old firs scattered
among the smaller timber. Huckleberry bushes and salal grow
densely on the ground. This is an excellent place to pick huckleberries, because in a good year they are abundant, and though
the distance from the road is not great, visitors are few.
       The trail ascends steadily, via short switchbacks, but
the gradient is not steep. As altitude is gained, the Skokomish
valley is glimpsed through the trees. Higher up the slope eases,
and the switchbacks end (ca. 3500 ft.), but the trail steepens
as it climbs directly along the top of Six Ridge.
       This long ridge, flanked by Six Stream on the south and
Seven Stream to the north, is somewhat serrated, knoblike

prominences alternating with notches or saddles. North and south across deep valleys are similar ridges. Patch logging in the Olympic National Forest scars distant mountainsides to the south. On the crest of Six Ridge, cool breezes murmur in the lichen-bearded mountain hemlocks, and as the afternoon sun slants low the ridge casts purple shadows in the forested valleys.

After several miles the trail breaks out into more or less open country on the south side of the ridge. This area, swept by fire in the past, is characterized by large, dead trees with blackened trunks. Here the trail switchbacks up a slope covered with brush and fire-killed trees. A touch of color is added by the red berries of mountain ash and the blue flowers of lupine. The trail now follows the ridgecrest through meadow-land and among rough outcroppings of rock. A few snowfields persist in late summer in shaded places.

5.4   Beyond a junction with the Mount Olson trail (5.4 mi.; 4400 ft.), the route drops into subalpine country on the south side of Six Ridge, where meadows alternate with groves of mountain hemlock. The trail crosses a small brook—the first water on the path since leaving Seven Stream—and soon crosses several larger brooks and two small, swampy meadows.

On the south edge of the second meadow stands the
6.4   broken down Belview Shelter (6.4 mi.; 4100 ft.), destroyed by an avalanche. The meadow is bordered on the north by a precipitous mountainside covered by Alaska cedar, and the snow avalanches from this slope onto the meadow, where it often remains until late summer and sustains a gurgling brook. On the horizon directly east of Belview is the Sawtooth Range.

Beyond Belview the trail drops slightly, then contours west along a steep mountainside where subalpine forest alternates with small, marshy meadows. Then the route climbs slightly through a stand of large mountain hemlock where undergrowth is lacking, and again contours west, crossing more marshy meadows. In many of the meadows the path disappears, but metal markers attached to trees or rocks indicate the way, and the trail can be picked up again on the opposite side. Small brooks are abundant beyond Belview, a marked contrast to their absence between Seven Stream and Belview Shelter.

The route crosses more subalpine forest, then breaks out into expansive mountain meadowlands that are dry, not marshy. Two small lakes on a bench below the trail are sometimes mistaken for the McGravey Lakes.

The trail continues to alternate between subalpine forest and dry meadowland flecked with rocky outcroppings. The route climbs over a spur, then descends to the larger of 8.5   the two McGravey Lakes (8.5 mi.; 4000 ft.).

This alpine lake lies in a bowl beside a small, domelike outcrop of smooth rock, and is surrounded by meadows dotted with solitary mountain hemlocks. Bear grass waves in the mountain breezes, murmuring brooks flow into the murky green lake, and bees hum busily in surrounding fields of mountainheath. Nearby is the slightly smaller second lake, reflecting mountain hemlocks in its quiet waters.

Beyond the McGravey Lakes the trail is poor, with several missing links where the route crosses small meadows. The trail then enters a large meadow, and begins to climb. Cairns mark the route, indistinct in places, the path sometimes vanishing. Hikers should be alert for the markers, as the route 9.6   can be lost easily near Six Ridge Pass. The pass (9.6 mi.; 4650 ft.) marks the narrow ridgecrest. Mount Olympus and other peaks are visible to the northwest. Beyond the pass the route continues as the Graves Creek trail.

Mount Olson Trail

0.0   The Mount Olson or Lake Success trail begins where the Six Ridge trail drops over the ridgecrest to Belview Shelter. This route continues up Six Ridge through more or less open country characterized by scattered mountain hemlocks and an abundance of bear grass and mountainheath, and the views become even better. The ridge gradually narrows to a spine a few feet wide, the mountainsides falling sharply away, and one can look directly down either side to Six Stream or Seven Stream. Beyond this spiny ridge the trail crosses the upper edge of a large meadow, where the path is not well defined, then commences to switchback steeply, climbing about four hundred feet to a promontory (4900 ft.). Across the headwaters of Success Creek, Mount Olympus stands on the horizon, framed by Mount Olson and a neighboring peak.

The route then drops below the ridge on the north side and contours west beneath rock buttresses, where the trail crosses shale slopes, rock slides and snowfields, then ascends to a notch in the gap connecting Six Ridge with Mount Olson. The view down the valley of Seven Stream from this point is superb. The Sawtooth Range, Mount Skokomish and Mount Stone dominate the eastern horizon.

Beyond the notch the trail descends a few hundred
4.0   feet, then contours north about a mile to Lake Success,
a tiny alpine tarn on the divide between Success Creek and Seven Stream.

Chapter XV

The Quinault

The Quinault Valley

In the Olympic Mountains, the Quinault River has two branches—the North Fork, with its source on Mount Seattle near Low Divide, and the East Fork, nurtured by the Anderson Glacier on Mount Anderson. These two streams combine in the foothills, and the river then flows through a broad, level valley to Lake Quinault, about ten miles to the southwest. This lake lies on the mountain perimeter, midway between the river's source and the Pacific Ocean. Thus the Quinault drains a large segment of the southwestern Olympics. Below the lake the lower Quinault flows across lowlands to the sea.

An area of rough, broken country comprises the watershed of the North Fork. Near Low Divide several high, glaciated peaks stand between the valley and the Elwha. To the east, the North Fork is bounded by Mount Christie and the ridges extending from that peak around the head of Rustler Creek to Chimney Peak in the Burke Range. Rustler Creek, also known as The Rustler or The Rusher, is the largest tributary of the North Fork, and a high ridge lies between it and the East Fork Quinault. On the west the Quinault watershed is defined by the mile-high Queets-Quinault Divide extending from Mount Noyes to Finley Peak, and including Kimta Peak. Many small lakes dot the meadows at higher altitudes; the lower slopes are heavily clothed with dense stands of virgin forest.

The East Fork Quinault sweeps across a long, narrow valley bordered by heavily timbered mountain slopes. Below the Anderson Glacier, the river flows through the Enchanted Valley. Here the narrow bottomlands are enclosed by precipitous mountainsides, and the valley's upper end abuts against the base of Mount Anderson. The northwestern margin of Enchanted Valley, the sidewall of the Burke Range, is a cliff four thousand feet high. The less abrupt southeastern side is bordered by the ridge running north from O'Neil Pass to White Mountain and Mount La Crosse. The Burke Range, isolating Enchanted Valley from Godkin Creek and Hayes River, tributaries of the Elwha, includes Crystal Peak (6896 ft.), Chimney Peak (6911 ft.) and other high points. Muncaster Mountain (5910 ft.) lying between the East Fork and The Rustler, marks the western terminus of the Burke Range. Below Enchanted Valley the East Fork is bordered by high ridges. Along the north side of the river a long, narrow ridge extends from Muncaster Mountain toward the forks of the Quinault. Beyond the ridges south of the East Fork are the headwaters of several rivers that flow from the southern flanks of the Olympics. These streams lie outside the national park. The largest tributaries of the East Fork Quinault are O'Neil Creek and Graves Creek.

Lake Quinault lies less than two hundred feet above sea level, and is surrounded by low, forested mountains. The land north of the lake is included in the national park, that to the south in the national forest and Quinault Indian Reservation. The river flows into the lake's northeastern end, where it has built a delta, then leaves the lake on the southwest side. The lake, four miles long by two miles wide, is part of the Quinault Indian Reservation.

The narrow, winding North Fork road follows the lake shore and river for eighteen miles, to a campground and the North Fork Ranger Station. Here the Low Divide trail begins. Along the lake's north shore the road passes through old growth forest and cutover land, then enters rougher country as it con-

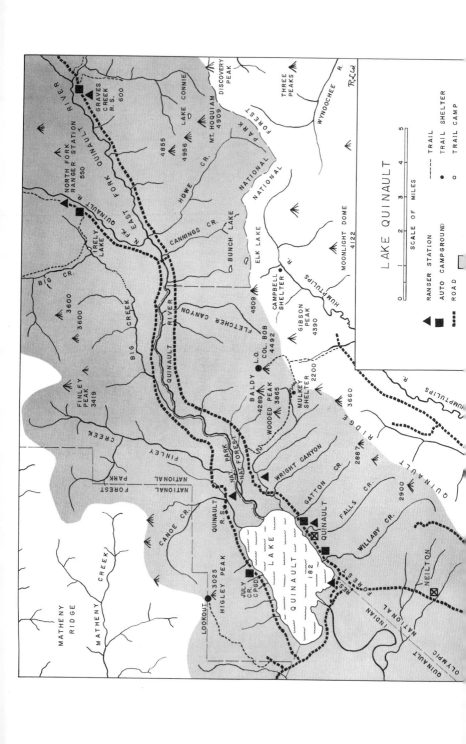

LAKE QUINAULT

SCALE OF MILES

RANGER STATION

AUTO CAMPGROUND

ROAD

TRAIL

TRAIL SHELTER

TRAIL CAMP

tinues up the Quinault valley. A spur road (14.0 mi.) leads right
to a bridge spanning the Quinault just below the confluence of
the two forks. Near the end of the road are heavy stands of large
Douglas fir.

The East Fork road begins near the lower end of Lake
Quinault, and passes summer homes built among the tall spruce
and fir trees that line the lakeshore. Beyond Quinault, a small
settlement on the south shore, the road follows the river about
twenty miles. The last ten miles penetrate dense rain forest
within Olympic National Park. Here are splendid stands of large
Douglas fir, and groves of bigleaf maple garlanded with luxuriant mosses. Near the park boundary at Bunch Creek the road
lies close to the river, and the bridge across the Quinault provides access to the North Fork. The East Fork road terminates
about three miles beyond the Graves Creek Ranger Station.

Low Divide Trail

An up-and-down route, this trail begins at the North
0.0   Fork Ranger Station (550 ft.) and follows the winding
North Fork Quinault to Low Divide, then descends
to the Elwha near Chicago Camp. Most of the route is through
dense stands of virgin forest. In the upper part of the valley,
above Francis Creek Shelter, stands of Pacific silver fir are
extensive.

2.5   From the ranger station to Wolf Bar Shelter (2.5 mi.;
630 ft.) the trail, bordered by splendid rain forests of
cedar, hemlock, fir and spruce, follows an abandoned road that
time has nearly obliterated. Beyond Rustler Creek, a major
tributary entering the river from the east, the trail traverses
broken country, ascending and descending as it crosses many
creeks, among them Elip, Three Prune, Stalding and Kimta,
that flow down from subalpine basins near the Queets-
Quinault Divide. The remnants of Halfway House
4.5   (4.5 mi.; 800 ft.) near Wild Rose Creek serve as a
7.0   trailside shelter, but Francis Creek Shelter (7.0 mi.;
1100 ft.) provides better accommodations. Near Kimta
Creek the trail passes the ruins of Bunch Cabin, mountain re-

treat of a Quinault pioneer who had a ranch in the valley near
the lake. Bunch Lake and Bunch Canyon, south of the Quinault, perpetuate his name. Beyond the cabin.the trail continues
up the rapidly narrowing valley which becomes a canyon where
the river flows between Mount Zindorf and Mount
12.0   Lawson. Big Fir Shelter (12.0 mi.; 1800 ft.) lies at the
base of Mount Zindorf, above the confluence of the
Quinault and Geoduck Creek. A half mile above Big
Fir the trail crosses the river to Sixteen Mile Shelter
12.5   (12.5 mi.; 2000 ft.). Nearby is the junction of the
Quinault and Promise Creek. The trail now climbs
steadily, paralleling the Quinault in a steep ascent around the
base of Mount Christie. The trail ascends through dense, gloomy
forests of hemlock and silver fir. The roar of the river—here a
continuous series of rapids and cascades—is ever present. Then
the trail climbs directly to the grassy, forest-rimmed
meadowland near Low Divide. Here is a junction
15.8   with the Skyline Trail (15.8 mi.).

Forest-clad slopes rise abruptly to rugged, snow-covered
16.0   heights on either side of Low Divide (16.0 mi.; 3662
ft.), the flat saddle between Mount Christie and
Mount Seattle. The tops of the two peaks are lost to view,
however, behind spurs and buttresses. Snowy, sharp-crested
Mount Zindorf stands directly in the line of sight down the
Quinault valley.

A shelter stands near the south edge of the meadow,
and the trail leads from here over a level, grass-covered expanse
and crosses the Quinault, now only a brook bordered by dense
growths of willow. The river's source is lodged in snowfields on
the east face of Mount Seattle. Another shelter is located at the
northern edge of the meadow. Nearby are a National Park
Service cabin and the desolate ruins of Low Divide Chalet, a
mountain hostelry destroyed years ago by an avalanche that
swept down the side of Mount Seattle.

North of the meadow the trail crosses the divide and
skirts the two mountain lakes discovered and named by the
Press Expedition in 1890. Lake Margaret (3600 ft.) has water
lilies, usually found only at lower altitudes. On its southeast
shore is a junction with the trail to Martins Park. From the

lake, Mount Seattle is visible—a broad, massive peak with two sharp pinnacles connected by a snow-covered ridge. The other tarn, Lake Mary, is considerably smaller and slightly lower in elevation. A vantage point here provides a view for many miles down the upper Elwha or Press Valley. Lake Mary is relatively warm for a subalpine pool, and hikers sometimes bathe here. Both lakes are surrounded by mountain hemlock and Alaska cedar. Elk, bear and cougar tracks are often imprinted in the soft mud near the shorelines. Bears are particularly common in this area, and in 1890 the Press explorers were saved from starvation by dining on dehibernating bears at Low Divide.

Beyond the lakes the trail descends sharply to Chicago
19.0   Camp (19.0 mi.; 2185 ft.) on the Elwha, where it joins the Elwha trail. On the way down the steep mountainside, one can look occasionally across the Elwha to forested slopes, and also view the cascades of nearby Delabarre Creek, which plunge noisily down the side of Mount Christie. The route avoids the cliffs climbed by the Press Expedition from the upper end of Press Valley.

Martins Park Trail

The spur trail from Low Divide to Martins Park is less than two miles long but climbs a thousand feet above the divide, up the northern slopes of Mount Christie. The
0.0   trail begins near the southeast shore of Lake Margaret (3600 ft.) and ascends forested slopes, first through a lush, marshy area, then over a small spur, and drops
1.0   into Martins Park (1.0 mi.; 4000 ft.), one of the loveliest mountain meadows in the Olympics. Along the way Mount Seattle is glimpsed through the trees.

Martins Park, a flat, grassy meadow with many flowering plants, is surrounded on three sides by rugged spurs of Mount Christie. This peak was named for the leader of the 1890 Press Expedition. Overlooking the eastern side of the meadow are shiny cliffs bearing on their crest the Martins Lakes, hidden from view here. Scattered over the meadows are large, angular boulders, and two clear, rock-bottomed brooks flow across the basin, sunlight glinting on their waters. Black bears roam here, in this idyllic wilderness setting. Among the flowers are shooting stars, mountain buckwheat, buttercups, yellow monkeyflower, pink heather, marshmarigolds, violets and elephanthead. Clumps of large-leaved falsehellebore add an artistic touch. Sometimes the trail across the meadow is covered by snow that has avalanched from the steep cliffs of Mount Christie.

Although the view higher up is better, Martins Park is a more pleasant place than the lakes. The meadow is well-watered, and swept by cool breezes. In the warm sunshine, however, the hiker can sun himself on one of the big boulders like a lazy marmot and listen to the murmuring of the brooks and the humming of bees.

The trail climbs the slope high above but parallel to the creek into the big basin (4400 ft.) below the Christie Glacier. Rocks, heather and snowfields lead up to the rugged higher slopes. The trail climbs steadily to the small
1.5   Martins Lakes (1.5 mi.; 4650 ft.) near the crest of a spur extending north toward the Elwha. A rocky outcropping above the first lake presents a splendid view of Mount Seattle, Mount Queets, Mount Meany, and the upper ramparts of Mount Christie, as well as such historic points of interest as the Elwha snowfinger, Mount Barnes and Dodwell-Rixon Pass.

The Martins Lakes are aquamarine. The north lake is bluer and is round, whereas the greener south lake is long and narrow. At the western margin of the lakes is the crest of the shiny vertical cliffs that drop several hundred feet and are visible from the meadow below. Both lakes are deep. On warm days a multitude of small frogs sun themselves on the lake shore, jumping into the water if disturbed.

Three Lakes Trail

0.0   The trail to Three Lakes begins a mile south of the North Fork Ranger Station and follows Big Creek valley to the lakes on the Queets-Quinault Divide, where the Skyline and Tshletshy Creek trails terminate.

The trail meanders through rain forest in a swamp-
1.0   like area to Irely Lake (1.0 mi.; 540 ft.), a popular fishing spot during the summer. About a mile beyond

the lake the trail climbs out of the Quinault bottomlands and ascends gradually as it traverses mountainsides above Big Creek. The forests of fir and cedar here are dense and tall, and in some places unusually beautiful—big firs rising high above a ground cover of sword ferns. A few of the old cedars are very large. Fallen logs are decorated with bracket fungus, exhibiting vivid shades of red, orange and yellow; alongside the trail are huckle-berry and trailing blackberries.

Leaving Big Creek, the trail follows a tributary about a half mile, then crosses to the west side and switchbacks up a steep, forest-clad spur to the divide. The route passes through stands of large Alaska cedar just before reaching Three Lakes.

6.6   Near the largest of these small subalpine pools is a junction with the Skyline trail (6.6 mi.; 3200 ft.). The grass-rimmed lakes are located in a swampy meadow where pale violets bloom among the grasses in the summer.

6.9   Beyond the lakes the trail climbs steeply to Three Lakes Shelter (6.9 mi.; 3400 ft.), located in a tiny meadow surrounded by forests of mountain hemlock and Alaska cedar. Bear grass splashes white on the slopes above.

7.1   The trail continues, climbing to the ridgecrest (7.1 mi.; 3600 ft.); then, becoming the Tshletshy Creek trail, drops into Paradise Valley on the Queets side of the ridge.

The Three Lakes region is noted for many little mead-ows, some so small as to resemble miniature football fields. Surrounded by subalpine trees, they are quite picturesque. From the ridgecrest one looks down into Paradise Valley, the remote, seldom-visited region at the head of Tshletshy Creek, where coyotes may be heard barking in the distance. The view encom-passes heavily timbered ridges and mountain spurs; fleeting glimpses of peaks to the north lure the hiker to the Skyline trail.

Skyline Trail

The Skyline trail, a scenic but strenuous route, follows the mile-high Queets-Quinault Divide nearly twenty miles from Three Lakes to the head of Seattle Creek Basin, then descends to Low Divide. From Three Lakes to Kimta Peak, the midway

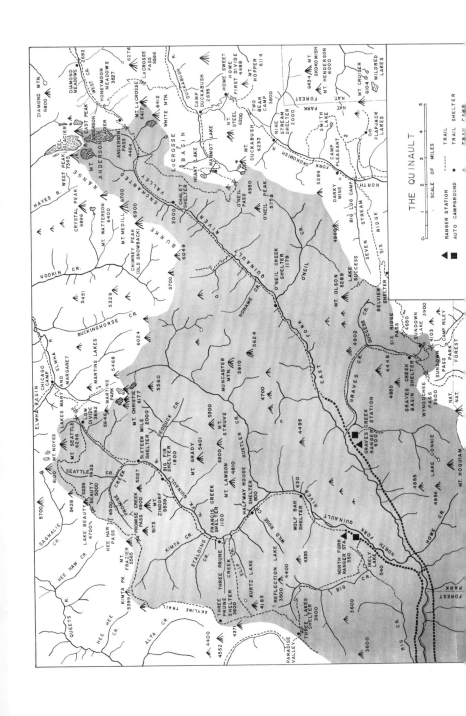

THE QUINAULT

SCALE OF MILES
0 1 2 3 4 5

▲ RANGER STATION   TRAIL
■ AUTO CAMPGROUND   • TRAIL SHELTER

point, the trail shifts back and forth from the Quinault to the Queets side of the divide, sometimes following the ridgecrest but usually contouring just below. Beyond Kimta Peak the ridge is higher, with wide expanses of country above the timberline.

This trail traverses a primitive, little known region as wild and beautiful as any part of the Olympic Mountains. Hikers should come prepared for inclement weather, however, for this is on the windward side of the mountains. Because winter snowfall is heavy, the route is usually blocked until late summer. The trail is a regular pathway for wild animals, and the tracks and droppings of elk, deer, bear and wildcat are commonly observed, as are the animals themselves on occasion. Elk congregate in the meadows in late summer; bears roam the slopes when the huckleberries ripen.

0.0   From its point of origin at Three Lakes (3200 ft.), the trail contours northward on the Quinault side of the ridge, passing alternately through small, forest-rimmed meadows and dense stands of large silver fir, mountain hemlock and Alaska cedar. Miniature lakes and pools grace the lush meadowlands, where violets and buttercups nestle among the grasses, adding subtle touches of color. To the right of the trail,

2.0   tiny Reflection Lake (2.0 mi.; 3500 ft.), little more than a snow pond, is glimpsed through the forest. The lake is situated in a semimeadowy, marshy area. Flowers are common, including avalanche lilies, shooting stars and elephanthead, and the seed stalks of the western anemone or "mouse on a stick" sway gently in the soft breezes.

Beyond Reflection Lake the trail climbs over a spur— an open meadow at the head of Elip Creek—where masses of red mountainheath carpet the mountainsides, and bees buzz continuously in the warm sunshine while they gather nectar. This is wild, lonely country, with splendid views up the Quinault to snow-capped Mount Seattle, Mount Christie and Muncaster Mountain. Tiny, scenic lakes dot the luxuriant expanses, mirroring the surrounding country, and clear brooks meander from lake to lake. The trail climbs over a low ridge, only to descend sharply on the other side through mountain hemlock forest to the basin at the head of the south

4.0   fork of Three Prune Creek. The Elip Creek trail (4.0 mi.; 3800 ft.) descends to the Quinault from here. The

Skyline trail contours north through forest and open meadow
    at the head of the basin, then rounds another jutting
5.0   spur. From this point Three Prune Shelter (5.0 mi.;
    3600 ft.) is glimpsed on the far side of Three Prune
Basin. This campsite received its name on the 1913 summer
outing of The Mountaineers. The pack train carrying the food
failed to keep up with the hikers, resulting in their spending
the night with an allowance of three prunes each for dinner.

North of Three Prune Basin, a series of little meadows,
the trail climbs steadily through dense forests of large Alaska
cedar, silver fir and mountain hemlock, then rounds a mountain
spur and enters the meadows of Stalding Creek Basin. The
route stays just below the divide, criss-crossing from one side to
the other, but most of the time remains on the Quinault side.

Beyond Stalding Creek Basin the trail climbs over another
spur, then drops to the Queets side of the ridge. Here the
mountainsides are extremely precipitous, falling abruptly to
the depths of Alta Creek valley. The trail soon recrosses to the
Quinault side and traverses forested slopes above South Kimta
Basin, where an old way trail leads down into the valley.

The Skyline trail continues northward, following the top
of the ridge, with views of both the Queets and Quinault valleys
through trees covered with staghorn lichen. Now the route
climbs sharply toward Kimta Peak, returning to the Queets side
of the ridge, where it traverses broad, open meadows that overlook the heavily timbered Alta and Queets valleys, as well as a
spur of the Mount Olympus Range. The trail crosses back over
the ridge into North Kimta Basin, a tangle of snowfields even in
late summer, and circles the head of the basin to Kimta Peak.
Elk tracks are common on the snow.

Because the trail in North Kimta Basin is often covered
with snow, the route is marked by blazes and blobs of orange
paint on pieces of tin tacked to trees. The trail keeps high,
just beneath the ridgecrest, and hikers should be alert, so as
not to be misled by the numerous game trails. The trail can
be lost easily here in the confusion of sharp spiny ridges and
rocky spurs of upturned shale shaved smooth by ancient
    glaciers.

11.0   Kimta Peak (11.0 mi.; 5399 ft.) has been called the
    "fog capital" of the Olympics. Cloud banks often hang

over the peak and along the ridge, obscuring the view, but on clear days a glorious panorama is revealed. Far below, the Queets River meanders through virgin rain forests, and the mountainsides are clothed with mountain hemlocks bearded with staghorn lichen. Mount Olympus, only five miles distant, dominates the northern scene, its sheer southern face of inaccessible cliffs streaked with snowfields and glaciers. This least glaciated side of the mountain is seldom viewed. The whole sweep of the Mount Olympus Range is visible, as is the heavily forested Queets valley, bordered by ridges, timbered from base to crest, that extend endlessly toward the distant Pacific. Queets Basin lies to the northeast, with some of the Bailey Range peaks poking above the encircling cliffs. Many distant mountains are visible to the south and east.

This remote country, one of the wildest parts of the Olympic Mountains, has few human visitors, thus adding to its charm. The shrill, piercing whistles of marmots occasionally break the solitude, and the deep surging sound of Kimta Creek rises from the forested depths.

The trail traverses east through heather meadows at about the five thousand foot level beneath the summit of Kimta Peak. Springs gush from the well-watered mountainside below the trail. The view down the valley of Kimta Creek is splendid, with craggy peaks on the skyline. The route descends gradually into the forest, where the trail crosses many small streams and is in poor condition. Several hundred feet of elevation are lost beyond Kimta Peak before the trail climbs steeply by

12.5   switchbacks to Promise Creek Pass (12.5 mi.; 4900 ft.)

at the head of Promise Creek. Here it suddenly breaks over the divide and a spectacular view unfolds. Occupying the foreground is Promise Creek Basin, a large snow bowl, with rugged Mount Zindorf on its eastern rim. Other peaks—Mount Seattle, Mount Chistie, Mount Noyes and Mount Meany—are visible in the distance, but Low Divide is hidden by a mountain spur. An old way trail leads from here into Promise Creek Basin, dropping a thousand feet to Cold Springs Camp, then continuing through the damp and gloomy depths of Promise Creek canyon to the Quinault.

Beyond Promise Creek Pass the Skyline trail becomes more a way than a trail. The route, marked by cairns, leads left over fields of snow and heather meadows near the crest of the divide between Promise Creek and Hee Haw Creek. Outcroppings of sharp shale are common, the strata turned on end or at high angles, and mountain hemlocks sprawl along the ridgecrest. The unobstructed view from this divide includes Mount Olympus and the upper basin of Hee Haw Creek, where large snowfields with schrunds (i.e., breaks in the snow) appear to be a glacier in the process of creation. In addition to the Mount Olympus Range, the rugged peaks surrounding Elwha Basin are visible from here, as well as an excellent panorama of the eastern Olympics. This splendid high country is reminiscent of the Bailey Range, with sweeping views for miles, and rugged, snowy peaks in all directions. A convenient campsite is located on the meadow near the ridgecrest, a vantage point for watching fogbanks rise out of the Queets valley and roll over Mount Kimta into North Kimta Basin. Also visible is the "Queets Burn"—several hundred acres of devastated, fire-killed forest on the north side of the Queets opposite Hee Haw Creek.

Beyond the campsite the route descends about five hundred feet in Promise Creek Basin to avoid a buttress on the ridge. The trail is almost non-existent, but the way, mostly over snowfields and upturned shale worn smooth by Ice Age glaciers, is marked by cairns. The route crosses a narrow, steep-walled ravine, then climbs sharply up the mountainside toward the divide. The trail again descends in order to round another spur, climbs up and contours cliffs only to descend a third time to meadows dotted with groves of mountain hemlock. In all, the way loses about seven hundred feet of altitude beyond Promise Creek Pass, and crosses several deep ravines, 14.5   before climbing to Hee Haw Pass (14.5 mi.; 4500 ft.).

This meadowy saddle in the ridge provides a superb view of Mount Tom. The trail crosses the pass to the Hee Haw Creek side of the ridge, then climbs through dense timber to the lower edge of a meadow beneath a large slide. Here the poorly marked trail is easily confused with a multitude of game paths, but the route enters meadows and climbs again.

15.5   Lake Beauty (15.5 mi.; 4700 ft.), surrounded by snow-fields and luxuriant meadows, is slightly off the route. The lake, cupped in a deep hollow, is intensely blue, and ice and snow still float in its shaded waters in late summer. Mount

Noyes and Mount Meany rise to the northeast, beyond the upper basin of Saghalie Creek; Mount Olympus and Mount Tom stand to the northwest. A campsite is located near the western end of the lake. The stillness of this remote place is unbroken save for the croaking of black ravens and the murmuring of soft breezes in the lichen-bearded mountain hemlocks. Sunsets are colorful from the lake, for the sun disappears behind the jagged silhouette of the Mount Olympus Range.

An old trail leads northwest of Lake Beauty to a smaller lake. This subalpine pool is very deep, and often contains snow and ice. The tarn is surrounded by snowfields and meadows dotted with clumps of lichen-covered mountain hemlocks. Some of the clumps are massive, five to ten trees growing in a thick cluster, and in one of them are remnants of an old Air Force cache, probably of World War II vintage.

East of Lake Beauty the route crosses Beauty Pass (5000 ft.) into another part of Promise Creek Basin. The view from the pass, which is marked by a cairn made of smooth river rocks that someone must have packed up the mountain, encompasses the entire width of Olympic National Park. Westward one looks through a gap in the Mount Olympus Range to the distant Pacific; on the eastern horizon the Sawtooth Range marks the national park boundary.

Below the pass the trail drops beneath rock cliffs studded with pentstemons, then contours the mountainside northeastward toward Mount Noyes through open meadows and stands of mountain hemlock. Across the valley of Promise Creek stands Mount Zindorf, a broad peak with many snowfields and crags. As the trail progresses, the view of Promise Creek Basin gradually unfolds, then the path rounds a bend and overlooks the upper Seattle Creek Basin. Mount Seattle, at the head of the basin, stands atop a wide meadow that in turn surmounts a broad, tree-covered basin. This massive peak, with its many snowfields, and rock towers, turrets and walls, resembles a medieval castle. Mount Christie and Mount Noyes also are in full view, and the tip of Mount Meany shows through a gap.

The trail crosses meadows threaded by clear brooks, and descends via switchbacks several hundred feet through mountain hemlock forest. The route crosses two precipitous

gorges, then enters the upper Seattle Creek Basin, where the trail traverses beneath the towering southern face of Mount Noyes and a spur of Mount Seattle. Bears roam these meadows, where gentle breezes riffle avalanche lilies and the plumes of squaw grass, and the stillness is broken by the roar of
18.0   Seattle Creek (18.0 mi.; 4200 ft.). The trail contours through rolling, rock-strewn meadows on the south-west side of Mount Seattle, then rounds the south buttress of the peak and again drops into mountain hemlock forest. On hot afternoons walking from the sunny meadows into the shaded coolness of the forest is almost like entering an air-conditioned home on the desert.

20.5   The trail loses elevation rapidly in the forest, and joins the Low Divide trail (20.5 mi.; 3550 ft.) just south of Low Divide.

Elip Creek Trail

0.0   The Elip Creek trail begins in the Quinault valley (1000 ft.) between Elip and Three Prune creeks, and climbs directly up a steep mountain spur through forests to
4.0   the Skyline trail (4.0 mi.; 3800 ft.). This route makes loop trips possible utilizing parts of the Low Divide and Skyline trails.
The trail provides a glimpse of Kurtz Lake through the forest, then emerges rather abruptly from the dense forest into meadows dotted with little "frog ponds." The transition from shaded forest to sunny meadow is so abrupt it is like walking into the bright outdoors from a dark room. Mount Lawson and Mount Christie, framed by a wall of trees, are visible from the meadows.
The trail merges with the Skyline trail about one mile south of Three Prune Shelter.

Higley Peak Trail

0.0   This trail leaves the Kiwanis Camp road near the west boundary of Olympic National Park, about a half mile

east of U. S. 101 north of Lake Quinault. The trail climbs
through forests to the lookout atop Higley Peak
3.0   (3.0 mi.; 3025 ft.), which marks the park boundary
north of the lake.

This peak, named for a pioneer family who settled on
Lake Quinault, provides a view of the lake, the Quinault valley,
and the forested foothills to the north and south that lead up
to the snowy peaks of the interior Olympics.

Enchanted Valley Trail

0.0   The Enchanted Valley trail begins where the East Fork
road ends (1178 ft.) and follows the East Fork
Quinault to Enchanted Valley and Anderson Pass. Beyond the
pass the route is known as the Anderson Pass trail.

Initially, the route follows an old roadbed through
stands of large Douglas fir where Devil's-club, adorned with
red berries, is conspicuous. The trail then descends to the river,
and crosses over the Pony Bridge (903 ft.), where clusters of
maidenhair ferns sheath the nearly vertical banks of the shaded,
rock-walled gorge through which the Quinault plunges.

The valley is pleasant, and gentle breezes, cooled by
glaciers and snowfields at the river's source, are usually present.
The trail winds through shadowy forest aisles as it follows the
meandering river. A few large Douglas firs are scattered among
the alders and maples on the bottomlands. Many of the broad-
leaved trees are festooned with mosses and liverworts. In the
early morning the shallow river has a light green color, except
for a show of white where it plunges over boulders, creating
rapids. The stream becomes turbulent on warm summer afternoons from the increased volume of silt-laden meltwater descending from the glaciers.

Opposite the point where O'Neil Creek flows into the
Quinault stands O'Neil Creek Shelter (4.7 mi.; 1179
4.7   ft.). Beyond the shelter the trail continues upriver, and
after several miles crosses the river, entering Enchanted Valley.
Here the river flats, covered with lush grasses and alder groves,
are enclosed by cliffs that rise four thousand feet in less than a

mile, and the Quinault splits into a multitude of small braided channels. In the cold water, fresh from the snowfields and glaciers of Mount Anderson, ouzels bob up and down. At dawn, the air is sharp and chill. In early summer, when snowdrifts on the Burke Range are melting, hundreds of filmy cascades plummet thousands of feet down the almost vertical cliffs that form the valley's northwest wall. These are responsible for another name, "Valley of a Thousand Waterfalls." Even in late summer, after most of the snow has melted, a number remain, and minute icefields, undermined with tunnels, cling to recesses in the mountain wall. In the winter and spring avalanches sweep down these cliffs, too steep to retain a forest cover.

The charm of Enchanted Valley is enhanced by isolation from highways. On the valley floor near the river 10.9 stands Enchanted Valley Chalet (10.9 mi.; 2000 ft.), a two-story log building formerly operated as a hostelry, but now used as a trail shelter.

Above Enchanted Valley the river, constricted between steep, forested slopes, cascades over boulders and rocks. The largest known western hemlock stands by the trail, its status proclaimed by a sign tacked to its trunk. The tree's diameter at breast height is eight feet eight inches.

The valley again widens as the trail gradually climbs. Springs gush from the mountain slopes, and just below a waterfall the trail crosses White Creek, a stream flowing from White Mountain. Near the creek is a junction with the O'Neil 14.5 Pass section of the Duckabush trail (14.5 mi.; 3200 ft.). Wild raspberries and blueberries grow profusely in this area.

The trail switchbacks as it climbs steadily toward Anderson Pass. Occasionally on warm summer afternoons the stillness is broken by the rumbling of glaciers and crashing of ice plunging down cliffs. Torrents of water from the unnamed glacier on the west side of Mount Anderson pour down the mountainside.

16.5 From Anderson Pass (16.5 mi.; 4464 ft.) one can look east down the valley of West Creek, a branch of the Dosewallips; west down the Quinault. A steep spur trail climbs above the pass to Anderson Glacier, one of the largest ice streams in the eastern Olympics, and source of the East Fork Quinault.

Graves Creek Trail

0.0   The Graves Creek trail begins just east of Graves Creek, one-half mile beyond the campground, in a setting of western red cedar. This creek has a steep gradient, with many falls and cascades, and after heavy rains or when the snow melt in the high country reaches its peak, the booming of the stream is pronounced.

The trail climbs abruptly about one hundred feet to a point overlooking the creek, then crosses an almost level bench forested with small hemlock and large fir and cedar. Maidenhair and sword ferns cover the ground. After following the bench some distance, the trail again emerges on a slope above Graves Creek, and traverses upstream. Near the one mile marker, a mountain torrent tumbles into the creek from the opposite mountainside, forming a series of cascades and waterfalls. Graves Creek roars away in the depths of its canyon, and much of the time can not be seen. Now and then a view unfolds up the canyon, where steep, heavily timbered mountainsides encroach from either side of the gradually narrowing gorge.

The trail begins to climb on a rising traverse high above the creek, where occasionally white water shows. Wisps of fog cling to the mountainsides, and rain clouds gather down the valley. The trail then descends to the brink of the gorge, a hundred feet or so above the thundering and booming creek, but the stream remains hidden in the depths of its narrow cleft canyon. From an unobstructed viewpoint, however, the creek can be observed ribboning over a rock barrier and falling into the deep gorge.

3.0   Just below the confluence of Success Creek (3.0 mi.; 1900 ft.), the trail crosses Graves Creek and, because a bridge is lacking, the hiker must take off his boots and wade. In late summer the water is only ankle deep. On the other side of the creek the trail climbs several hundred feet through forests of hemlock and silver fir, as it switchbacks up the mountainside, then traverses southward.

Graves Creek Basin consists of a series of small openings in the forest. At the lower edge of the first meadow are 5.3 the remnants of the Graves Creek Basin Shelter (5.3 mi.; 2500 ft.). Near the head of the basin the trail 6.1 forks (6.1 mi.; 2700 ft.). The right branch ascends to Wynoochee Pass (1.5 mi.; 3600 ft.), then descends the headwaters of the Wynoochee River and crosses into the Olympic National Forest; the left branch climbs toward Sundown Pass, switchbacking up the mountainside. Higher up the trail crosses a large expanse of grassy subalpine meadows with views down the canyon of Graves Creek. Scattered mountain hemlocks and subalpine firs grace the meadows, luxuriant with false-hellebore and larkspur. Rocks are covered with lichens 7.4 and mosses. In another meadow is a junction (7.4 mi.; 3800 ft.) with the South Fork Skokomish trail which climbs to Sundown Pass (0.5 mi.; 4103 ft.), then descends to Camp Riley and enters the Olympic National Forest, where it follows the South Fork for many miles.

The Graves Creek trail crosses the meadow to a gap in a little ridge, then contours to Sundown Lake Shelter 7.8 (7.8 mi.; 3900 ft.), on the shore of Sundown Lake.

This deep, subalpine lake lies at the bottom of a steep-sided bowl, an old glacial cirque. The slopes above the lake are covered in part by scattered trees, in part by meadows. A snowfield at the head of the lake often persists into late summer. Sundown Lake is oriented such that its outlet, and the only view from the cirque, is toward the setting sun in summer, hence the name.

Beyond Sundown Lake the trail climbs through forest, traverses a steep slope beneath low cliffs, then crosses expansive subalpine meadows made picturesque by mountain hemlocks, angular boulders, and wildflowers, including the rare white lupine. The common lupine, bear grass and falsehellebore are abundant. A sweeping view to the west and north into the interior Olympics is dominated by Mount Olympus on the far horizon. Occasionally the trail switchbacks upward along steep forested slopes that alternate with meadowland, as the route

9.3 climbs to Six Ridge Pass (9.3 mi.; 4650 ft.), on the narrow ridgecrest where mountain hemlocks murmur faintly.

The route beyond Six Ridge Pass is known as the Six Ridge trail.

Mount Colonel Bob Trail

The trail to the summit of Mount Colonel Bob, a peak
0.0 standing about five miles east of Lake Quinault, begins seven miles up the East Fork Quinault road from the Olympic Highway. This trail is entirely within the Olympic National Forest, but has been included in this book because this area—the south slope of the Quinault valley between the national park boundary and the lake—consists of magnificently timbered mountains rising steeply above the bottomlands, and should have been included within the Olympic National Park.

The trail climbs from the bottomlands (300 ft.) along
3.5 the west side of Mount O'Neil (Baldy) to the Mulkey Shelter (3.5 mi.; 2200 ft.), then switchbacks up to the ridge between Colonel Bob and Gibson Peak. Here is a junction with a trail leading down into the Humptulips valley. The Colonel Bob trail skirts the west side of Gibson Peak, then traverses across to the summit of Colonel Bob
6.5 (6.5 mi.; 4492 ft.).

This peak presents an outstanding vista of the Quinault country—the lake, the valley, the foothills, the snowy peaks to the north and east surrounding the headwaters of the North and East forks of the river.

Chapter XVI

The Queets

The Queets Valley

The Queets River flows along the northern side of a valley that is narrow near the river's headwaters, but broadens considerably downstream. Most of the watershed is drained by three large tributaries entering from the southeast: Tshletshy (Chileechee) Creek, Sams River and Matheny Creek. These streams are paralleled respectively by Tshletshy, Sams and Matheny ridges. The Queets-Quinault Divide constitutes the eastern and southern limits of the valley; the Mount Olympus Range and Kloochman Ridge the northern and western.

The glaciers and snowfields surrounding the Queets Basin east of Mount Olympus are the source of the Queets River. Meltwater from the Queets Glacier on Mount Queets, and the Humes and University (Jeffers) glaciers on Mount Olympus, together with that from extensive snowfields in the upper basin below Dodwell-Rixon Pass combine to form the river, one of the largest on the peninsula.

Queets Basin is a wild subalpine region of snowfields and rolling, flower-strewn meadows. The river flows from the basin through a narrow canyon that gradually widens. Below the confluence of Alta Creek the valley has the typical u-shape that results from glaciation, and the floor is broad and level. As in the Hoh Valley, the bottomlands are covered with spruce-hemlock rain forest, and the bordering mountainsides rise steeply upward, heavy with western hemlock and silver fir.

The Queets River road leaves the Olympic Highway seven miles east of Queets, an Indian village near the mouth of the river. For fourteen miles it follows the river through the Queets Corridor, ending where the corridor joins the main body of the park. Near the road's beginning is an excellent upriver view of snow-covered Mount Olympus shining in the distance.

Queets Corridor

The Queets Corridor, a narrow strip of land along both sides of the lower Queets River, is part of Olympic National Park, and almost connects the mountainous part of the park with the coastal strip. The Queets River road traverses the corridor's entire length.

The corridor was created to protect one river valley on the peninsula from the mountains to the sea. However, the last five miles of the river flow through the Quinault Indian Reservation.

Fishing is the main attraction of the corridor, but the rain forest scenery is excellent, and elk may be observed in these lowlands, especially in the winter.

Queets River Trail

The Queets River trail follows the river up the valley about fifteen miles to Pelton Creek Shelter. Because the road lies on the south bank, the river must be waded to reach the trail, on the north side. Boots with non-skid soles should be worn, for the current is swift, the water cold, and the bottom of the river covered with slippery rocks. The crossing is plainly marked at a place near the end of the road where, in late summer, the water is shallow. In other

0.0

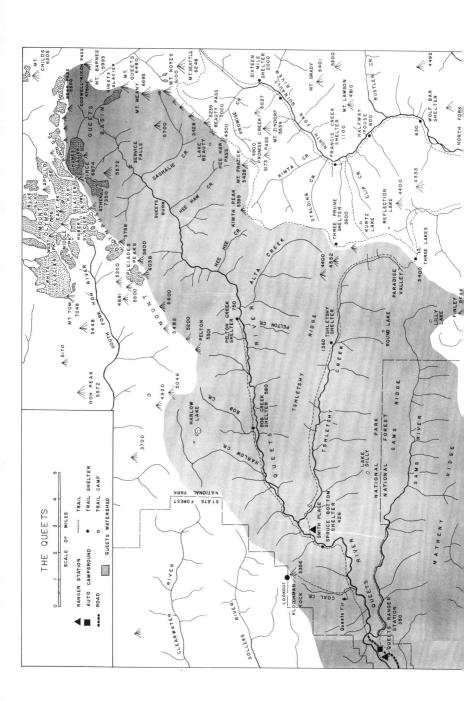

seasons, however, the river is deep and swift, and the crossing treacherous.

The Queets is famous as a steelhead stream, and anglers come from near and far to try their luck. Yet that part of the Queets valley accessible only by trail is essentially a place of solitude. On the bottomlands the trail goes through splendid rain forests where giant spruce, hemlock and bigleaf maples mantled with mosses tower above a jungle of vine maple. Elk live in the valley, their peculiar-sounding "bugle" sometimes ringing through the forest.

2.3   Near Coal Creek the Kloochman Rock trail (2.3 mi.; 350 ft.) branches to the left and ascends the mountainside on the north. Before making the upriver trek, the hiker should climb to this vantage point for the sweeping view it provides of the Queets valley.

Beyond the trail junction the river route crosses a small clearing where the forest was logged years ago. The lookout cabin perched atop Kloochman Rock, three thousand feet above the valley, catches the eye. The trail again enters the forest, and not far beyond the clearing is the lower Tshletshy ford

3.9   (3.9 mi.) where the river may be crossed and the Tshletshy Creek trail found on the other side.

The river trail continues along the north side of the Queets through very dense forest, then drops to pic-

4.9   turesque Spruce Bottom Shelter (4.9 mi.; 426 ft.). The shelter stands on the river bank, surrounded by immense spruce trees and bigleaf maples luxuriantly adorned with mosses. Spruce Bottom is popular with backpackers, and fishermen often take giant steelhead from deep pools in the Queets. The quiet is unbroken except for the mesmeric roar of the river.

Beyond Spruce Bottom the trail follows a slope high above the Queets, only to descend again to the bottom-

5.6   lands. Here is the upper Tshletshy ford (5.6 mi.), another place where the river may be crossed to reach the Tshletshy Creek trail. The route crosses Bear Creek, then enters Harlow Bottom (600 ft.), a large flat covered by splendid stands of Sitka spruce, possibly the finest in the park. Beyond Harlow and Camp creeks, the trail continues through

11.0   dense rain forest to Bob Creek Shelter (11.0 mi.;
15.4   580 ft.) and Pelton Creek Shelter (15.4 mi.; 750 ft.),
the termination point.

Above Pelton Creek the almost impassable Queets canyon extends about ten miles to the Queets Basin. The canyon
—one of the wildest areas in the Olympic Mountains—is very
rugged, with steep mountainsides rising almost directly from
the river's banks. Points of interest here include Hee Hee and
Hee Haw creeks, Kilkelly Rapids and Service Falls.

Queets Basin, a remote and particularly attractive "back
country" area, is almost inaccessible by way of the Queets
River trail. The normal approaches are to climb over the
glaciers of Mount Olympus; hike the Elwha trail and cross
Dodwell-Rixon Pass; or traverse the Bailey Range southward
from Mount Carrie or Ludden Peak. The basin, an excellent
base camp for climbs of nearby glacier-clad peaks, is characterized by rocky, rolling meadowlands and cliffy outcroppings
sprinkled with red and white mountainheath, the whole accentuated by clusters and lines of mountain hemlocks. Little
brooks cascade down from the snowfields that cover the upper
basin near Dodwell-Rixon Pass, and the roar of the Queets
River in its timbered canyon far below contrasts with the
twittering of birds, the buzzing of bumblebees and the sighing
of mountain winds. Wildflowers clothe the hillsides—bear
grass, daisies, paintbrush, avalanche lilies, yellow monkey flowers and mountain buckwheat. Jeffrey shooting stars sparkle in
patches of marshland.

Below Dodwell-Rixon Pass is an excellent campsite on
a shelf where polished glacial rocks rise from a flat meadow and
impound a mountain brook, thus creating a small lake that
overlooks the basin. Mountain hemlocks rise from rocky knolls
on either side of the lake's outlet, framing a view of Mount
Olympus that includes the Humes Glacier and Middle and
East peaks. Marshmarigolds and shooting stars line the edge of
the tarn in August, alongside remnant snowfields. Down the
Queets canyon toward the Pacific rise green-timbered mountainsides, their detail lost in purple shadows. Fog often drifts up
the valley, enclosing the peaks and basin in gray mist.

The upper basin, below Dodwell-Rixon and Bear passes,

is mostly a series of terraces and undulated slopes covered by snowfields. Elk herds are sometimes observed crossing the snow toward Dodwell-Rixon Pass, on their way to the Elwha Basin. On the high, open slopes of Bear Mountain, above the deep snowfields of the upper basin, lush grasses grow knee deep, and gentians, lupine and buttercups nod in the cool breezes. A few elephanthead pedicularis and strawflowers add touches of purple and pink. Along the ridgecrest sprawling mountain hemlocks struggle for existence, and juniper spreads dense mats along the ground.

This is the beginning of the Bailey Range traverse from the south.

Kloochman Rock Trail

A spur of the Queets River trail, this route begins on 0.0   the valley floor (350 ft.) and climbs to the lookout 3.0   cabin atop Kloochman Rock (3.0 mi.; 3356 ft.). This peak, called Boulder Hill on some old maps, rises sharply above the bottomlands, and is clothed with dense forest except for the cupola-like mass of rock capping the summit. The word "kloochman" is from the language of the coast Indians, and is synonymous with "squaw."

Near the trail's beginning a short path to the left leads to the Queets fir, the largest known Douglas fir. The massive trunk, seventeen feet thick at the ground, towers above the neighboring hemlocks and is covered on the north side by tiny hemlock seedlings. The tree's original height is unknown because the top is broken off, and the diameter at the break is four feet. Storms have probably broken the top off more than once during this tree's long life in the rain forest, estimated at more than a thousand years. Apparently the tree is the lone survivor of an ancient Douglas fir forest that has been replaced ecologically by hemlock.

In 1962 the Queets fir centered in a controversy between Oregon and Washington, each state claiming to have the largest Douglas fir. Oregon put forth as its challenger the Clatsop fir, near Seaside, Oregon. An impartial panel of foresters measured the trees to end the dispute. Final figures gave the Queets tree the greatest bulk (14,065 cubic feet of wood to 10,095) and height (202 feet to 200 feet 6 inches), but the Oregon tree had the greatest diameter at breast height (15 feet 6 inches to 14 feet 6 inches). A few months after these findings were made, a storm with hurricane force winds toppled the Clatsop fir, and the Washington tree remained unchallenged.

Winding through hemlock forest, the trail crosses Coal Creek, the last place where water can be obtained. Huckleberries grow in profusion at various points along the trail, and ripen in late August or early September. Beyond the creek the path switchbacks up the southern spur of the mountain, gaining three thousand feet of elevation in less than three miles, a seemingly endless climb through forests of hemlock and silver fir. Near the base of the rock mass capping the peak, one can glimpse through the trees the lookout cabin, perched atop the summit rocks like a tiny bird cage, and anchored by cables for protection against the shock of winter storms. The final ascent is via wooden ladders up the steep rock face, and caution must be exercised because the timbers have rotted.

The vista is spectacular—a panorama of untouched virgin forest. Three thousand feet below lie the Queets bottomlands, clothed with virgin fir and spruce, and the braided channels of the meandering Queets flow through the forest like intertwined silver ribbons. Mount Tom, Mount Olympus, and the snowy peaks studding the Queets and Elwha basins, twenty miles to the northeast, loom above timbered foothills. The view of Olympus is of its least glaciated side. All else is an unbroken expanse of forest, hemlock-covered mountains extending to the far horizons.

More than half the country visible from the lookout lies outside the national park, and logging operations have begun to invade this region, especially to the south, in the Olympic National Forest.

Tshletshy Creek Trail

0.0   A long route linking the Queets River and Skyline trails, this trail begins at Smith's Place, a ranger cabin on the east side of the river near Spruce Bottom

Shelter. The trail follows Tshletshy (Chileechee) Creek, a steelhead stream, to its headwaters in Paradise Valley, then climbs to the Queets-Quinault divide.

9.2   Most of the distance is through spruce and hemlock forest. Beyond the Tshletshy Shelter (9.2 mi.; 1360 ft.), where the trail crosses to the south side of the creek, the route becomes a way trail, and is hard to follow.

15.0   Paradise Valley (15.0 mi.; 3000 ft.) is a lush expanse of meadow surrounding a small, triangular tarn, and enclosed by forested mountainsides. This remote valley is an elk haunt, and coyotes are sometimes heard barking.

16.0   Above Paradise Valley the trail climbs to the divide, where it merges with the Three Lakes trail, near the southern terminus of the Skyline trail.

Chapter XVII

The Hoh

The Hoh Valley

The Hoh valley is oriented toward the Pacific, and extends deep into the mountains to the foot of Mount Olympus, where the elevation is less than one thousand feet above sea level. The upper valley, above the confluence of the South Fork, is long and narrow, with the pronounced u-shape that results from glacial sculpturing, and is bordered for miles by steep, withdrawing mountainsides. The precipitous Bailey Range lies between the upper Hoh canyon and the Elwha valley. West of Olympus heavily forested spurs rise between the Hoh and the South Fork, the major tributary. The Mount Olympus Range, extending southwest from Olympus, constitutes the watershed between the South Fork and the Queets. On the north a high ridge connected to the Bailey Range divides the Hoh from the Bogachiel and Soleduck valleys.

The name Hoh is a condensation of the Indian word Ohalet, meaning "fast moving water," an apt designation for the river that gathers four-fifths of the Mount Olympus drainage. The Hoh is a glacial stream, milky because of the presence of "rock flour." The Hoh Glacier, deeply entrenched on the east side of Olympus, is the river's source, and the Hoh emerges as a large stream from the glacier and flows to the northeast, collecting the waters of many small creeks. Throughout its upper course, where it sweeps to the northwest around Olympus, the Hoh flows through a deep canyon paralleled by the steep-walled Bailey Range.

Glacier Creek joins the Hoh at the base of Olympus. This stream, sustained by the Blue and White glaciers, is as large as the river at this point. The Hoh then flows west to the park boundary, fifteen miles distant, its braided channels meandering on the level valley floor. The bottomland gradually widens, averaging approximately a mile across within the park. Many smaller creeks add to the river's volume, the largest being Mount Tom Creek. Beyond the park boundary the river is joined by the South Fork, and flows through low, broken country to the Pacific.

The valley of the South Fork is of similar configuration, but on a lesser scale. In its upper course the bottomland disappears entirely, very steep mountainsides rising directly from the river's banks.

The upper Hoh River road extends nineteen miles up the valley from the Olympic Highway to the Hoh Ranger Station, six miles inside the park. The road parallels the swift-flowing river. During the winter sportsmen come long distances to fish the river for steelhead. Outside the park the road is bordered by cutover lands, but patches of luxuriant rain forest hint of what lies ahead. Cows, dwarfed by giant stumps, graze peacefully in lush pastures. These stumps, ten to twelve feet in diameter, are the remnants of enormous spruce trees that once covered the land.

Westward Hoh (6.0 mi.) is the sole supply point in the valley. The South Fork road (10.3 mi.) branches to the right and crosses the river over a wooden bridge, providing access to the South Fork trail and the homestead of John Huelsdonk, the "Iron Man of the Hoh," a pioneer settler who became almost legendary because of his enormous strength.

Twelve miles from the Olympic Highway the main road passes the last settlement, then enters the national park. Here it penetrates some of the finest rain forest, where virgin fir and spruce rise above an understory of moss-laden vine maple. The

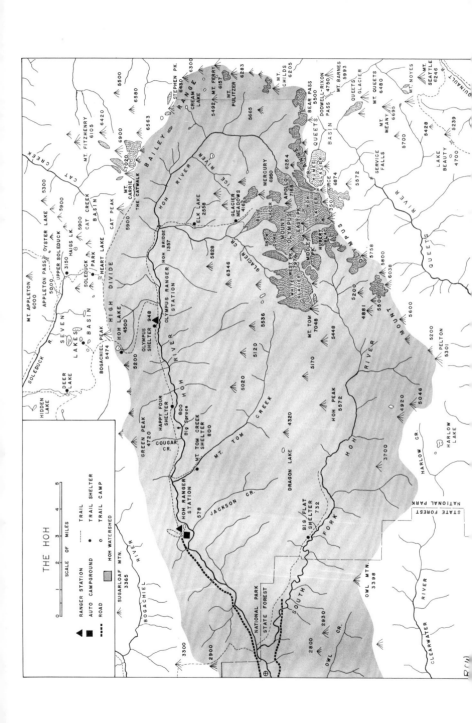

THE HOH

SCALE OF MILES
0 1 2 3 4 5

RANGER STATION
AUTO CAMPGROUND
ROAD
TRAIL
TRAIL SHELTER
TRAIL CAMP
HOH WATERSHED

largest conifers are more than 250 feet tall, twelve or thirteen feet in diameter, and more than five hundred years old. Wildlife in the valley includes elk, deer, chipmunks, squirrels, flocks of Oregon jays ("camp robbers"), and an occasional black bear.

The Hoh Ranger Station (19.0 mi.; 578 ft.), shaded by towering spruces, stands in the midst of luxuriant rain forest. Nearby are commodious campgrounds in groves of black cottonwoods, spruce and alder. Directly across the river, along the lower course of Jackson Creek, is an almost pure stand of large, old growth Douglas fir, one of the finest examples of this species in the park. A mile north of the ranger station the ridge bordering the valley reaches heights in excess of three thousand feet.

Hoh Nature Trail

The Hoh Nature trail, two half-mile loops forming a figure eight near the Hoh Ranger Station, was designed primarily for visitors who wish to see the rain forest without hiking very far. Points of interest along the route are indicated by markers. A printed guide to the trail can be obtained at the visitor center where the route starts.

The pathway crosses Taft Creek over a wooden footbridge. The upper trail loop, lying north of the Hoh River trail, crosses a bench covered with stately Douglas firs, then traverses forests of hemlock and spruce to the "Hall of Mosses," a colonnade of bigleaf maples adorned with luxuriant growths of selaginella and feather moss. The trail then circles east and south, winding among large spruce trees whose bases are almost hidden by dense growths of vine maple, and returns to its point of origin.

South of the river trail, the lower loop meanders among giant spruce trees and particularly fine displays of moss-draped vine maple and bigleaf maple near the Hoh River.

Hoh River Trail

The Hoh River trail, the main artery of travel to Mount Olympus, extends eighteen miles from the Hoh Ranger Station to the Blue Glacier. The first eleven miles of trail traverse bottomland covered with dense rain forest, where the elevation increases imperceptibly, gaining only five hundred feet. A radical change occurs, however, at the base of Mount Olympus, as the trail begins the steep climb to the Blue Glacier. Beyond the moraine, where the path ends, the route to the summit of Olympus lies over fields of ice and snow.

0.0   The trail begins at the visitor center near the Hoh Ranger Station (578 ft.), crosses tranquil Taft Creek, and plunges immediately into primeval forest where the wind-swept crowns of giant fir and spruce tower above a jungle of ferns and moss-covered vine maple. The trail on these bottom-lands is not stony and rough, like the mountainside paths, but meanders smoothly among spruce, cedar and fir, and occasionally crosses grassy glades. The fragrant scent of the evergreens pervades the atmosphere.

For several miles the route goes through spruce-hemlock forest, but occasionally crosses groves of moss-covered alder by the river, only to again enter gloomy stands of conifers. This is a multi-storied forest. Above a myriad of plants covering the ground—chiefly ferns, mosses, lichens and liverworts—is a tangle of vine maple, huckleberry and elder, shaded in turn by bigleaf maples festooned with selaginella and ferns. Above all are the conifers—the slender hemlocks and the giant spruces, six to twelve feet in diameter. Fallen trees are padded with cushions of moss and tiny conifer seedlings.

Near Mineral Creek, where the unpleasant odor of
2.7   hydrogen sulphide gas sometimes permeates the air, is a junction (2.7 mi.) with the Mount Tom Creek trail. The Hoh trail continues upriver. Near Cougar Creek the path passes an immense Sitka spruce, once thought to be the largest specimen of this species. The tree is fifteen feet in diameter, 220 feet tall, and large burls adorn its base. Then the trail enters a grove of giant cedars.

Near Happy Four the forest changes gradually to Doug-las fir, but spruce is common as far upvalley as the
5.3   Olympus Shelter. Happy Four Shelter (5.3 mi.; 800 ft.), surrounded by heavy growths of large Douglas fir, stands

near the river's edge, at a point swept by mountain and valley breezes, and is an excellent campsite. Beyond Happy Four the trail continues through the changing patterns of the rain forest, with periodic views of the Hoh River. The Olympus

8.6   Shelter (8.6 mi.; 948 ft.) stands in a grassy meadow approximately midway between the Hoh Ranger Station and the Blue Glacier. The meadow is rimmed by large spruce trees. In addition to a small, rustic cabin—an old guard station built by the Forest Service—are two lean-to shelters. The buildings harmonize well with their surroundings. Behind the cabin is a clear, icy brook. Above Olympus Shelter

9.2   the Hoh Lake trail (9.2 mi.; 1000 ft.) splits away from the river trail and climbs the northern side of the valley, following a mountain spur to Hoh Lake, then traverses steep mountainsides to Bogachiel Peak.

Douglas fir becomes dominant beyond the trail junction, but spruce, hemlock and cedar are still present. For several miles the trail winds through a forest of ancient firs. A few of the trees are twelve feet in diameter, many eight to ten, and the tallest reach heights of three hundred feet. The great shafts, covered with coarsely ribbed bark, rise limbless for a hundred feet or more, like classic Doric columns, and the summer breezes murmur softly in the crowns far above the trail. In the midst of this forest the trail edges a small meadow and the Bailey Range is visible. The ruins of an old Forest Service cabin stand near the center of the meadow.

11.0   Eleven miles above the Hoh Ranger Station the trail reaches the end of the level bottomland, climbs gradually for a mile, then turns to the south and crosses the river just above the confluence of Glacier Creek. Here the Hoh,

12.0   spanned by a high wooden bridge (12.0 mi.; 1357 ft.), surges through a rock-walled gorge one hundred fifty feet deep, and turbulent Glacier Creek flows through a similar canyon. Delicious huckleberries grow in the vicinity, and hikers often pause at the bridge for lunch.

The trail now climbs the north side of Mount Olympus,

14.0   twisting up heavily forested slopes to Elk Lake (14.0 mi.; 2558 ft.), where two shelters are maintained.

Water lilies grow in the warm water. As late as 1935 the lake had no fish, never having been stocked, but trout are plentiful today. The fir forest extends to the lake, then is replaced by higher altitude species, primarily silver fir.

Beyond Elk Lake the trail climbs sharply through dense forest, then contours a precipitous mountainside overlooking Glacier Creek fourteen hundred feet below. Vantage points provide views of the Snow Dome on Olympus and the White Glacier. The former extent of the glacier is indicated by sharp lines of demarcation between brush-covered moraine and virgin forest.

16.6 The trail meanders through subalpine forests to Glacier Meadows (16.6 mi.; 4200 ft.), where the dense forest ends, leaving small trees scattered up the mountainsides and on the rocky moraine above. The area of meadowland is not extensive. Two shelters stand in the forest's margin, near the lower edge of the meadows, where the trail forks. Both paths lead to the Blue Glacier.

The trail to the left, the old route, winds through dense groves of subalpine trees, then crosses the upper meadow to a ravine, snow-filled in early summer, about a mile above the glacier's terminus. This trail climbs to the top of the lateral moraine, and cairns mark the way. The terrain is deceiving, and 18.0 the distance from the shelters is much farther than it appears. The trail ends (5000 ft.) where the moraine abuts a steep mountainside. The moraine is a knifelike ridge of loosely consolidated boulders and dirt, and rises almost perpendicularly from the glacier's edge. The view is one of the finest in the Olympic Mountains. Below is the sweep of the lower glacier; beyond are the East, Middle and West peaks of Olympus, the Snow Dome, Glacier Pass, and the icefall plunging over cliffs from the upper fields of névé (granular snow which accumulates and compacts into glacial ice).

17.5 The other trail, the newer route, is more direct, crossing Jemrod Creek behind the shelters and climbing over broken, angular rock and debris to a notch in the moraine just above the glacier's terminus. The view of the heavily crevassed glacier is excellent, but the peaks of Olympus are hidden by the Snow Dome.

Mount Olympus

The ascent of Mount Olympus is normally made between Memorial Day and Labor Day, and starts from a base camp at Glacier Meadows or a higher one on Caltech Moraine, across the Blue Glacier. During favorable weather the climb is not difficult, but hazardous nevertheless by reason of the crevassed glaciers that must be crossed. When Olympic National Park was created, an average of only twenty-five people climbed the peak each year, but the ascent has since become increasingly popular, and climbers now number in the hundreds.

The climbers retire early in the evening, then arise about 3 A.M., prepare a light breakfast, and begin the ascent an hour later with the aid of flashlights. The air is cold, and the climbers move briskly in order to keep warm. The purpose in leaving this early is to gain the summit before the peaks are obscured by afternoon clouds.

On the moraine members of the climbing group pause to admire the morning alpenglow on the upper slopes, then descend to the glacier's edge, where they tie themselves into rope teams. Patches of snow on the glacier are hard and firm, but soften rapidly under the warm sun. The glacier's appearance varies from year to year, depending on the amount of snowfall the preceding winter and the warmth of the summer. By early August the lower glacier is usually free of snow, and the dense, crystalline ice is revealed. This ice is deep blue, and glows intensely in the depths of yawning crevasses. The cold air chills the climbers, making warm clothing a necessity. Occasionally a warm breeze from the valley sweeps across the glacier.

The glacier, broken by deep, crescentic crevasses, has a gentle gradient, and the climbers make rapid progress across the ice to the base of the Snow Dome, about a mile away. Here the climbers pause to daub their faces with sunburn ointment, and put on colored glasses. Parties planning to make several ascents in the area often camp here on a small lateral moraine, thus

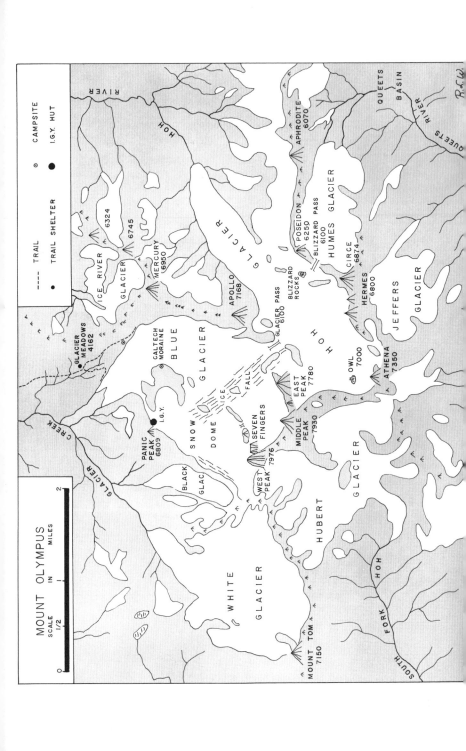

avoiding the trek up and down the glacier each day. This site, used by the California Institute of Technology as a base camp for its glaciology studies, is free from insects and has a splendid view and plentiful supply of water, but fuel is lacking.

Here the climb steepens, but numerous resting spots are found on rock outcroppings looking across to the icefall. This wall of jumbled ice blocks plunging down from the upper cirque is a thousand feet high and a mile wide, extending from the Snow Dome to Glacier Pass. East, Middle and West peaks rise from the névé slopes above the icefall.

The climb continues up steep snow toward the top of the Snow Dome, revealing an ever widening panorama of the surrounding country. The Snow Dome, actually part of the névé fields supplying Blue Glacier, is a mile long by a half mile wide. Outlined against the blue sky, it appears immaculate. Near the crest of the dome, but slightly off the climbing route, stands the IGY hut, used by scientists during the International Geophysical Year. Not a permanent structure, it will be removed when the studies are concluded, thus leaving the mountain unmarred by man-made structures.

Beyond the crest of the Snow Dome (6850 ft.), the route zigzags to avoid crevasses, and ascends to The Notch (7200 ft.), a gap in the rock ridge leading down from West Peak. A large bergschrund twenty to thirty feet wide and more than one hundred feet deep guards the approach. This bergschrund changes from year to year. Usually, however, a substantial snow bridge eases the climbing problem.

The ascent continues across upper névé fields that nourish the icefall. Straight ahead are East and Middle peaks, beyond them a myriad of snow peaks on the horizon, with Mount Rainier shining above the distant haze. Middle Peak can be climbed from this point by crossing the upper cirque to the peak's west side and climbing the rocks directly to the summit. The route to West Peak, however, swings right beneath Five Fingers Peak (7880 ft.). An easy rock scramble leads to the top of this false summit. The view is splendid, but the scene to the west is blocked by West Peak, a slightly higher wedge-like mass of rock rising perhaps one hundred fifty feet above the summit snows. The summit route traverses left, avoiding Five Fingers Peak, and crosses a steep slope of rotten rock to Crevasse Pass, the notch between West Peak and Five Fingers. A precipitous snow slope, the loftiest in the Olympic Mountains, leads to a ledge on the side of West Peak, or one can rock climb directly from Crevasse Pass. The route traverses the ledge across the east face of the peak to a sixteen-foot vertical cliff, the last obstacle before the summit (7976 ft.) is attained.

Once on top the climber finds the crest of Olympus to be a knife-edge ridge of broken rock surrounded by a sweeping view of the Olympic Mountains. Hundreds of snow-streaked peaks and ridges surround this vantage point. Some have razor-edge crests, others are rounded, but all are splotched with snowfields or glaciers. The lower slopes are heavily timbered. Canyons and valleys, often filled with fog, wind away in all directions through the tangle of peaks. The view is of unmarred wilderness, and no houses, roads or other man-made works are visible, with the sole exception of the tiny IGY hut.

On all sides the slopes of West Peak drop vertically: north to the Snow Dome, west to the White Glacier, south to the Hubert Glacier, and east down the route just ascended to Crevasse Pass. Across the broad upper cirque tower East and Middle peaks; beyond the South Fork Hoh, the Mount Olympus Range dwindles into forested foothills; enclosing the White Glacier is the bulk of Mount Tom, outlined against timbered ridges that stretch endlessly toward a band of misty blue, the distant Pacific.

Upon this pinnacle, the top of the Olympic Peninsula, the climber can easily loosen the reins on his imagination, and picture in his mind the seafarers, Perez and Meares, sailing along the coast nearly two centuries ago. He appreciates why, when Meares looked at this high point where he now stands, he declared Olympus the home of the New World's gods.

The descent from the summit to Glacier Meadows is rapid, taking perhaps half as long as the climb. A brief but swift glissade on the snow slope at the foot of West Peak is followed by a much longer one down the Snow Dome to Blue Glacier. There the hot afternoon sun creates rivulets that flow over the ice in constantly changing patterns, and deep within the glacier unseen streams roar ominously. Many hollows, pools and crevasses in the ice reflect brilliant shades of blue, as do the bottomless moulins, vertical "wells" extending deep into the glacier.

After heavy rains, short-lived glacial fountains sometimes play like miniature geysers.

To climb East Peak (7780 ft.), mountaineers make the same approach to the Blue Glacier, but instead of ascending the Snow Dome follow the eastern edge of the glacier to Glacier Pass (6100 ft.), the u-shaped notch between the Blue and Hoh glaciers. The route then traverses beneath hanging ice on the cliffs of East Peak, and climbs the steep slopes of the upper Hoh Glacier.

Because it lies between East and West peaks, Middle Peak (7930 ft.) can be climbed by either route.

Mount Tom Creek Trail

0.0 The Mount Tom Creek trail begins near Mineral Creek, less than three miles above the Hoh Ranger Station, on the river trail. The Hoh can be forded just above the mouth of Mount Tom Creek, the largest tributary between Glacier Creek and the South Fork.

On the south side of the river the trail follows the east side of the creek across the Hoh bottomlands, through dense rain forest. Mount Tom Creek Shelter (1.0 mi.;
1.0
800 ft.) stands on the west side of the creek. Beyond it
2.0 the trail continues up the valley another mile. This trail is used mostly by fishermen.

Hoh Lake Trail

0.0 This trail begins a half mile east of Olympus Shelter, and ascends a steep mountain spur forested with hemlock and silver fir to Hoh Lake, then continues across high, open slopes to Bogachiel Peak.

The trail has a gentle gradient where it meanders through rain forest on the bottomlands, but it soon begins to climb abruptly, via long switchbacks, and is shaded by
5.5 dense stands of tall hemlock. Near Hoh Lake (5.5 mi.; 4500 ft.) the forest thins and the trees are smaller.

The deep, round lake occupies an old saucer-shaped glacial cirque. The steep surrounding slopes are covered with heather and clusters of subalpine firs. High above the Hoh valley to the south loom Mount Olympus and Mount Tom. A rustic shelter is located beside the lake's outlet. Fishing is good, but the lake often remains frozen until mid-July, and sometimes well into August. When the snow melts, rolling meadows appear, colorful with bear grass and lupine. On the northern, shaded sides of the steep ridges, the snowdrifts remain until late in the season, when south-facing slopes are covered with mountain flowers.

Sunrises and sunsets are especially beautiful viewed from Hoh Lake. Mount Olympus is a soft, velvet white in the morning, but more colorful at sunset. Then the mountain assumes various shades of pink, gold and purple. While the summit snows are swathed in bright sunshine, the hemlocks near the lake form black silhouettes against satin snowfields.

Between Hoh Lake and Bogachiel Peak, where the trail traverses high, open country, the view of the upper Hoh valley, the Bailey Range and Mount Olympus is impressive. In early summer the mountains are completely covered with snow, contrasting with the dark green forests and the river far below.

6.5

The trail ends at a junction (6.5 mi.; 5200 ft.) with the High Divide and Bogachiel River trails, just below the summit of Bogachiel Peak.

South Fork Hoh Trail

Access to the trail up the South Fork Hoh is via a logging road that branches from the Hoh River road about ten miles from the Olympic Highway. This logging road is several miles long, and parallels the Hoh and the South Fork. Floods frequently render it impassable. The road goes across cutover country and through stands of virgin forest. On the South Fork Hoh are remnants of an old bridge that has been destroyed by floodwaters.

0.0

One must scout around for a log spanning the river in order to cross to the north side, where the "trail" can be found. The first few miles of the route are a continuation of the road through logged-off lands outside the park. Beyond the park boundary, however, the trail penetrates virgin rain forest.

0.9   Big Flat Shelter (0.9 mi.; 732 ft.) is located near the river, and beyond this campsite the route continues several miles up the valley to an old patrol cabin. Above this point, near the base of Hoh Peak, the bottomland disappears, and steep mountainsides rise from the river's banks, creating a wild, rugged canyon.

The source of the South Fork is the Hubert Glacier on Mount Olympus.

Chapter XVIII

The Bogachiel-Calawah

The Bogachiel and Calawah Valleys

The Bogachiel valley lies largely on the outer slopes of the Olympic Mountains, and is of comparatively low elevation. Except for meadowlands near the river's source, virgin forests cover the entire watershed. Timbered ridges divide the valley from the Hoh on the south; from the Calawah and Soleduck on the north. As the river emerges from the mountains, the bottomland widens, but is not as level as that along the Hoh and Queets. Within the park the North Fork, a major tributary, joins the river at the base of Sugarloaf Mountain. The snowfields on the steep western side of Bogachiel Peak are the river's source. Glaciers are absent, consequently this is a clear stream, despite the Indian name meaning "muddy water." Thus the Bogachiel contrasts with the Hoh, a river that is milky from glacial silt.

The Calawah River is the largest tributary of the Bogachiel. The valley of the Calawah's South Fork above the confluence of the Sitkum River lies within Olympic National Park. This valley parallels the Bogachiel, and a trail over Indian Pass provides access from one valley to the other.

Superlative rain forest is found in both the Bogachiel and Calawah. Although these valleys lie on the perimeter of the park, they are primitive and undeveloped, and isolation gives them a special appeal. The trail over Indian Pass is the only one entering the Calawah valley. The bottomlands along both rivers are the winter range of the elk herds that roam during the summer on the uplands of the High Divide and Seven Lakes Basin.

When Olympic National Park was created, the Bogachiel was considered the least spoiled wilderness on the peninsula, and this valley still retains its primitive landscape, unmarred by the works of man.

The Bogachiel road extends about six miles east of the Olympic Highway, and follows the north side of the river almost to the park boundary. However, the last three miles are often impassable for conventional vehicles. Little of interest is found along this road, bordered as it is by stump ranches and logged off country.

Bogachiel River Trail

Undisturbed solitude awaits the hiker of the Bogachiel River trail, a route that traverses the heavily forested western slope of the park. The trail parallels the Bogachiel River for ten miles, then follows the North Fork to its source, and climbs to the meadows at Little Divide. Beyond this point it follows the Soleduck-Bogachiel divide to Bogachiel Peak.

0.0   The trail begins at the park boundary (350 ft.), near the site of the destroyed Bogachiel Ranger Station. The cabin burned down, and all that remains is the foundation. The trail traverses luxuriant bottomlands, but shortly enters an area of cutover land, where giant stumps are silent reminders of the great spruce trees that once grew here. Beyond the logged area the trail enters virgin forest, and crosses Mosquito Creek. Here is rain forest typical of the western side of the Olympics: spruce and hemlock, with a dense undergrowth of moss-draped vine maple. The terrain is uneven, and the trail rises and dips slightly as it progresses up the valley.

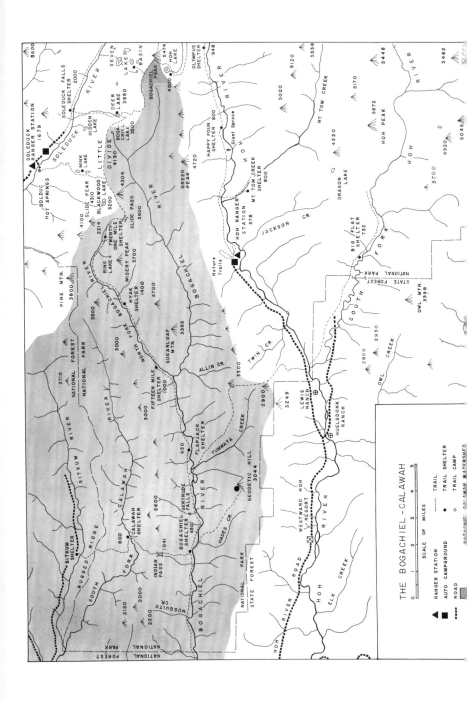

THE BOGACHIEL - CALAWAH

SCALE OF MILES

0   1   2   3   4   5

▲ RANGER STATION   —— TRAIL
■ AUTO CAMPGROUND   ● TRAIL SHELTER
···· ROAD   ○ TRAIL CAMP

4.0   The picturesque Bogachiel Shelter (4.0 mi.; 450 ft.),
       and an old ranger station cabin and horse stable,
surrounded by giant, bell-bottomed spruce trees, stand near a
junction with the Indian Pass trail. Beyond this point the river
trail, penetrating rain forests that become increasingly
       luxuriant, continues up the valley, past a junction
6.0   with the Tumwata Creek trail (6.0 mi.) to Flapjack
8.0   Shelter (8.0 mi.; 650 ft.), where optimum conditions
       exist for maximum rain forest development. Splendid
stands of Douglas fir cover the benches and mountainsides
north of the river; vigorous growths of tall spruce and hemlock
are found on the bottomlands, where elk roam during the
winter and spring months.

       Three miles above Flapjack Shelter, the North Fork
Bogachiel, a large branch of the river, flows from the
       northeast. Beyond the juncture of the two streams
11.0   (11.0 mi.), the trail follows this tributary to Slide Pass,
       then crosses back to the Bogachiel. Fifteen-Mile
12.0   Shelter (12.0 mi.; 1000 ft.), surrounded by magnificent
       Douglas firs, stands on a bench near a picturesque falls
and rapids in the North Fork. Above the shelter the trail crosses
to the south side of the North Fork, where the stream flows
through a small gorge lined with conifers. Ferns decorate clefts
in the moist banks of the river, and the ground beneath the
evergreens is covered by dense undergrowth. The bridge spanning the river is old, with axe-hewn side rails, and its floor,
about fifty feet above the water, is covered with moss, an
indication of the dampness of the rain forest and the lightness
of trail traffic in the upper Bogachiel valley.

       Across the river the trail meanders among spruce trees
on flats covered with sword ferns. The trail continues up the
valley of the North Fork. Less than a mile beyond the bridge,
however, the route climbs a mountainside high above the river
and contours through forests of tall Douglas fir. The North
Fork is visible in the depths of the valley, and its noisy chatter
can be heard on the trail. Then the route descends again to
       the bottomlands.

15.0   Hyak Shelter (15.0 mi.; 1400 ft.) and an old Forest
       Service guard station cabin stand near the south bank

of the river at the edge of a beautiful meadow that is covered
with grass and bracken fern and surrounded by big trees. This
opening in the dense forest permits views of the ridges defining
the northern and southern limits of the valley. About four
hundred yards east of the meadow the trail crosses Hyak Creek.
Here, along the river and creek, are flats covered by lush undergrowth; then the trail traverses low on the mountainsides
above the North Fork. For several miles the forest appears to
have been "manicured" by nature. The tall, straight trees—
mostly hemlock, but also Douglas fir, cedar and silver fir—raise
their canopy above a carpet of oxalis, vanillaleaf and ferns. The
parklike appearance is accentuated by the absence of dead and
fallen trees and brushy ground cover.

18.0   Twenty-One-Mile Shelter (18.0 mi.; 2214 ft.) marks
         the end of this groomed forest and the beginning of
the climb out of the valley to Slide Pass, the route switchbacking through forests of western hemlock. Previously the
trail gained elevation gradually as it followed the river through
the lowlands.

19.5   Near Slide Pass (19.5 mi.; 3600 ft.), the cross-over
         point from the North Fork to the Bogachiel, are dense,
almost pure stands of silver fir, as well as western hemlock and
mountain hemlock. Here the trail climbs the ridge, alternating
from one side of the narrow spine to the other. Through the
lichen-festooned trees are tantalizing glimpses across the
Bogachiel valley.

         The route breaks out into a meadow where the ridge
widens. Sweeping views extend across the upper Bogachiel to
Mount Olympus and the distant Bailey Range. Eleven hundred
feet below the ridgecrest, on the north slope, Blackwood Lake is
cupped picturesquely in a bowl, and is surrounded by dense
forests. The view to the north is down the valley of Blackwood
Creek, with timbered ridges extending to the Strait of Juan de
Fuca, on the horizon. Slide Peak stands to the left, northwest of
the lake.

         A few mountain hemlocks are scattered over the
meadows, and the ground is covered with low, sprawling
juniper, huckleberry, bracken fern, heather, strawberries,
Columbia lilies, stonecrop and mountain azalea. A Corps of

Engineers benchmark, set in a concrete post projecting six inches out of the ground, indicates the elevation is 4304 feet.

The trail descends slightly from the meadows and 20.5 follows the ridge to Little Divide (20.5 mi.; 4130 ft.).

The small meadow here, covered with bracken fern and wild strawberries, provides a view of Mount Olympus, Mount Tom, Hoh Peak and Bogachiel Peak. On warm summer days, the meadow is bright with lupine, and bumblebees buzz sonorously from bush to bush.

Beyond a junction with the Mink Lake trail at Little Divide, the route contours through dense forest along the ridge between the Bogachiel and Soleduck valleys. Bogachiel 23.0 Lake (23.0 mi.; 3500 ft.) lies four hundred feet below the trail, at the foot of a steep slope. The trail contours above and beyond the lake to a notch in the ridge, then crosses to the north slope and descends to the meadow on the 24.2 upper side of Deer Lake, where it merges with the Canyon Creek trail (24.2 mi.; 3550 ft.).

Above Deer Lake the path climbs gradually back toward the Bogachiel-Soleduck divide, meandering up forested slopes. As the trail gains altitude, the forest thins, giving way to meadows and scattered clumps of mountain hemlock. The vista of softly outlined ridges to the north and east widens with every upward step, and Deer Lake appears as a blue disk in the forest below.

Along the ridge the trail crosses fields of avalanche lilies, then crosses to the south side and enters dense stands of contorted subalpine fir and mountain hemlock, but shortly breaks out into the upper Bogachiel Basin. Here the path gradually gains elevation as it traverses the steep mountainside. Bogachiel Peak looms straight ahead on the horizon.

Wild flowers bloom profusely on the grassy slopes of the basin: glacier and avalanche lilies in early summer; lupine, phlox, daisies and mountain buckwheat later. Natural rock gardens on the mountainsides are colorful with lomatium, pentstemons, paintbrush, violets and stonecrop. Bears visit this area frequently to dine upon the plentiful blueberries, and marmots live in small colonies in the rock slides, their shrill whistles punctuating the mountain stillness.

Near Bogachiel Peak, where the terrain becomes more
rugged, the trail skirts a boulder-strewn notch in the
27.5   ridge (27.5 mi.; 4900 ft.). This vantage point overlooks
Seven Lakes Basin, discovered and named by Chris
Morganroth, an Olympic Peninsula pioneer. He counted seven
glittering lakes when he viewed the glacier-scoured basin from
a distance. The lakes, actually about a dozen in number, varying in size from small pools to tarns four hundred yards across,
are renowned for their eastern brook, Montana black spot and
rainbow trout. The largest lakes are Morganroth, Soleduck,
Bunch, Lunch, Round, Long and Lake Number Eight. A
steep way trail descends from the notch into the basin.

The elk herds that range the Bogachiel and Hoh valleys
during the winter inhabit this high country in the summer. On
hot afternoons bands of the animals congregate on the extensive
snowfields of the upper Bogachiel and Seven Lakes basins, and
the high land of Soleduck Park to the east.

Beyond the notch the trail contours beneath Bogachiel
Peak, the western terminus of the High Divide and the hydrographic apex of the Soleduck, Hoh and Bogachiel watersheds.
The south slope of the mountain is dotted with rock outcroppings and clusters of subalpine firs; the north slope is
covered by permanent snowfields. A fire lookout cabin once
topped the peak, but it has been destroyed.

The trail ends on the south side at a u-shaped pass
28.4   (28.4 mi.; 5200 ft.), the common meeting point of the
Bogachiel, Hoh Lake and High Divide trails. The view
of the upper Hoh valley, the Bailey Range and Mount Olympus
is superb.

The panorama from Bogachiel Peak (5474 ft.), reached
by a way path from the pass, includes virtually the entire
northwest corner of the Olympic Peninsula. Westward the
upper Bogachiel River winds in sweeping curves toward the
foothills, and the trail disappears over the ridges. On the horizon the distant Bogachiel valley, clothed with shining virgin
forest, fades into a purplish haze; on exceptionally clear days the
Pacific is sometimes discernible as a band of blue high on the
horizon. The view north includes the Soleduck high country
and Seven Lakes Basin; east are the slopes of the High Divide

and the snowy Bailey Range, and south, across the deep valley of the Hoh, tower the peaks of Mount Olympus.

Sunsets are spectacular from this viewpoint. As purple shadows in the valleys slowly creep up the mountainsides, the icecap of Olympus catches the last rays of the sun and reflects a rosy alpenglow. This fades quickly, however, and when the darkness deepens, beacon lights along the coast blink intermittently. Later the moon appears to sink in the sea beyond Destruction Island.

Cold winds buffet the peak during the night, and fog forms over the lowlands, then moves up the valleys like probing white fingers. Stars, their brilliance undimmed by lowland haze, parade across the heavens. Then, as the approaching sun drives night from the mountains, Mount Olympus looms above the fog-filled canyons like a giant pearl. A soft, almost hushed whisper precedes the dawn, as the night winds diminish to gentle breezes with an elusive touch of winter.

Dawn comes suddenly as the sun tops the Bailey Range. Sunshine, streaking across the High Divide while the valleys remain in dark shadow, silvers the dew on the prostrate juniper; patches of snow glitter with countless points of light and a blinding sheen. Wild flowers glow in the morning sun: the gentian, with unopened buds that resemble blue flames; showy white and red mountainheath; myriads of bluebells and pink bluebells; low-growing stonecrop and gaudy paintbrush; the western anemone, and thick mats of white phlox. Chipmunks scurry over rocks and snow in search of food, prowling supplies left unattended by the careless camper. A lone grouse calls from a clump of trees, repeating its message at regular intervals.

Indian Pass Trail

The route over Indian Pass, part of the old Snider-Jackson trail of the Olympic National Forest, leads northward from the Bogachiel River to the Calawah River, then climbs to the national park boundary on Rugged Ridge.

0.0   The trail begins near Bogachiel Shelter (450 ft.), on flats covered by old spruce trees of large diameter.

Beneath the trees the ground is carpeted by sword ferns. The trail soon leaves the bottomlands, however, and climbs immediately up to a benchland covered with dense stands of hemlock, with some Douglas fir. The trees are not of large diameter, but are very tall, and the stands are quite dense, resulting in a perpetual gloom. The wind whispers in the tops of the hemlocks, and cool breezes near the forest floor are welcomed by hikers. Beneath the trees is a ground cover of sword ferns and other low-growing plants.

Near Indian Pass the forest changes to silver fir. The trees are tall and slim. A few remnants of an older forest are present. Left of the trail stands a giant Sitka spruce about thirteen feet in diameter at the base and more than 250 feet tall. This tree appears to be very old, and its large limbs trend downward, then elbow upward, giving it a hoary appearance strikingly similar to the famed Grizzly Giant, a sequoia in Yosemite National Park. Nearby a Douglas fir of comparable size stands beside the trail.

1.8   Indian Pass (1.8 mi.; 1041 ft.), marks the watershed between the Bogachiel and Calawah rivers, and is covered with stands of silver fir. North of the pass the trail descends gradually, traversing mountainsides, to the South Fork Calawah River, which is not bridged. In late summer, however, the stream is shallow enough that the hiker can boulder-hop with care from one side to the other. Across the valley rises heavily forested Rugged Ridge. On

3.5   the north side of the river is the Calawah Shelter (3.5 mi.; 800 ft.).

Beyond the river the trail climbs to the national park

6.2   boundary on Rugged Ridge (6.2 mi.; 1300 ft.) and continues in the Olympic National Forest as a way trail to the Sitkum River.

Tumwata Creek Trail

The Tumwata Creek trail, part of the old Forest Service trail from Snider Ranger Station on the Soleduck to Jackson Ranger Station on the Hoh, begins on the Hoh River road (436 ft.) a half mile inside the park, opposite the confluence of the South Fork Hoh. The trail climbs to a north-south ridge—a jog in the divide between the Hoh and Bogachiel—and follows this ridge north, then descends to the Bogachiel along a spur ridge paralleling Tumwata Creek. Water is not available on this trail.

0.0   Where it begins the trail climbs a mountainside overgrown with moss-covered alders, small hemlock and a few old Douglas firs. Within a short distance, however, the path reaches a level bench and meanders through a dark rain forest of spruce and hemlock. Although not maintained by the National Park Service, the trail is in fair condition because elk and deer use it regularly. The bench is part of the valley floor, and its north edge abuts the base of the steep ridge dividing the Hoh and Bogachiel valleys. Here the trail angles eastward up the mountainside through hemlock forest mixed with the spectacular remnants of ancient Douglas fir forest. Some of the firs are more than ten feet in diameter, and appear to be very old, their gnarled crowns weatherbeaten from the storms of centuries. The Hoh River, glimmering in the morning sun like molten silver, is glimpsed through the trees. As the trail gains elevation, the slopes drop sharply on the right to the upper Hoh, inside the park; on the left to the lower Hoh, outside the park.

Higher up the Douglas fir is left behind and the route climbs through forests of western hemlock and Pacific silver fir. The trail attains the end of the north-south ridge 3.7   (3.7 mi.; 2900 ft.) and follows this ridge north above the head of Tumwata Creek. The ridge is forested, but one can look out among the trees; from a couple of points Mount Olympus is visible.

6.0   At the north end of the north-south ridge (6.0 mi.; 3200 ft.), the trail turns west along a spur ridge paralleling Tumwata Creek, and begins to descend into the Bogachiel valley. The upper part of this spur is covered with young stands of silver fir so dense that the forest floor is barren for lack of sunlight. The trees are tall and slender, with only a few limbs forming a compact bushy crown, like the tip of an artist's brush. This young forest is soon replaced, however, by mature stands of silver fir on the shaded north side of the ridge. Here the ground is carpeted with oxalis. As the trail loses altitude, the forest becomes almost exclusively western hemlock. Unlike on the Hoh side of the ridge, Douglas fir is absent here. The undergrowth of ferns and oxalis is luxuriant. Young hemlocks a few feet high have grown up beside the trail so densely that the path is literally hidden; in places the hiker can not see his feet as he walks along the trail where it traverses a steep mountainside.

11.6   Upon reaching the foot of the mountain spur, the trail crosses the bottomlands to a point on the Bogachiel River about two miles below Flapjack Shelter (11.6 mi.; 650 ft.). The river must be forded here in order to reach the Bogachiel trail.

Geodetic Hill Trail

The trail to the summit of Geodetic Hill (3044 ft.) was constructed during World War II, and an airplane spotter cabin was built on the summit. The trail has not been maintained and is now overgrown with small hemlock trees, and is covered with windfalls, thus making the hike to the lookout a strenuous one.

0.0   This route begins across the river from the Bogachiel Shelter, and winds up the mountain spur east of Hades Creek, most of the way through forests of large hemlock and silver fir. Just above the river flats the trail passes by one of the finest examples of western red cedar in Olympic National Park. The tree, about twelve feet in diameter, is solid and rises with very little taper to a great height. Higher up the mountainsides the forest is mostly silver fir, and includes the largest known example of this species. About half way to the lookout cabin are the remnants of an ancient Douglas fir forest—several enormous firs that have been badly damaged by lightning. On the ridgecrest, the ground is covered in many places with a solid carpet of elkhorn or lycopodium.

4.0   When the lookout cabin (4.0 mi.) was built, the trees on the summit were cut down, but young trees have since grown up and are obscuring the view.

Chapter XIX

The Soleduck

The Soleduck Valley

The Soleduck is one of the largest rivers on the peninsula, with its source in the northwest part of the mountains. Near the sea this stream combines with the Bogachiel to form the Quillayute. Most of the drainage basin of this system lies outside the mountains, and the Soleduck does not drain the loftier Olympics. The highest peak that contributes to its flow is Mount Appleton (6000 ft.). The upper part of the valley, within the national park, is bordered by ridges about five thousand feet high—Aurora, Happy Lake and Boulder ridges to the north and east; a long, sinuous ridge on the south dividing the valley from the Bogachiel. The High Divide and the western spurs of Cat Creek Ridge enclose the headwaters of the Soleduck. Beyond them are the Hoh and Elwha valleys.

Creeks and rills flowing from snowfields in Soleduck Park, a rolling meadowland on the northern slopes of the High Divide, collect to form the river. The stream then rushes tumultuously into dense evergreen forests. Never quiet as it flows through the mountains, the Soleduck dashes down rocky canyons, leaping and tumbling over boulders shaded by low-

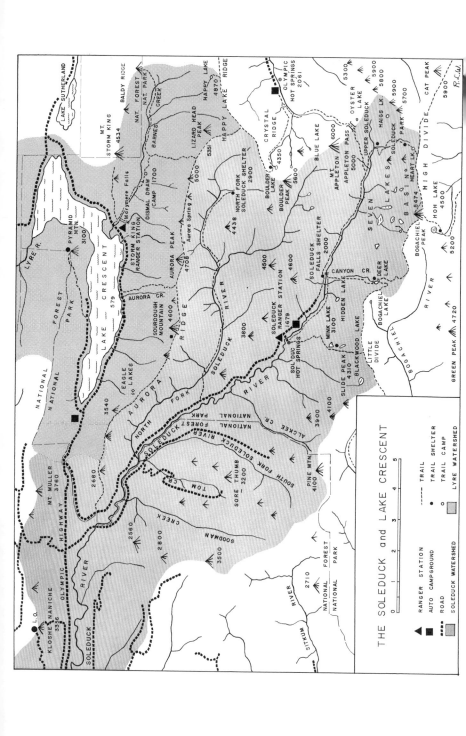

THE SOLEDUCK and LAKE CRESCENT

RANGER STATION	▲
AUTO CAMPGROUND	■
ROAD	▬▬▬
SOLEDUCK WATERSHED	

TRAIL	------
TRAIL SHELTER	●
TRAIL CAMP	○
LYRE WATERSHED	

R.C.W.

hanging limbs of fir and hemlock. Below the confluence of Canyon Creek, however, the valley floor broadens and is heavily forested with Douglas fir and hemlock. Only one major tributary, the North Fork Soleduck, is within the park, but many large creeks flow into the river. The Soleduck abounds in cutthroat and rainbow trout, and during the winter is often fished for steelhead. *Sol Duc* (or *Soleduck*) is an Indian word meaning "sparkling water," and the river's clarity justifies the name.

Although rugged, the Soleduck country is a region of soft outlines. The high country drained by the river is primarily meadowland jeweled with dozens of subalpine lakes. Noteworthy is the Seven Lakes Basin, harboring some of the largest mountain lakes in the Olympics.

The Sol Duc Hot Springs road leaves the Olympic Highway at the park boundary west of Lake Crescent, and follows the river through cutover land and stands of old growth Douglas fir to the picturesque Soleduck Ranger Station (12.3 mi.; 1679 ft.). The road continues up the valley, passes a campground a half mile above the ranger station, and ends on a bench (14.2 mi.; 2000 ft.) above the Soleduck River.

Across the river from the ranger station are the Sol Duc Hot Springs, with a store, cabins, baths and swimming pool. Chemicals present in the mineralized water range from such common elements as iron and aluminum to rarer ones like strontium and barium. Supplies for trail trips are available at the resort.

According to Indian legend the Sol Duc and Olympic Hot Springs are the tears of two dragons who fought a duel on one of the mountain peaks. The combat ended with neither victorious, and the dragons crawled back into their caves and wept from mortification.

Soleduck River Trail

This trail follows the river to Soleduck Park and the High Divide, where it merges with the High Divide–Bailey Range trail.

0.0   The path winds through forest from the end of the
0.9   road to Soleduck Falls Shelter (0.9 mi.; 2000 ft.) and a junction with the Canyon Creek trail. Above

Soleduck Falls the route up the valley is through dense stands of tall Douglas fir and western hemlock. Silver fir gradually replaces Douglas fir, however, as the trail penetrates deeper into the mountains. The trees in this valley are relatively uniform in size—an even-aged forest, a somewhat unusual phenomenon in the Olympic Mountains. Luxuriant glades are found in the wetter places.

4.9   Near the head of the valley is a junction (4.9 mi.; 3100 ft.) with the Appleton Pass trail, a route that leads across the ridge to Olympic Hot Springs. Beyond this junction, the trail crosses the river to the Upper Soleduck

5.4   Shelter (5.4 mi.; 3150 ft.). This lean-to, almost obscured by thick brush, stands on a level spot beside the river. The trail now climbs through higher altitude forests where Alaska cedar and true firs predominate. Although the elevation is not high, subalpine conditions exist at a lower altitude here than in many parts of the Olympics because of heavy winter snowfall. Near the upper limit of dense

7.0   forest is a small, ramshackle shelter (7.0 mi.; 4200 ft.) housing a tiny stove in one corner.

Emerging from the forest, the trail enters the high, open country of Soleduck Park, where undulated meadows stretch upward to the High Divide. In the lower part of the meadowland, near Bridge Creek, stands the Soleduck

7.7   Park Shelter (7.7 mi.; 4500 ft.). The observant hiker who camps here is likely to see elk or bear on mountainsides across the valley, or perhaps close by the shelter itself.

With each upward step the hiker's view of the Soleduck valley grows more impressive. Heart Lake

8.1   (8.1 mi.; 4750 ft.), a small, heart-shaped tarn surrounded by meadows and clumps of small trees, mirrors the surrounding ridges. Above the lake the trail ascends to the crest of the High Divide, and a junction with

8.5   the High Divide–Bailey Range trail (8.5 mi.; 5050 ft.). Soleduck Park lies on the northern slope of the High Divide between Seven Lakes and Cat Creek basins. The south slope of the divide, on the Hoh River side, is timbered to the ridgetop, but deep snows on the shaded northern side keep the timberline several hundred feet lower. The altitude of the rolling meadows of Soleduck Park varies from about forty-five hundred to five thousand feet. One of the finest examples of subalpine country in the Olympics, this area is an excellent base camp for trips to the snowfields and glaciers of the nearby Bailey Range. During the winter Soleduck Park is covered by deep snow.

On clear days, when the haze is not pronounced, the distant Pacific is visible as a bluish band above scattered trees that fade away on slopes to the northwest. The peak terminating Cat Creek Ridge looms over Soleduck Park on the northeast; to the south and east are the Mount Olympus and Bailey ranges. Between Olympus and the High Divide, however, lies the deep Hoh valley.

Several times in the past advocates of developments for winter sports have proposed building a road into Soleduck Park and construction of lodges and mechanical ski lifts. Such developments would be incompatible with the purpose of a national park. Furthermore, if permitted, they would destroy the superlative wilderness character of the northwest quadrant of Olympic National Park.

North Fork Soleduck Trail

0.0   This trail, used primarily by fishermen, leaves the Sol Duc Hot Springs road (1475 ft.) eight and one-half miles above the Olympic Highway. The trail climbs over a low ridge (1800 ft.) into the valley of the North Fork
1.0   Soleduck (1.0 mi.; 1475 ft.).

Here the trail follows the North Fork through forests of Douglas fir and western hemlock. The route leaves
6.0   the North Fork at the confluence (6.0 mi.; 2075 ft.) of the river and a large, unnamed tributary, and follows this tributary to the east. The North Fork Soleduck
9.0   Shelter (9.0 mi.; 2900 ft.) marks the end of the trail.

Lovers' Lane

     Lovers' Lane is a level trail along the south side of the
0.0   Soleduck River from Sol Duc Hot Springs to the Can-

2.8   yon Creek trail (2.8 mi.; 2000 ft.) near Soleduck Falls.
           The trail begins behind the swimming pool at the hot
springs. About a mile above the resort the path enters stands of
magnificent Douglas fir, and crosses several luxuriant glades
scattered among the big trees. Beyond Canyon Creek the trail
continues through the forest, with occasional views of the river,
including an outstanding vista where a waterfall plunges vertically a hundred feet into the Soleduck.

Mink Lake Trail

0.0   This trail begins at Sol Duc Hot Springs (1679 ft.) and
           ascends past Mink Lake to Little Divide, the watershed
between the Soleduck and Bogachiel valleys.
           The first half-mile of trail crosses logged off land cov-
ered with second-growth fir and hemlock. Then the trail enters
the virgin forest, where the ground is shaded and mossy. As the
trail climbs higher, hemlock predominates, and the tall Douglas
firs gradually disappear. This is Canadian zone forest, with a
           dense understory of huckleberry.

2.5   Forest-rimmed Mink Lake (2.5 mi.; 3100 ft.) is half
           choked with vegetation, and is gradually destroying
itself. A shelter cabin stands near the south edge of the lake,
and the camper who awakens early is likely to hear the weird
call of the loon.
           Between Sol Duc Hot Springs and the lake, water is
not available, but just above the lake the trail crosses several
brooks. Beyond Mink Lake the trail traverses forests of hemlock
and silver fir, and during the last mile below Little Divide the
route switchbacks up through a mixture of meadowland
           and stands of mountain hemlock. On Little Divide
4.3   (4.3 mi.; 4130 ft.) is a junction with the Bogachiel
           River trail.

Canyon Creek Trail

0.0   Canyon Creek trail originates at Soleduck Falls Shelter,
           one mile beyond the Sol Duc Hot Springs road. Here

the river plunges over a precipice, then surges through a deep, close-walled canyon. Mist sprays over a wooden footbridge that spans the river below the falls.

The trail follows aptly named Canyon Creek, which has carved a deep canyon in its short course. Vegetation on the forest floor is luxuriant. Bunchberry often forms dense carpets; Devil's-club grows rank in moist clefts. The well kept trail climbs, rather sharply in places, through the dense forest to Deer Lake (3.5 mi.; 3100 ft.), one of the many small mountain lakes found in the Olympics. The lake is surrounded by forests and meadows covered with lush grasses. The white plumes of bear grass are conspicuous along the shore. Shooting stars, elephanthead, marshmarigold and other wildflowers grow profusely on the marsh at the head of the lake. Frogs, orange-bellied newts and water ouzels are abundant in the marshy edge of the lake.

3.5

Near the upper end of Deer Lake the trail merges with the Bogachiel River trail, which leads to the Seven Lakes Basin, Bogachiel Peak and High Divide. (See Bogachiel River trail).

High Divide–Bailey Range Trail

The High Divide–Bailey Range trail provides one of the most impressive high country vistas in the Olympic Mountains. This route follows the crest of the High Divide east from Bogachiel Peak, then skirts the southwestern side of the Bailey Range at the five thousand foot level. The trail ends abruptly on a rock face below the col or depression on the ridge between Cat Peak and Mount Carrie.

0.0

The High Divide is the watershed between the Soleduck and Hoh valleys. This ridge extends from Bogachiel Peak to Cat Peak, approximately four miles, and has an average elevation of five thousand feet. A succession of spectacular views unfold from the trail, because the divide overlooks the upper Hoh, Soleduck and Bogachiel valleys, and the basin of Cat Creek, a tributary of the Elwha. Steep mountainsides descend sharply on the south into the mile-deep valley of the Hoh, where fog often blankets the bottomlands. Across the valley the densely forested lower slopes are topped by Mount

Olympus, a massive pile of rock and ice. The Blue Glacier is clearly visible, its pronged snout projecting over a cliff. East of Olympus is the Bailey Range, a long, curving chain of snow-clad peaks paralleling the upper Hoh canyon. The precipitous slopes of this range extend to the river's edge. North of the High Divide lie the uplands at the head of the Soleduck, with Soleduck Park and the glacier-scoured Seven Lakes Basin in the foreground. Subalpine lakes and ponds are sprinkled over this area. Elk frequent this region during summer and autumn, and often congregate near the pools, or on the snowfields. During the summer the High Divide is clothed with profusely blooming wild flowers: avalanche lilies, lupine, mountain buckwheat, bluebells, columbine, monkey face, daisies, gentian, bear grass, and both the red and white mountainheath.

2.0   Two miles east of Bogachiel Peak the High Divide trail merges with the Soleduck River trail; beyond this point the route is known as the Bailey Range trail. About a mile east of the junction the path climbs over a spur of Cat Creek Ridge, then descends through meadows. The view of Olympus and the Blue Glacier from here is noteworthy. The trail drops six hundred feet to the gap at the head of Cat Creek, where it passes through dense stands of subalpine fir and mountain hemlock. The trees shade the hiker from the hot sun, and cool, refreshing breezes are often present. Beyond the gap the trail climbs slopes covered with huckleberry and blueberry bushes. Exposed to sunshine for long hours during the summer, the berries ripen to a delicious sweetness. Bear grass is also found here in abundance, in places blanketing the meadows like fields of white cotton.

Then the trail, blasted from solid rock, contours the steep slopes of the Bailey Range. The precipitous mountainsides, cut by the paths of snow and rock avalanches, descend sharply to the canyon of the upper Hoh far below. A few feet below the trail a rivulet of clear water emerging from a crevice in the rocks is the only source of water along this portion of the route. The trail rounds a promontory offering a spectacular view up and down the Hoh valley, then ends abruptly,

5.5   without warning (5.5 mi.; 5000 ft.). Here a vertical cliff confronts the hiker. This is the sidewall of *The*

Catwalk, the rugged, exposed arête or sharp ridge connecting Cat Mountain and Mount Carrie.

The trail hiker should not proceed beyond this point, but experienced mountaineers can continue cross-country along the Bailey Range, one of the finest high country traverses in the Olympic Mountains. First, however, one must backtrack a dozen steps or so and climb a faint way trail about two hundred feet up the steep side of Cat Mountain to the western end of The Catwalk.

This narrow, spinelike ridge of jagged rock is covered by contorted subalpine trees that have been twisted into fantastic shapes. The ridge, high on both ends and sagging in the middle, widens near the Mount Carrie end, where one may rest after struggling over the sharp, angular rocks and through the thick-branched trees. A pool alongside a melting snowbank provides water, an old rusty skillet is hidden in a hollow tree, and nearby is a circle of rocks used as a rudimentary fireplace.

Near this campsite The Catwalk ends abruptly. The route now crosses open meadows on the flanks of Mount Carrie, where flowers bloom profusely: blue and white lupine, daisies, phlox, stonecrop and violets. Gentians grow in clumps, and the unopened blue flowers look like cone-shaped Christmas lights. Lomatium and the alpine yellow monkeyflower splash color on the shale slides; juniper bushes, covered with glaucous blue berrylike fruits, sprawl along the cliffs. Mount Carrie's upper slopes consist of seemingly endless shale slides, and bands of broken, razor-sharp slate set on edge and streaked with veins of quartz. Scattered among the shale slides are snowfields, icy hard in early morning.

From the slopes of this peak one can see, in a sweeping glance, the Hoh valley from Mount Olympus to the park boundary. Below the confluence of Glacier Creek, the u-shaped valley extends west toward the Pacific, clothed with primeval forest as far as the eye can see. On the level bottomlands the river's channels resemble braided strands of silver. The only sign of civilization is the old Forest Service cabin above the Olympus Shelter, a tiny speck almost lost in the vast rain forest.

The vista from the summit includes not only the impressive view down the valley, but also the upper Hoh canyon, nearly encircled by the Bailey and Mount Olympus ranges. The glaciers near Bear Pass are visible; beyond them rise the snowy summits of Queets, Meany and Christie and, on the far horizon, other snow-covered peaks.

16.0   Between Mount Carrie and Bear Pass (16.0 mi.; 5600 ft.), the route traverses the wild, isolated Bailey Range. This country is deceptive, and the distance between peaks is less than it appears. Because the range is remote, visitors are few, but this primitive region lures the dedicated backpacker. The mountains are quiet and peaceful, the stillness broken infrequently by the wind, the whistles of marmots or the barking of coyotes on distant mountainsides. Sometimes the peaks are bathed in brilliant sunshine; more often fog drifts across the ridges to create eerie patterns. Rock, snow and ice dominate near the crest of the range, but lower down are meadows sheltering cold, blue lakes nurtured by brooks that flow from sun-cupped snowfields. Bees buzz in the heather; elk and bear roam the meadows.

This is the backbone of the wilderness Olympics, where from high vantage points the mountains appear to circle upon themselves in a confusion of peaks and ridges that extends for miles in every direction.

Book III

By the Sea

The Olympic Mountains were created in the mysterious depths of the sea, where life originated. Crustal movement of the earth pushed peaks high above the level of the sea, but the materials composing them were already formed on the ocean bottom, the product of sediment deposition and flows of basaltic lava during millions of years.

The unrestrained surges of the Pacific against the Olympic coast demonstrate that the restless sea still seeks to establish contact with the mountains. Similarly, the mountains are slowly returning to the sea. The elements of erosion constantly pluck and tear at the peaks, and the material broken loose is transported, via the swift rivers, to the ocean floor. Eventually, unless further uplift occurs, the mountains will disappear.

The western coast of the Olympic Peninsula extends a hundred miles from Cape Flattery to Grays Harbor. Half of this, including the wildest, most primitive portion, is contained within Olympic National Park. This narrow ribbon of land facing the Pacific, commonly called the Olympic Ocean Strip, comprises less than four per cent of the park. This area along the coast was the last addition to the park. In 1953 President Truman declared it part of Olympic National Park by presidential proclamation.

The northern two-thirds of this strip is the longest stretch (about thirty-five miles) of roadless coast on the Pacific between Canada and Mexico. Thus is preserved for present and future generations a representative portion of the peninsula's coast, an unspoiled seascape of the type that has become increasingly scarce with the pressure of civilization for more development. This seacoast, largely uninhabited wilderness, is one of the few places unmarred by civilization where land and sea meet close to highly populated regions. Here one is reminded that the sea, not the land upon which we dwell, is the dominant environment on the planet earth.

Chapter XX

Beachwalking

Beachwalking

Olympic National Park's ocean strip extends from the Quinault Indian Reservation northward approximately fifty miles to the mouth of the Ozette River near Cape Alava, the peninsula's westernmost point. This strip varies in width from a quarter mile to almost three miles, but is generally from one-half to one mile wide, and is divided into three sections of almost equal length. Each area is bounded at either end by a river and an Indian reservation. The southern third of the strip is traversed by the Olympic Highway, thus is easily accessible to the casual tourist, and cannot be called wilderness. The middle and northern thirds, however, are more isolated, and remain almost as primitive as when seafaring explorers sailed along the coast in the eighteenth century.

Hiking along this remote shoreline is a rewarding experience, but is not difficult because the beach is a natural trail. Driftwood is available for campfires; good campsites are easy to find. Securing fresh water is sometimes a problem, but it can be obtained from streams entering the sea. Those planning beach hikes should remember that the annual rainfall on this coast exceeds one hundred inches, and thus take appropriate clothing. Good hiking boots or shoes should be worn because some headlands must be climbed over via rudimentary trails, and the beach is often rocky. Other points can be rounded only at low tide, therefore the hiker should check tide tables before going on an excursion in this region. Since undergrowth is heavy in the forest back of the beaches, constituting an impenetrable barrier, low tide must be awaited in order to go around certain steep cliffs.

Because the peninsula lies in the path of the prevailing westerlies, cyclones occur regularly during winter and spring. These storms strike the western coast with great impact, their winds churning and strengthening incoming waves. For centuries wind and rain have played a significant role in developing the character of this seashore. The coastline is rugged, subject as it is to the ceaseless assault of breakers that march from the sea and pound against the beaches, as they have since primeval time, like even-ranked platoons attacking a fortress. Wave shock is tremendous. Breakers crash against jagged rocks and cliffs, and thunder in rocky coves and caverns, spraying saltwater high in the air and leaving a wake of inert foam as they recede. In winter the white froth of spindrift often covers the beaches like enormous masses of beaten egg white.

As the sea erodes the peninsula, cutting ever inland, left behind are resistant remnants of the former coastline. These offshore rocks, known as seastacks, are steep-sided islands and islets that form jutting pinnacles. Some taper to sharp points; others are rounded or flat-topped. Dense brush and conifers cap some; others are barren. Most of the stacks stand like giant stumps in the sea, and are seldom visited because of their isolation and inaccessibility. Thus they serve as havens for many kinds of shore and sea birds, and often are splattered with guano.

The coastline included within the national park consists of rugged headlands that alternate with quiet coves and storm-battered beaches. Bluffs from one hundred to three hundred feet high border the ocean for miles. Between them and the sea are narrow beaches—a succession of long, sandy stretches with intervening rocky areas marked by huge boulders or multitudes of cobblestones and gravel. Most of the stones, polished smooth and lacking sharp corners, are flattened and exhibit circular or elliptical shapes. On headlands composed of more resistant rock the sea has carved tunnels and caves, some with a spiral configuration.

No sharp line of demarcation exists between land and sea. Like everything in nature, the two blend into each other. The tidal range on this coast is about ten feet, and the division line is best defined by erosional debris. Drifting tree trunks, carried to sea by the swift Olympic rivers, are washed onto the beaches or pushed against onshore rocks. Here they are battered by the hammering surf until the limbs and branches are torn away. Fragments of wood litter the beaches. These bits have been polished to satin smoothness, and their corners rounded, from the constant abrasion. Enormous quantities of driftwood line the shore for miles, on open beach and secluded cove alike. Jumbled piles form at the high tide line near the mouths of rivers and the larger creeks.

On the landward side, forming a backdrop to the drift-wood-lined shore, is the silent, wind-lashed forest. Everywhere, but most pronounced on the bluffs, the forest displays evidence of the fury of winter storms that roar their opening octaves along the Washington coast. Dead trees and broken snags, silvery gray and bare of bark, together with the upturned roots of fallen trees, relieve the monotony of green timber. Many living trees have limbs only on their leeward sides. This wind-torn forest, an integral part of the natural scene, accents the primitive wildness of the region.

The most common species growing close to the ocean include Sitka spruce, western hemlock, and western red cedar, but some Douglas fir, lodgepole pine and Pacific yew are also present. The largest known western red cedar is located in this park strip, south of Ruby Beach. Generally speaking, however, the trees immediately fronting the sea are smaller than the giants of the rain forests. Red alder is the most common decidu-ous tree. The tangled underbrush is composed of various shrubs: willow, salmonberry (twenty feet high), salal, and the false and evergreen huckleberries. Less common are crabapple, Devil's-club, elder and dogwood.

Although the forest facing the ocean is silent, the sea itself is never still, for the currents and drifts respond to the pulsating rhythm of tide and wind, as well as upwelling of cold water from the depths. Always the surging boom of breakers is present, and the waves crash against the rocks to the accompaniment of complaining cries by the seagulls. The seashore is also a place of strong odors—the fresh tang of salt spray, the fragrance of seaweed, the scent of spruce and hemlock. On the quietest days the breezes are fresh, and the salt air clean and pure. The skies present continuously changing patterns of fog and cloud, reminding one that nothing is permanent, although implying that everything endures as an unending interplay of cosmic forces, with the ultimate meaning beyond the comprehension of mankind.

Beachcombing at low tide becomes the preoccupation of almost every shorewalker on the Olympic coast. Included among the things to be found are glass floats, fishing plugs, buoys, bottles, parts of wrecked ships, driftwood, seashells, agates, colorful stones, and perhaps a vertebra from the backbone of a whale. Much of the material washed up on the coast has been brought from afar by the Kuroshio Current. Fishnet floats from the Orient are sometimes left stranded at the high water mark, hidden in the debris of winter storms. These glass balls can be found most easily at night with the aid of flashlights.

The incoming tide agitates the material on the beaches, but during the tidal recession everything settles again. Thus the beach sands are flooded when the tide is high, left bare as it ebbs. The accumulation of fine sand on many of the beaches results from the smaller waves of summer; the fiercer storms of winter wash away the sand, revealing the bare rock. Low tide is the time, of course, to explore tidepools and rock reefs, because many living things in the ecologically complex community of sea life are then exposed to view. Crabs, shellfish, sea anemones, starfish, barnacles, snails, mussels, sea urchins and numerous other seaforms are then easily observed. Clams can be dug when the tide is low, and cooked over a driftwood fire on the beach.

Most of the plant life in the sea consists of minute planktonic organisms. The largest sea plants are the giant kelps, but several other varieties of seaweed are present. Some of the smaller species cling to rocks, and resemble smears of grease or mineral incrustations. The larger common seaweed looks like an enormous tadpole with an extremely elongated tail. Kelp, rich in iodine, carries on the photosynthetic process and absorbs minerals from seawater. The plants undulate among the waves, swaying rhythmically like ballet dancers in slow motion.

Animal life in the sea is equally interesting. Whales swim along the coast during spring and fall migrations, and the spectacle of their mating off Shi-Shi Beach a few miles north of the park strip has become as much an attraction to tourists as to biologists. These huge mammals summer in Arctic waters, winter in the tropics. Species present on the Olympic coast include the valuable sperm whale and six baleen whales—the gray, blue, piked, humpback, finback and sei whales. Also present are the Baird beaked, Pacific beaked and goosebeak whales; the Pacific killer whale or sea wolf, the predator of the sea; and several kinds of dolphins and porpoises. Bones from dead whales are commonly found on the beaches. Occasionally a carcass washes ashore, to be quickly devoured by scavengers like the black bear.

Smaller mammals include the northern sea lion and the Alaska fur seal. These animals also migrate along the coast. The sea lions are gregarious marine animals that occasionally enter the rivers. They are polygamous and sometimes gather in herds on nearby islands. However, the fur seals, found on this coast only during the winter, usually are too far to sea in their migrations to be observed by beach hikers. The common harbor seal of the northern hemisphere is a resident of the reefs and coastal islands, where it rests and suns itself on the rocks. This animal is shy and elusive, the result of persecution by man in the past. Sea otters formerly inhabited the Olympic coast, but none has been observed for years.

Among the mollusks common in offshore waters are snails, clams, oysters and octopi.

Land animals inhabit the bordering forests and often come down to the beaches at night where they leave evidence of their nocturnal visit imprinted in the wet sand. The tracks of elk, bear and deer are common. Skunks and raccoons prowl the tidepools in the evening, searching for crabs or other crustaceans. During the day sea lions bask off shore, and elk and deer sometimes visit islands connected at low tide to the mainland by sandspits. Elk are plentiful along this coast, but likely will disappear because of the logging roads being built close to the park boundary.

The Olympic coast, with its multitude of sea life, is the natural home of many species of sea and shore birds. Most conspicuous are the gulls. These birds carry clams high above the ground, then drop them onto rocks to break the shells. Gulls also line up in regular ranks at the surf's edge, facing the incoming breakers, to catch the smelt that spawn upon the sandy beaches. Each bird has its own station and respects the position of his neighbors. The long black "sea ravens" or cormorants also feed upon smelt. These birds, commonly called "shags," are known for their voracious appetites. Usually, however, they take fish that are worthless or of little value from man's standpoint. Bald eagles winter on the Olympic coast, and some of the birds are resident throughout the year, nesting along the wildest parts of the coast. These birds are often pestered by ravens when searching for their food, largely fish.

Many of the islets and seastacks on this coast are included in the Flattery Rocks and Quillayute Needles national wildlife refuges, where such sea birds as auklets, cormorants, murres, petrels and gulls breed by the thousands. On the shore live oyster catchers, sandpipers, turnstones and other species.

Life in the sea, both plant and animal, is commonly divided into three classes, the benthos, nekton and plankton, and it exists in such abundance that tremendous competition takes place among the various forms for food, space and light. In some places, however, marine life is not abundant. These "deserts of the sea"—rare at this latitude—appear as the areas of bluest water. The specific gravity of organisms living in the oceans is not much different than that of the sea itself. They have, therefore, less need for supporting structures than do plants and animals that live on the land or in the air. Sea plants do not have stiff stems and trunks, and only a few of the animals that live in the ocean have legs for walking. In fact, many sea animals resemble plants more than they do land animals.

The benthos includes life forms on the shallow bottoms near the water's edge, where sunlight penetrates to the sea floor. In this category are plants and animals that "cruise with the currents" for a brief period in their youth. Once they attach themselves to rocks or other objects, or burrow in the sand—to prevent their destruction by the pounding surf—they become stationary and remain in one place for the rest of their life. These are the barnacles, kelps, hydroids, oysters, piddock (boring) clams, shipworms and similar organisms. Some live near the low tide line and are submerged most of the time. Others, whose habitat is higher up the beach, are covered for short periods only, or perhaps merely splashed occasionally by the waves. The thick-shelled oysters and barnacles cement themselves to firm surfaces. The benthos also includes certain creeping and crawling creatures (starfish, conchs and crabs, et cetera) that are not actually tied down but live within restricted areas. This is possible because the seawater circulates continuously and replenishes the supply of nutriments.

Much benthonic life is found among the tidepools and rocks of the reef exposed at low tide on the Olympic shore: anemones, brittle stars, giant chitons (orange-colored), Dungeness crabs, purple shore crabs, sea cucumbers, hermit crabs (one large claw), sea lemons, purple starfish, sea urchins, and plumed worms called "feather dusters." On mudflats and areas of fine-grained sand live razor and littleneck clams, mussels, cockles, mud shrimps and sand dollars. Often the smooth, sandy beaches are littered with comb jellies that have been blown from the sea by the wind. These marble-sized translucent spheres with eight longitudinal lines are primitive animals related to the jelly fish. Among the rocks containing wet pools in their scooplike hollows are the isopods, sea snails (limpets), periwinkles, snails and ubiquitous barnacles. Some forms cling to the rocks beneath the kelp, because this helps them to retain moisture when the tide is low. However, rocks near the sandy beaches are generally relatively free of organisms because the waves pick up the sand and blast the rocks.

In the high intertidal zone, the sea life exhibits increased abundance and more varied forms with increasing depth. High on the rocks is a band of rockweed, mussels and barnacles; below it a lower band of rockweed. Thus, in the ocean is found a vertical zonation of plants and animals similar to that found in the mountains; only here the zonal range is only about ten feet. This zonation is determined by how much drying out and how much sunlight the plants and animals can withstand when exposed at low tide. Green seaweed occurs only high on the rocks, because if it is covered by more than two or three feet of sea water it can not photosynthesize. The brown algaes of the high intertidal zone occur out to depths of twenty-five feet; the red algaes to considerably greater depths.

The nekton consists of marine animals that have loco-motive powers and wander widely by swimming against the currents. This is life of the open sea, just beneath the surface, where no hiding place exists and survival depends upon speed and agility, camouflage or pure luck. Actually, nektonic organ-isms are not completely independent of the currents. Because their precise locations are controlled by their internal energies, however, their movement is either with or against the drifts. Life in this category is primarily the fishes (noted for stream-lined bodies, backbones, and ability to breathe in water), but also included are whales, porpoises, seals, turtles, and a few invertebrates such as squid and shrimp.

Fish inhabit the sea adjacent to the peninsula in great numbers. Salmon swim up the rivers to spawn; halibut, ocean perch, black sea bass and rockfish are taken offshore by fisher-men. Vast numbers of smelt spawn on the beaches in early summer, brought to shore by the incoming waves. Fishermen obtain them by dipping nets in the breakers on moonlight nights. The smelt runs occur on gravel beaches with a low gradient, like those at Kalaloch and Ruby Beach.

Although most of the animals and plants normally noted by the casual observer are included in the benthos and nekton, the bulk of sea life falls within the group known as plankton, "that which is made to wander." The plankton con-sists of uncountable numbers of tiny microscopic organisms, both plant and animal, that drift freely at the mercy of the currents because they have only feeble powers of locomotion. Most of these organisms are only about a thousandth of an inch in diameter. Sixty per cent of the plankton are single-celled algae called diatoms, but nearly one hundred thousand varieties of invertebrates and vast numbers of microscopic plants are included in this classification. These constitute the base of the complex pyramid of sea life, wherein smaller organisms are ruthlessly devoured by larger ones, until finally the limit of size is reached. The plankton also includes some life forms that are neither plant nor animal but have characteristics of both; for example, dinoflagellates. Like plants, these organisms make their own food, but they also devour other creatures after the manner of animals. A few larger life forms such as jellyfish are also included with the drifters.

A phenomenon occurs in the sea that is comparable to "timberline" on land. This is the level below which plant life is not found on the seabottom. In the ocean it occurs only a few hundred feet down, and therefore is unlike the upper limit of vegetation on land, usually high in the mountains. In the sea this line appears to be determined by the point where sunlight fades away along the slopes of the continental shelf.

Chapter XXI

Queets-Hoh

The southern section of the Olympic Ocean Strip is about twelve miles long and extends from the Quinault Indian Reservation near the mouth of the Queets River to the tiny Hoh Indian Reservation, on the south side of the Hoh River.

This part of the strip is easily accessible, and is not wild and rugged like the areas to the north. Here the coast is paralleled by the Olympic Highway for its entire length except for about a mile between Ruby Beach and the Hoh Indian Reservation. The sea is seldom visible from the highway, however, for the terrain, unlike that of the southern Oregon coast, is not conducive to looking out. But through openings where the highway crosses ravines, and from a few vantage points along the crests of bluffs, the ocean can be observed. Historic Destruction Island, supporting a lighthouse and Coast Guard station, stands about five miles offshore.

This is an area of straight, smooth beaches bordered by high bluffs, thus unlike the rugged coastline from the Hoh River to Cape Flattery where the beaches are crescent-shaped and bounded by projecting points and headlands. Kalaloch Beach, a broad expanse of sand near the south end of this section, exhibits a phenomenon called "shingle beach"—an area covered with smooth, rounded stones. Spruce trees capping the bluffs here have burls and swellings on their trunks. Their cause is unknown. A resort, including lodge, restaurant, cabins, grocery and service station, are located at the mouth of Kalaloch Creek. On the sandy beaches seagulls wait patiently for the incoming smelt, and pipestem-legged sandpipers, light-footed as ballet dancers, run rapidly at the surf's edge. Sometimes a flock will run down the beach together, and if one bird reverses its direction the others will turn and follow.

Ruby Beach is near the northern end of this section of the coast strip, where the highway turns inland and leaves the sea. The wide, sandy beach here is known for its smelt runs, and tourists often stop to watch fishermen take the fish in dip nets. Offshore are seastacks and low rocks harboring tidepools and caves. The beach is free of obstacles, and an easy walk leads to the mouth of the Hoh, about three miles north. The last mile, along the south side of the Hoh estuary, is within the Indian reservation. Baskets can sometimes be purchased at the small village located at the river's mouth.

The National Park Service has constructed seven "beach trails" in this section of the coast strip. From the highway paralleling the shore these paths switchback down steep bluffs to the ocean, sometimes following the gullies of small creeks. The trails are only about two hundred yards long, and are numbered consecutively one to seven from south to north. However, trail number five is no longer maintained.

These spur trails give the tourist quick access to the beaches. Some of the attractions include tremendous piles of driftwood at the end of trail number two; stratified rocks at the terminus of trail number four, where the creek has carved a channel by removing a soft layer of rock; and a rust-colored creek that flows alongside trail number seven. Most picturesque of all is trail number three with its sandy beach below cliffs where matted conifers have been contorted by fierce winds. Stacks are in the process of formation here from sandstone rocks streaked with color and containing concretions, and holes filled with loose rocks that are rolled and pounded by the waves until smooth and round. Coarse black sand sometimes covers the sandstone, but on occasion is washed away at low tide.

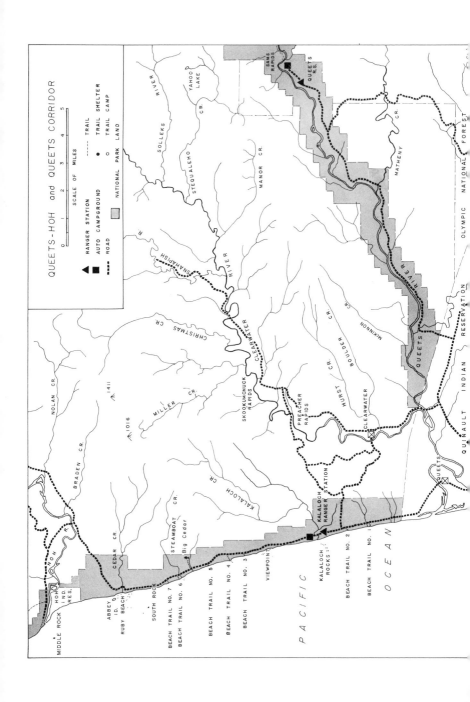

QUEETS-HOH and QUEETS CORRIDOR

SCALE OF MILES
0 1 2 3 4 5

▲ RANGER STATION   ••• TRAIL
■ AUTO CAMPGROUND   ● TRAIL SHELTER
••• ROAD   ○ TRAIL CAMP
▨ NATIONAL PARK LAND

Trail number four is also scenic, the path following a creek that divides and flows around a knoll covered with low, windswept trees. This is a popular beach for taking smelt. Driftwood is scarce, and the beach across which the creek meanders is mostly an expanse of coarse, black sand. Beyond the sand are tidepools. Sandstone near the bluffs contains scoops and hollows eroded by the sea.

The smooth beaches of this section of the Olympic Ocean Strip attract primarily the casual tourist, or the family with small children. Experienced hikers prefer to visit the wilder region lying north of the Hoh River.

Chapter XXII

Hoh-Quillayute

The middle section of the Olympic Ocean Strip, fifteen miles of rugged coastline as the seagull flies, is bounded on the south by the Hoh River and Hoh Indian Reservation; on the north by the Quillayute Indian Reservation and Quillayute River. This coast trends generally in a northwest direction, and most of the beaches are pronounced crescents bounded by steep, rough headlands.

Access is provided from the Olympic Highway by the Oil City and LaPush roads. The Oil City road parallels the Hoh, ending near its mouth. The name Oil City is misleading; the designation is all that survives of the hope once prevalent that commercial oil wells could be developed in the vicinity of Hoh Head. The LaPush road begins one mile north of Forks, the largest settlement between Grays Harbor and Port Angeles, and crosses logged off land to the Indian village of LaPush. Here the Quillayute flows into the sea. The name LaPush is derived from the French words *la bouche* ("the mouth"), referring to the river's outlet into the sea.

LaPush, the only port between Grays Harbor and Cape Flattery, has a man-made breakwater. A Coast Guard station is located here, and the village is the headquarters of a fleet of tall-masted fishing boats. For a fee, Indians will give visitors a ride through the surf in a dugout canoe. Baskets are for sale at the village. Offshore is James Island, once utilized by the Indians as a fortress. The island has a large cove on its seaward side.

First Beach

Fronting LaPush is First Beach, a crescent of smooth sand extending about a mile from the Quillayute estuary to Quateata Point. James Island stands offshore near the northern end of this easily accessible beach, a popular one with tourists who come to LaPush. Men, women, children and dogs clamber across huge piles of driftwood left by winter storms, in order to reach the beach, where they can walk on the smooth sand and enjoy the rush of waves toward the shore, or watch the fishing boats sail between the mainland and James Island.

Second Beach

Between Quateata Point and Teahwhit Head is Second
0.0 Beach, reached by a half-mile trail that leaves the La-
Push road less than a mile south of the village. The trail winds through dense forest containing old, broken snags and thick underbrush, and climbs to a high point where the booming of the breakers is pronounced, sounding like the roar of a passing train. Then the trail drops steeply to the beach.

0.5 Second Beach is smooth and sandy, a favorite of beach-
combers searching for glass fishing floats that have drifted to the coast from the Orient during winter storms. On the smooth sand are clusters of small, beautifully colored rocks; scattered at intervals are buttonlike stones, flat and rounded, with streak marks in the sand where water flows from each side toward the sea. Offshore are the Quillayute Needles, a group of steep-sided seastacks. Some are broad; others form sharp pinnacles. The largest ones are small, tree-capped islands.

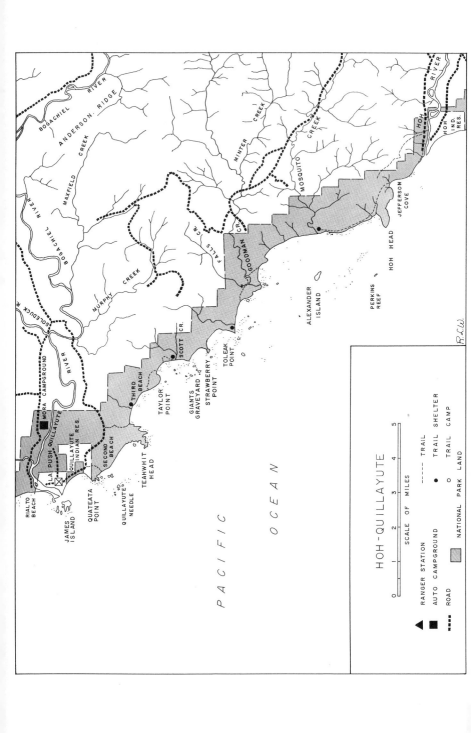

HOH-QUILLAYUTE

	SCALE OF MILES				
0	1	2	3	4	5

▲	RANGER STATION
■	AUTO CAMPGROUND
▪▪▪	ROAD
-----	TRAIL
●	TRAIL SHELTER
○	TRAIL CAMP
▨	NATIONAL PARK LAND

R.F.W.

South Wilderness Beach

The South Wilderness Beach comprises the ocean strip between the Hoh and the Quillayute (including Second Beach just described), and is characterized by broad, curving beaches, abrupt headlands, and many offshore seastacks. This coast is accessible from either the north or the south. A trail leads from the LaPush road two miles southeast of LaPush to Third Beach and provides access from the north. Second Beach is rarely included in a hike along this coast because rugged Teahwhit Head is between it and Third Beach. This promontory can not be rounded, and no trail crosses over. At the southern end of the South Wilderness Beach a muddy trail from the terminus of the Oil City road follows the Hoh River to the beaches opposite a cluster of houses on the Hoh Indian Reservation.

This stretch of primitive coast presents no serious problems to experienced hikers, but the trip is strenuous enough for beginners to find it trying. Several good campsites exist, and water can be obtained from creeks flowing into the sea. No bridges span the creeks, but all the streams are small enough to be easily waded, including Goodman Creek, the largest. Hikers should consult tide tables to avoid rounding doubtful points during incoming tides.

The trail to Third Beach, the northern gateway to this wilderness coast, runs along the edge of a forest bounded by a logged area; or one may drive a half mile down a rough logging road and find the trail there. At this point the path enters a dense stand of tall hemlocks that shade a ground cover of deer ferns and other low growing plants, crosses a picturesque ravine edged by sword ferns and large trees, and passes the rusting remains of an old donkey engine. The trail climbs to a high point overlooking the sea, then drops sharply to the beach, switchbacking down a steep bank through a luxuriant growth of elderberry and sword ferns.

Third Beach, a crescent of smooth sand more than a mile long, is bounded on the northwest by Teahwhit Head, on the southeast by Taylor Point. Waves break ceaselessly, restlessly against the shore, and shimmer like molten silver in the morning sun. Tidepools are found where the beach abuts Teahwhit

Head. Near Taylor Point a number of sharp seastacks stand offshore, and huge boulders of gray conglomerate lie on the beach. These have fallen from the cliff because the sea has undermined the rocks. Near the boulders a ribbonlike waterfall films down the rock wall.

Because Taylor Point can not be rounded safely it must be climbed over. The attractions of Third Beach, however, detain many from making the southward trek. The ease of access and closeness to LaPush have not impaired the sense of isolation. The pulsation of the sea is ever present: the roar of breakers alternates with a stillness punctuated by the gurgling backwash and, where the beach is rocky, the noise of rolling rocks. As the seawater floods over the smooth sand, erasing the footprints of man and animal, the receding breakers make a hissing noise similar to the sinister sound that accompanies the snow avalanche. Sandpipers run near the surf, taking to the air when necessary to escape an incoming wave. Occasionally a lone seagull flies overhead.

2.0   The route over Taylor Point leaves Third Beach near the waterfall that plunges down the cliff face. The way trail climbs sharply through trees and thick undergrowth to a flat bench covered with alder and clumps of sword fern. Then it meanders in the forest, cutting through dense underbrush and often crossing old logs. Some of these have notches chopped for footholds. The way path drops sharply to a curved beach that is nearly enclosed by two headlands. Here are many rough rocks, some covered with seaweed. Numerous stacks stand in the water, and high, yellow banks bound the far side of the crescent. For about four hundred yards the beach is strewn with large, smooth rocks, some covered with mustard-colored marine plants. Among the rocks are intertidal pools that swarm with sea life. Gradually, however, the beach changes to smooth sand, and breakers pound against the unobstructed coast. Offshore from Scott's Bluff is the Giants' Graveyard, a jumble of immense seastacks that stand like sentinels guarding the rockbound coast. During low tide one can walk along them.

Hiking around Scott's Bluff at beach level is unsafe because the breakers crash against the base of vertical cliffs. One

3.0   must climb up and over, via a short trail that leads to a campsite and shelter near Scott Creek, south of the bluff. Here the hiker may relax, and observe life in action on the wilderness coast. Offshore is a seastack, wooded on its landward side. In the top of the tallest tree is an eagle's nest, and a bald eagle often perches on a dead limb of the tree, and looks out to sea. Sometimes one of these birds is observed sitting in the dead top of a tall tree on the crest of Scott's Bluff. Porpoises cavort in the sea, rolling with the waves and occasionally jumping from the water. Overhead, a heron may fly by, its wings flapping slowly and ponderously. These ungainly birds appear to make a great effort to fly, in marked contrast to the effortless soaring of the eagles and gulls. When the tide is low at Scott's Bluff, clams can be dug from the smooth sand. Starfish cling to the rocks of the intertidal pools; seaweed sways in the undulating seawater. Always the beaches are strewn with the debris of the sea and the artifacts of man. Here, as elsewhere along the coast, the sea ceaselessly cuts away the land. South of the bluff is a point where the ocean dashes against jutting rocks and stacks, and the beaches here are littered with material cast overboard from ships: old gloves, bottles, boards, deck lumber, and plastic items ad infinitum.

4.3   Offshore from easily rounded Strawberry Point is a large seastack that is covered with dense vegetation on its landward side. However, on the seaward side, which can be explored at low tide, are tidepools and interesting "sea caves"—actually a tunnel and fissure in the rocks. The walls of the tunnel are almost completely covered with red algae. On the rocks south of this seastack, seals bask in the sunshine.

5.5   Toleak Point, one mile south, is marked by many seastacks. Two old cabins perched above the high tide line provide shelter during inclement weather, although sometimes they can not be used because of skunks and rats living beneath them.

This part of the coast is characterized by seastacks, tidepools and broad beaches. Beyond Toleak Point the beach is wide and sandy, and strewn with seaweed. The sand is so smooth it has a glasslike appearance. Beyond Jackson Creek the beach is still smooth, but composed of coarser sand.

The route now goes inland, away from the ocean beaches, in order to cross Goodman Creek above the sheer-walled gorge through which it flows into the sea. Because the tidal effect extends inland beyond the head of the gorge, this detour is necessary. The way trail over the headland begins about a mile east of Toleak Point, at a point where colored rocks mark the high water line. The path climbs sharply through a hemlock and cedar forest garlanded with 7.5 ferns. The route descends to and crosses Falls Creek near a scenic waterfall about forty feet high, then crosses Goodman Creek. At low tide the creek is shallow and easily crossed at this inland point. Undergrowth is very luxuriant, and moss-draped alders and maples overhang the stream. This bottomland is quite swampy.

(A side trip to the mouth of Goodman Creek can be taken from this point. Where the creek enters the ocean the scenery is quite picturesque. A number of rugged seastacks rise above the water, one of which contains a "sea cave" through which the waves crash.)

Beyond Goodman Creek the route climbs the opposite hillside to a benchland covered with hemlocks and ferns. Huge snags, rotted and covered with young hemlocks, stand among the smaller trees. As the path winds through the forest and again approaches the sea, the booming of the surf becomes audible, sounding much like a distant artillery barrage.

8.3 The trail descends to the Pacific at Jefferson Cove, where many seastacks stand offshore. The largest of these remnants of a mainland that once extended further west are flattened on top and covered with trees, but the smaller ones have been eroded to sharp pinnacles. These serve as observation posts for gulls.

Between Goodman and Mosquito creeks the beaches are smooth and sandy, often strewn with debris, both natural and man-made. Battered driftwood, shells, starfish (dead and alive) and kelp lie beside deck planking from ships, bottles, cans, and other paraphernalia of civilization. Some of the seaweed tossed upon the beach resembles elaborately fringed ropes. The sand is often marked by the tracks of seagulls, and occasionally those of a bear or deer that has come down to the water's edge. Cormorants sit on rocks, resting between fishing excursions.

10.6   Ankle-deep Mosquito Creek, a meandering stream, flows to the sea through a picturesque valley bordered by green-clad hills. Here a trail takes up over the mainland from behind a shelter on the south bank of the creek. This pathway, known locally as the "high tide route," descends to the sea again several miles below Hoh Head.

Seagulls by the hundreds congregate at the mouth of Mosquito Creek, or along the beach, where they search the incoming tide for a meal. The birds walk on the sand in a stately manner, and are indifferent to people unless they come too near. Eagles also scout the beaches for food. In the forest behind the Mosquito Creek Shelter is an eagle's nest in the top of an old tree. This is a "live" nest, one still being used by the birds, and should not be disturbed.

A mile offshore is Alexander Island, a big block with steep rock walls. When fog rises from the water along its black sides, in early morning, the island is grim and forbidding.

Near the edge of the bluff south of Mosquito Creek is a large seastack. Beyond it the broad sandy beach
11.0   continues several hundred yards to a headland that cannot be rounded but can be climbed over in five minutes. The view from the crest of the way trail over this point reveals a picturesque cove—a crescent-shaped beach of smooth sand bounded by vertical cliffs to the north and a rocky spur to the south. Stacks guard the entrance. The route drops down into the cove and follows the smooth, sandy beach, then
11.4   winds among rocks near the base of Point Four, the rocky spur on the south end of the crescent. Colorful starfish cling to barnacle-encrusted rocks that stick out of the glassy smooth sand at medium low tide.

For nearly a mile south of the cove the beach is
12.2   smooth and sandy, then another point must be rounded at low tide. The large rocks, covered with barnacles and kelp, are slippery. Beyond this point is another that can
12.7   not be skirted. However, a trail climbs steeply up from the beach to a lookout point. Hoh Head is visible to the south. This jutting, steep-sided promontory pokes out into

the sea like a fat thumb, and is covered with dense forest. The trail coalesces with the "high tide route" and meanders over a forest covered bench. Ferns carpet the ground. The trail continues through rain forest; the hiker must clamber over rotten logs and cross muddy areas, as he makes his way through a dense growth where the stillness and closeness are claustrophobic, arousing an intense longing to return to the breeze-swept beach. The trail is not long, but the way through this dense growth seems interminable.

13.0   The path drops sharply to the beach south of Hoh
13.8   Head, where a short stretch of sandy coast extends to a point that can be crossed almost any time, but best at low tide. A massive jumble of huge boulders composed of conglomerate lies at the base of a steep cliff. The breakers crash against these rocks, tossing spume and spray high into the air.

South of this point the beach again widens and becomes sandy. Driftwood is abundant, including many
15.0   huge logs piled along the shore. At the mouth of the Hoh River a long sandspit or gravel bar extending into the sea is used by fishermen surfcasting for ocean perch. Across the river is the small settlement on the Hoh Indian Reservation.

The route now follows the north bank of the river to the trail leading to the end of the Oil City road.

Chapter XXIII

Quillayute-Ozette

The northern part of the Olympic Ocean Strip is wild and primitive like the middle section, and extends twenty miles from the Quillayute River and Indian reservation to the Ozette River just beyond the Ozette Indian Reservation. Near Cape Alava the strip broadens to about two miles, and is bordered on the east by Lake Ozette. This lake, the largest on the peninsula, is eight miles long, from one to two miles wide, and is surrounded by low, forest-clad hills. A ranger station is located at the north end of the lake near the outlet into the Ozette River. Before Alaska and Hawaii became states, Cape Alava and the nearby offshore islands were the westernmost point in the United States.

This is a rugged coastline. The ocean constantly rolls against the land, at high tide covering the beaches and rushing in among the rocks. Plumes of white water spray over the outlying rocks as the sea gushes rhythmically through deep gashes in the seastacks and cliffs. At night phosphorescent waves mark the shoreline, and flickering lights on the horizon reveal the presence of ships sailing along the Washington coast.

Two roads give access to this section of the park strip, one at either end. The Rialto Beach road branches from the

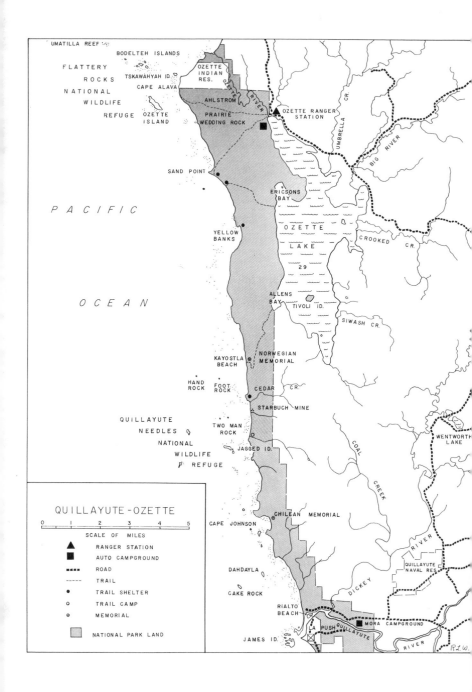

UMATILLA REEF
BODELTEH ISLANDS
OZETTE
INDIAN
RES.
FLATTERY
ROCKS
TSKAWAHYAH ID.
NATIONAL
CAPE ALAVA
WILDLIFE
AHLSTROM
REFUGE
OZETTE
ISLAND
PRAIRIE
WEDDING ROCK
OZETTE RANGER
STATION
UMBRELLA CR.
BIG RIVER

SAND POINT
ERICSONS
BAY

PACIFIC
YELLOW
BANKS
OZETTE
LAKE
CROOKED CR.

29

OCEAN
ALLENS
BAY
TIVOLI ID.
SIWASH CR.

KAYOSTLA
BEACH
NORWEGIAN
MEMORIAL

HAND
ROCK
FOOT
ROCK
CEDAR CR.

QUILLAYUTE
STARBUCH MINE
NEEDLES
TWO MAN
ROCK
NATIONAL
WENTWORTH
LAKE
WILDLIFE
JAGGED ID.
REFUGE

COAL
CREEK

CHILEAN MEMORIAL

CAPE JOHNSON
RIVER

QUILLAYUTE
NAVAL RES.
DAHDAYLA

CAKE ROCK
DICKEY
RIALTO
BEACH
MORA CAMPGROUND
LA PUSH
QUILLAYUTE

JAMES ID.
RIVER

R.L.W.

QUILLAYUTE-OZETTE

0   1   2   3   4   5
SCALE OF MILES

▲   RANGER STATION
■   AUTO CAMPGROUND
▬▬▬ ROAD
----- TRAIL
●   TRAIL SHELTER
○   TRAIL CAMP
⊙   MEMORIAL
▨   NATIONAL PARK LAND

LaPush road eight miles from the Olympic Highway, and crosses the Soleduck River above its union with the Bogachiel, the beginning of the short Quillayute. Within the park strip this road traverses a scenic forest, then follows the north bank of the Quillayute to Rialto Beach (4.9 mi.). The sandspit extending from the beach toward James Island marks the southern terminus of the coast strip's northern section. The Lake Ozette road provides access to the northern end of the strip from the Strait of Juan de Fuca near Sekiu and Clallam Bay. The road crosses logged off country and ends where the Ozette River emerges from the north end of the lake (20.0 mi.).

Four trails lead to the ocean from Lake Ozette. Two of these begin at the north end of the lake, one going to Cape Alava, the other to Sand Point. The other paths, accessible only by boat, extend to the sea from bays on the western side of the lake.

Cape Alava Trail

0.0   The Cape Alava trail begins in a dense forest of hemlock and cedar. Thick, almost impenetrable underbrush forms a jungle beneath the trees. Skunk cabbage grows profusely in the swampy areas, and the air is filled with its pungent aroma. Midway to the Pacific the trail crosses a prairie about ninety acres in extent, once the home of Lars K. Ahlstrom, a bachelor who for many years claimed the distinction of being the "most westerly resident in the United States." Ahlstrom died in 1960 at the age of 88, but he had not lived on the ranch for several years prior to his death. Old buildings, deteriorating from the ravages of time and the damp climate, stand near the western edge of the prairie.

The trail reenters the forest, and near the sea traverses a timbered hillside where the ground is covered with large clumps of sword fern. The path ends at rocky Cape
3.3   Alava (3.3 mi.), near the south boundary of the Ozette Indian Reservation. This reserve covers slightly more than one square mile, and is bounded on the west by the sea, on all other sides by national park land. The last of the Ozette Indians has died and controversy has arisen in regard to disposi-

tion of the land. The Makah Indians claim the reservation, and the suggestion has also been made that the land be added to the national park and an Indian museum and memorial established there. An Indian village once stood on the reservation near Cape Alava.

(For description of the scene at Cape Alava, see section on the North Wilderness Beach).

Sand Point Trail

0.0   The Sand Point trail also begins at the outlet of Lake
3.0   Ozette, and crosses the park strip to Sand Point, a
      promontory three miles south of Cape Alava. Because this route traverses a swampy area, most of the way the trail is covered with planking. The route is through forests of cedar and spruce. In the spring the yellow of skunk cabbage is conspicuous; in summer bunchberry creates a showy display of white blooms.

A large quantity of driftwood has collected at Sand Point, but immediately to the east is a smooth, sandy beach more than a mile long. When the tide is low the depth of the beach is more than six hundred yards.

Ericson's Bay and Allen's Bay Trails

Near the south end of Lake Ozette two trails lead to the ocean, one from Ericson's Bay, the other from Allen's Bay. These trails, accessible by boat from the upper end of the lake, are each about two miles long, and pass through dense forest. Ericson's Bay trail reaches the sea a half mile south of Sand Point; Allen's Bay trail enters an open area before emerging onto the beach just south of the Norwegian Memorial.

North Wilderness Beach

The North Wilderness Beach extends from the Quillayute River to the Ozette River, approximately twenty miles.

This is the part of the coastal strip that juts farthest into the Pacific, and many ships have been driven by storms onto the jagged rocks. In the vicinity of Cape Johnson are two memorials marking the graves of the crews of wrecked ships.

Experienced hikers have no difficulty walking the length of this wilderness coast. Elevated terrain can be reached at all points in the event one is overtaken by a high tide. However, low tide must be awaited in order to round Yellow Banks and Cape Johnson. Several other headlands can be crossed by using old Coast Guard trails. The points should be rounded on outgoing tides.

Smooth, level beaches of fine sand, washed daily by the sea in its eternal ritual of the tides, alternate with areas strewn with rough, broken boulders and coarse gravel. Slippery rocks predominate in the southern part, contrasting with the sandy beaches to the north. The unhurried hiker can explore tidepools along the reef, relics of gold mining equipment lying along the shore, and old miners' cabins perched high above the beaches.

0.0   If one goes from south to north, the trip begins at the National Park Service picnic area on Rialto Beach. Upstream on the Quillayute, and somewhat back from the coast, is a campground. South of the picnic area is the sandspit on the Quillayute estuary, from where the village of LaPush is visible. At low tide a man can wade across to James Island.

Gravel alternates with broad stretches of smooth sand on the beach at Rialto. Smelt fishing is popular with both men and birds. Gulls stand in groups near the surf's edge, waiting for the fish, and their tracks are imprinted in the wet sand.

North of Rialto the beach gradually becomes more sandy, with less gravel. James Island appears as a prominent sea-mark to the south; a mile to the west is steep-sided Cake Rock, flat on top with a slight hump in the middle. The beach is glassy smooth in an area of large seastacks accessible at low tide. These pinnacles appear to be composed of good climbing rock, but are so steep and overhanging as to offer serious challenges to the best climbers. A huge, jutting promontory here resembles an elephant with its trunk buried in the sand, thus forming an arch through which the hiker can walk. A number

of tidepools with kelp-covered rocks are surrounded by the
smooth sand.

1.5   North of the stacks a point must be rounded, the first
in the series of five that culminates in Cape Johnson.
Barnacle-encrusted rocks, tidepools teeming with snails, and
slick, kelp-covered boulders afford precarious footing. Most of
the rocks are covered by seaweed, some of it moss-like. Air
bladders on the kelp burst with a popping sound when stepped
on; tiny rock crabs skitter among the tidepool rocks at the
approach of the hiker.

One of the attractions of this place is a large expanse of
smooth gray rock, flat as a table. The alternate bands of light
and dark upended strata have been shaved smooth by abrasive
action of the sea, resulting in wavy geometric patterns.

Beyond the point is a crescent beach of sand and
smooth stones. Offshore seastacks are numerous, standing like
minarets at either end of the crescent. Another headland juts
southward into the sea, and the large rocks at its base are
covered with kelp. At low tide a level "tableland" of rock—a
classic example of a wave-cut terrace—is exposed, much of it
covered with rockweed ("crabclaw kelp") growing in clumps
like maidenhair ferns. This wide expanse of level rock is broken
by deep, vertical-walled channels that have been carved in the
rock by the sea. Through these the tide surges, splashing white
foam high in the air. This is one of the larger points in the Cape
Johnson complex. James Island is visible to the south; Cake
Rock to the southwest.

Once this point is rounded the going is easier; smooth,
vari-colored rocks are mixed in the black sand. After rounding
another headland near several offshore stacks, the way leads
to a large cove immediately south of Cape Johnson. Here, in
the forest beside the beach, is the Chilean Memorial, marking
the grave of crew members of the W. J. Pirrie, a schooner
wrecked when it struck Cake Island on November 26,
1920.

3.0   Cape Johnson is northwest of the memorial. This point
cannot be climbed over, and must be rounded at low
tide. The cape is rocky; barnacles and kelp cover everything. A

half mile north of the cape is a similar headland, the last in the series. Hikers should allow at least an hour to pass the two points. At one time the Ozette Indians maintained a whaling station in this area. On a large rock to the north is an Indian carving of the thunderbird.

5.0   Beyond the last headland the beach is relatively smooth for a mile, and is marked at low tide by barnacle-encrusted rocks sticking out of smooth sand. Then another high point juts westward, as if challenging the sea. This point is in the process of becoming an island, for wave action is gradually cutting away the low ridge connecting it to the mainland. A trail leads over the ridge, but waiting for low tide is worthwhile; then one can round the point and view the overhanging cliffs undercut by the sea. The upper cliffs are bearded with bright green "sea grass," much in the manner that selaginella festoons vine maple in the rain forests. The southward view from the trail over the ridge includes Cape Johnson beyond a broad, curving bay and a high, vertical headland topped with dense forest. To the right are seastacks. The scene to the north includes the abrupt cliffs of the point, and, below, a broad sandy beach and driftwood. Jagged Island, a mile offshore, looks like a miniature mountain.

The beaches are delightfully smooth and sandy for about a mile north of the point, then change to gravel and small round boulders. Jagged Island is now seen to be not one but at least four seastacks. Several miles offshore is unsurveyed Carroll Island, a large blocklike mass. About one mile north of the point is a campsite; low tide here reveals rock formations and numerous tidepools. Many stacks rise from the sea, their lower walls plastered with starfish, some orange-colored, others purplish brown. Between this camp and Cedar Creek, a mile of smooth, sandy beach is bordered onshore by beautiful young forests. The ubiquitous tidepools are present; on offshore rocks, covered with kelp, sea lions sometimes bask in the sunshine.

6.8   Near the mouth of Cedar Creek, rusting equipment marks the site of the abandoned Starbuch Mine. Slip-

7.0   pery, kelp-covered rocks lie at the base of a headland
         north of the creek. Rounding this point at high tide is
         not feasible, but a primitive trail leads over the top.

7.5   The Norwegian Memorial, about five miles north of
         Cape Johnson, is mistakenly designated the Swedish
Memorial on some maps. On January 2, 1903, the crew of a
three-masted bark, the *Prince Arthur*, mistook lights shining in
a cabin for the Tatoosh Island beacon, and turned their ship
eastward, thinking they were at the entrance to the Strait of
Juan de Fuca. The ship was wrecked and eighteen men lost.
They lie buried beneath the memorial, an eight-foot-high
marker surrounded by bracken fern and young spruce trees.
Offshore are Hand Rock and Foot Rock.
         North of the Norwegian Memorial for several miles the
beaches are rocky mosaics of small colored stones, interrupted
now and then by piles of large boulders resembling glacial moraine. The rocks have been worn smooth, however, and lack the
sharp angles of moraine rock. The tidepools here support millions of tiny crabs; when a hiker approaches, they scuttle for
places of refuge, falling freely from the edges of the rocks into
         the water.

9.3   A headland of rough, wave-cut rock, together with an
         arch and deepset tidepools in an area of rocky head-
lands, marks the halfway point on the North Wilderness Beach.
Waves dash forcefully against scarred bedrock where stacks are
in the process of formation. Some of the cliffs contain caves.
One cliff, composed of hard rock, is pockmarked with countless
holes of various sizes. Below it, in the upturned strata, are
tidepools. The cliffs are streaked with green and white "sea
grass."
         Beyond the halfway point the beach changes gradually,
almost imperceptibly, from large rocks to smaller ones, then to
small gravel and sand. Driftwood is piled up in the coves, and
near the high water mark on the long stretches of sandy beach.
Rocks are exposed between sand and sea at low tide.
         This area is remote from roads, and wildlife signs are
therefore abundant. Animals, large and small, visit the beaches.
Occasionally a dead whale is cast ashore, and the black bears

come out of the forest to feast upon the carcass. Noisy crows sit on nearby snags, fussing and complaining while the bears gorge on the decaying whale.

13.5   At Yellow Banks the beach of glassy smooth sand is broad, but the point should be rounded at low tide; the cliffs of yellow mud bordering the beach are unsafe to scale. The smooth sand beach continues beyond Yellow Banks into Miner's Cove. Onshore, in the tangled jungle, stands a dilapidated miner's shack weathered by ravages of time. The point at the north end of the cove can be rounded on medium tide by going through a tunnel in a wet, mossy cliff. The rocks below are slippery, and are covered with seaweed that looks like green wool.

Beyond the point are small, picturesque coves, tidepools and low rocks. The sand changes to pea gravel and large, scarred rocks that are battered ceaselessly by the breakers. Several gravel cliffs are followed by a half mile of smooth, sandy beach. Driftwood in large quantity lies near the forest's edge.

15.0   A nondescript shelter built of lumber and plywood gleaned from the beach marks the termination of the Ericson's Bay trail from Lake Ozette.

15.5   Another shelter at Sand Point, a half mile to the north, marks the end of the Sand Point trail. As its name indicates, this point is characterized by sandy beaches. Raccoons and skunks prowl here at night in search of crustaceans. The point of low sand—a tombolo—is covered with grasses and leads out to a low, rounded seastack covered with brush. Immediately north of the point is a broad, curving beach of fine, smooth sand with much driftwood at the upper edge, tidepools at the lower. Offshore stacks stand to the north and west.

Beyond this beach the hiker must clamber for a mile over jumbled rocks that have fallen from cliffs. Crows caw incessantly in the nearby forest; foghorns sound on ships

17.0   sailing along the coast. Midway between Sand Point and Cape Alava is Wedding Rock, decorated with a number of Indian petroglyphs. These primitive, childlike carvings of face masks, killer whales and warriors are inconspicuous because weathering has made them indistinct. They can be photographed, however, by tracing the lines with chalk or graphite. Both pictorial and alphabetical drawings have been found. An especially interesting one of an owl and the full moon is sometimes covered beneath the shifting beach sand. North of Wedding Rock the beach is comparatively smooth and littered with "international debris"—artifacts cast from the ships of many nations and washed ashore by incoming breakers.

18.5   At Cape Alava several small islands and many offshore rocks rise from the sea. These are included in the Flattery Rocks National Wildlife Refuge. The largest is Ozette Island; the farthest west is triple-humped Bodelteh. These islands can be reached only by boat. Tskawahyah, also known as Indian or Cannonball Island, is accessible at low tide by crossing the sand. The beach at the base of this islet is covered with large sandstone rocks that look like cannonballs. These almost perfect spheres are concretions that have been eroded from the island's cliffs by the sea. From the top of Tskawahyah, reached by a steep, muddy trail, the view to the north includes Point of the Arches, Cape Flattery and Tatoosh Island.

The beaches at Cape Alava are rocky. Marine life is abundant in the tidepools, and includes hermit crabs, clams and seaweed. Bald eagles circle overhead, hunting for fish; crabs scurry beneath the eelgrass. At low tide the sand at Cape Alava is often patterned with crescentic ridges and depressions resembling miniature barchans, a type of sand dune.

An Indian village once stood near the cape, but little now remains to indicate its location. However, a half mile north of the Cape Alava trail is an old canoe dragway through the rocks, visible at low tide.

Between Cape Alava and the mouth of the Ozette River is a mile of smooth sand strewn with kelp. Several 20.0   interesting coves and caves are found here, near where the Ozette River empties into the sea. The river marks the northern limit of the park's coastal strip. The stream's current breaks the force of the breakers, and they are more like those of inland waters than the open sea. Offshore rocks and tidepools, characteristic of the Olympic coast, are also found here.

In 1958 William O. Douglas, Justice of the United States Supreme Court, led a large party of hikers down the

North Wilderness Beach from Cape Alava to Rialto in order to publicize the feeling of conservationists that the region should be retained in its primitive, roadless state. The threat is real, because from time to time various plans and proposals have been put forth advocating the construction of a road along the coast from Rialto to Lake Ozette.

Epilogue

The day ends at Cape Alava, farthest reach of the Olympic Peninsula. The sun has disappeared, but its last rays still glow on the summit snows of Mount Olympus. The scintillating sea has turned purplish gray, and is flecked with tinges of gold. In the forest edging the sea, where lengthened shadows linger, the tall evergreens form black silhouettes. Overhead a few stars twinkle in the darkening sky.

On the beach between forest and sea a dying campfire flares brightly for a moment, and a multitude of sparks splash upward through the blackness and vanish. The evening grows chill, and campers sitting close by the remnant of fire become philosophic. How fortunate, they conclude, that man has preserved the best of the Olympic Peninsula, this strange land of primitive mountains and wild seashore. And they express gratitude, also, to the men who conceived the national park idea—men whose spirits have gone, like those of the Indians buried on nearby Ozette Island, to the Happy Hunting Ground, but whose handiwork remains as a monument to their vision.

Offshore, the Umatilla Lightship blinks intermittently, and a lone seagull wings southward, its plaintive cry sounding above the mournful sea wind that rises fitfully.

INDEX

ROBERT L. WOOD

was born in 1925 in Springfield, Missouri, and spent his boyhood in the Ozark Mountains. After wartime service in the army he moved to Washington State, graduating from the University of Washington in 1950. Mr. Wood is now Official Court Reporter, King County Superior Court, Seattle, Washington.

An avid mountaineer, hiker, skier, and photographer, Mr. Wood has expressed his deep interest in protecting natural beauty through an active membership in several conservation organizations. He gained the sobriquet "Ol' Grizz" while serving as editor of The Mountaineer.

Mr. Wood is the author of ACROSS THE OLYMPIC MOUNTAINS: THE PRESS EXPEDITION, 1889–90, published jointly by the University of Washington Press and The Mountaineers in 1967. The book is a detailed account of the historic Press Expedition, the first party to cross the Olympics.

TRAIL COUNTRY: OLYMPIC NATIONAL PARK is the culmination of Mr. Wood's extensive experience on park trails. His knowledge of these trails is probably more complete than that of any other living person.

A NOTE ON THE BOOK

The text was set in Electra, designed for the Linotype by W. A. Dwiggins. The book was printed by offset.

Composed, printed, and bound by the Kingsport Press, Inc.

Typography, binding, and jacket design by Joyce Kachergis.

Executive editor—Murrell Boyd.

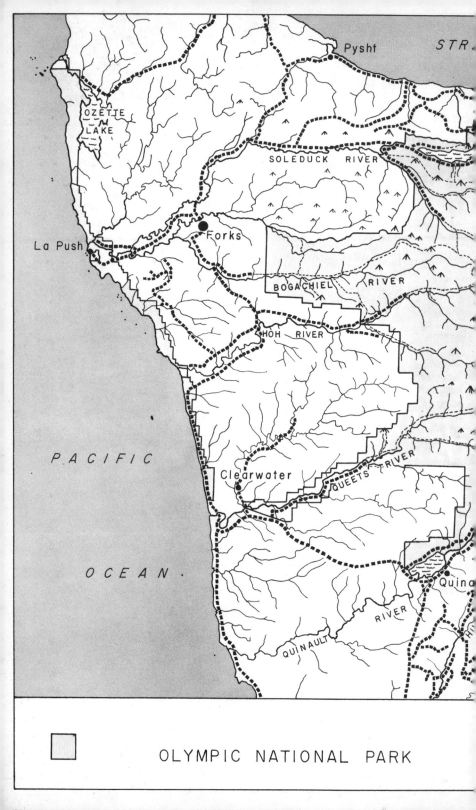